Advance Praise for *F*ck*

"Daniel Jupp has gained a deserved reputation for being one of the most insightful commentators on exposing the nefarious intentions and machinations of the Globalists and the woke Left. This is a thoroughly researched and clinical dismantling of everything that is wrong with the world. Inevitably it covers much of the madness of recent years including covid, election fraud, censorship and cancel culture, the destruction of traditional family values, and the move toward China-like total digital control. But the book also provides important advice on how to resist the changes that the globalists wish to impose on us."

–Professor Norman Fenton

"Daniel Jupp applies his incisive mind to modern politics. He dissects narrative politics piece by important piece, summing up in each section the salient facts. This book is important reading, not just for those who are interested in politics, but especially for those who have no interest in politics. 'It's all just the same, isn't it?' No, it isn't, as Daniel Jupp explains. The world we face today is one we must understand, to see the very real peril we are in. Then we can forge a future of a much better golden age for our children and grandchildren as we know what we are fighting against."

–John Le Sueur, Writer *The Conservative Woman*

Also by Daniel Jupp
*Gates of Hell: Why Bill Gates Is the Most
Dangerous Man in the World*

F*ck the Planet

HOW TO RESIST THE GREAT RESET IN THE TRUMP ERA

DANIEL JUPP

BOMBARDIER
BOOKS

Published by Bombardier Books
An Imprint of Post Hill Press
ISBN: 979-8-88845-906-5
ISBN (eBook): 979-8-88845-907-2

F*ck the Planet:
How to Resist the Great Reset in the Trump Era
© 2025 by Daniel Jupp
All Rights Reserved

Cover Design by Jim Villaflores

This book, as well as any other Bombardier Books publications, may be purchased in bulk quantities at a special discounted rate. Contact orders@bombardierbooks.com for more information.

This is a work of nonfiction. All people, locations, events, and situations are portrayed to the best of the author's memory.

No part of this book may be reproduced, stored in a retrieval system, or transmitted by any means without the written permission of the author and publisher.

Post Hill Press
New York • Nashville
posthillpress.com

Published in the United States of America
1 2 3 4 5 6 7 8 9 10

TABLE OF CONTENTS

Preface	ix
Introduction: It's a Mad, Mad World	xiii
The Pathology of Your Enemy: Globalists Are Often Cluster B Personalities	1
What is Globalism?	15
Turn Off Your Television	29
Live Not by Lies	43
Spreading the Truth	55
The Power of Your Pocket	65
The Digital Samizdat	75
Life Under Globalist Rule	87
Your Guns: The Second Amendment and Self-Defense on Globalist Streets	99
Is It Worth Voting?	111
Julian Assange and Hacking the System	121
The Censorship-Industrial Complex and Your Free Speech	129
Managing Your Interactions to Protect Yourself: The Police, Mainstream Media, and Social Media	143
We Care a Lot: Addressing the Lie of Globalist Compassion	163
From Compassion to Oppression: Beware of Globalists Bearing Gifts	173
From Dependence to Self-Reliance: Reclaiming Your Capacity for Independent Living	185
A Cautious Note of Optimism: The Red Pill Is Not the Black Pill	197
Appendix: Globalist Institutions	209
About the Author	255

Dedicated to the memory of Joanna Futerman. RIP.

PREFACE

Between the completion of this book and its publication something wonderful happened. An event occurred which offers hope to all of the people this book is for. In the book I say that this event is a possibility that would deliver a real chance of a better way and a better alternative to the insane policies Globalists support. That possibility is now a reality.

Because Donald Trump won the 2024 US election. Because it was "too big to rig." Because Trump won the Presidential race. Because he won the Electoral College vote *and* the popular vote. Because he won every Swing State. Because he won Congress, and he won the Senate too. The victory and the mandate was enormous. Better measures against fraud and a better and bolder team behind Trump (including excellent former Democrats like Tulsi Gabbard and Robert F. Kennedy Jr) ensured that victory.

And the world is changed for the better because of it.

The pace of the second Trump term has been astonishing. For the first time in my lifetime the Globalist project and the Great Reset is under serious assault. It wasn't this threatened by the first Trump term. It's not been this threatened by excellent but less influential populist leaders in Argentina, Hungary, and Italy. The US still has the power to lead the entire Western world in ways other nations cannot. One of the ironies now at play is that the Globalist accumulation of more and more power to the State and its agencies, which had been under the Biden administration united with billionaire interests and with unaccountable transnational organizations in a vast network of graft, corruption, and patronage destroying the Western world, now put the foes of Globalism in a position to unravel the network.

And this is what the second Trump term is doing. For the first time since 1946, a US President is tackling and confronting malign forces that enrich themselves at the nations expense. Executive Orders which confront the most obvious insanities, like LGBTQ+ and Trans activism via the State, are culturally of huge importance. But these alone don't offer the radical change that is needed. Only tackling Globalist networks of power and self-interest does that. All of these networks, from rogue government agencies and departments to external bodies like the UN or World Health Organisation, are finally being challenged in a real and substantial way.

Because the vast rivers of stolen money are being blocked. All of the crimes of Globalism have been built on taking money from ordinary citizens to do things those citizens would never, in the majority, vote for. To do things you are never given a choice about or asked to vote on. The UN only exists thanks to money given to it by nation states. The WHO only has power to dictate global responses on pandemics if nation states sign a Pandemic Treaty giving it that power. People are only forced to sit through racist lectures on the evils of whiteness because vast sums of public money are funnelled to the universities by people who want those evil lectures to be part of the deal. Globalists have controlled the narrative and steered the policies toward social engineering absurdities and toward a crooked system of twisted values enriching them because they have been the ones controlling the money and directing the spending.

What DOGE is doing exposes how the money was stolen, where it was sent, who is on the corrupt payroll, and what it was really for, instead of what Globalists have claimed it was for.

In this book I talk about not trusting the media and understanding just how much the mainstream media exists solely to lie, to invert reality, and to serve interests which are not the interests of ordinary people. Now DOGE is confirming what outsider voices such as mine already knew. We can see Reuters issuing an article critical of DOGE, but we can also for the first time immediately see why. Reuters has received millions of dollars of misdirected, essentially stolen public funding to put across Deep State arguments while pretending to be an independent, free press.

It wasn't free. It was purchased. With your tax dollars, to lie to you. With your vast national debt, to lie to you and brainwash you. One of the receipts even has the explanatory note "for large-scale social deception." And the corrupt network that has parasitized US power and spending did this globally, in Globalist (not US) interests.

This is the first time since World War Two that the power of the State has been turned against the Deep State, in service of the ordinary citizen. Magnificent as Reagan and Thatcher were in many ways, their primary enemy was the Soviet Union. They didn't get to fight and destroy the enemy within. They didn't fight a culture war except by example and some excellent and insightful rhetoric. Readers throughout the Western world will be familiar with just how useless mainstream conservative parties and politicians have been as Western values were perverted and as Western wealth was squandered and stolen.

Only populism actually fights back in a real fashion, and this second Trump term is hitting the Great Reset and the Globalist project where it hurts and effects lasting change, in the pocket. All the major strands of Trumpist policy assault key Globalist aims:

1. Trump is withdrawing from the Paris Accords and intends energy independence. This shatters the Globalist consensus on using climate change to enforce social change and massive theft.
2. Trump denies LGBTQ+ and Trans activism, threatening the Trans surgery industry and the diversity non jobs patronage system. The Globalist project of reshaping Western morality is also under threat.
3. Trump is doing everything he can in the Middle East and Ukraine to end the perpetual wars and the Globalist profit from them.

4. Trump is trying to force the administrative State to start serving the interests of ordinary people again. This offers far more real democracy and ends the kind of permanent "our direction only" tyranny that Globalists want.
5. Trump is protecting the borders but more importantly going after the NGOs and State empowered Globalists who used US funding to encourage and assist the migrant invasion.

But these fights are not yet won, and this has only just started. There are still 50,000 NGOs, almost none of which actually do good. We are still paying for a UN which employs terrorists, wants to become a global government, and pushes the most damaging and disastrous policies in the name of "sustainability" or "diversity." Corrupt Democrat judges have launched a new wave of lawfare, this time trying to desperately protect the stolen money system from DOGE. The Globalist enemies of our world, our freedom and our right to pick the policies we actually want, are not resting. They are challenged, but not yet vanquished.

And for people in Blue States in the US or served by institutions with Globalist or Democrat leaders, the madness is still in charge. A twelve-year-old relative of J.D. Vance, for instance, has been denied a heart transplant due to being unvaccinated. That's the kind of callous lunacy Globalism always offers to most of us.

Similarly, the people outside the US still suffer under Globalist governments. Canada has the euthanasia murder of the elderly, the poor, and the depressed as its fastest growing industry and may get a Globalist banker as its replacement of Justin Trudeau. EU leaders and NATO are still trying to provoke World War Three with Russia. And in Britain, my country, the people suffer under a Marxist Globalist leadership that is enacting as rapidly as it can everything that MAGA is dismantling in the US.

We have hope now, and we have leadership doing real things in the US. But millions of us are still living in the mad anarcho-tyranny that Globalists create. This book is about surviving until the Trump Effect, the actions and example of MAGA, saves us all.

INTRODUCTION

IT'S A MAD, MAD WORLD

One of the ways to distance ourselves from the madnesses of our times is to retain an interest in politics but not to rely on it as a source of meaning. The call should be for people to simplify their lives and not to mislead themselves by devoting their lives to a theory that answers no questions, makes no predictions and is easily falsifiable. Meaning can be found in all sorts of places. For most individuals it is found in the love of the people and places around them: in friends, family and loved ones, in culture, place, and wonder. A sense of purpose is found in working out what is meaningful in our lives and then orienting ourselves over time as closely as possible to those centres of meaning. Using ourselves up on identity politics, social justice (in this manifestation) and intersectionality is a waste of a life.

—Douglas Murray, *The Madness of Crowds: Gender, Race and Identity*

When parasitized by such a conspiratorial and delusional mindset, the bikini becomes a sexist tool of the patriarchy whereas the burqa is liberating and freeing since it averts the male gaze.

—Gad Saad, *The Parasitic Mind: How Infectious Ideas Are Killing Common Sense*

This book is addressed to ordinary people, to the average citizen of the nations of the West. It's for people in the US, the UK, Australia, Canada, New Zealand, the entire Anglosphere, and all the nations in Europe, too, that have been described as part of the "Free World."

It's not a book for the billionaires in these nations, for the professional political class, or for the kind of people who get paid huge salaries as they sit at the top of institutions and political organizations.

It is for people like me and people like you—those of us who have always obeyed the laws, always paid our taxes, always had to work or look for work, and who have tried to build ordinary lives while doing so.

It's for people who have had to worry about getting ahead and getting a home, rather than having had these things just handed to them. It's for parents and grandparents and people who grew up in liberal democracies inheriting and expecting a certain amount of basic freedom and opportunity.

And these people, whether they live in the United States, the United Kingdom, or any similarly developed and reasonably successful Western nation-state, have been thinking one thing. They have one thing, politically, in common, and it's a thought that's been occurring to all of them more and more. Essentially that thought is this:

Why has the world, my world, apparently gone insane?

That's the biggest question that the ordinary majority share. And it is, still, the majority of us. Most of us aren't so wealthy or so privileged that we feel protected from radical political changes and policies. Most of us know what it is to struggle or worry about money or pay the bills or maintain a mortgage. The people who don't have to worry about the ordinary everyday things are a minority.

All of us in Western nations were born in places we thought were more free, more developed, more democratic than other parts of the world. No matter how much we had to work and struggle, no matter what life and luck threw at us, we thought that certain things were long established and couldn't be taken away.

We thought that our elections were free and fair. We thought that our political differences were largely peaceful ones. We thought that the people in charge were limited in what they could do and were prepared to do. We might think that some of our parties and politicians got things wrong. We might think that there were different left-wing or right-wing approaches to the economy and to policy choices and to the things that matter to us.

But we generally did not think that the world was going mad, our leaders were reckless ideologically crazed lunatics, and our basic rights could be ignored by governments still claiming to be democratic, politically accountable, and free.

There are many different things happening that might seem crazy to you. There are so many of them that it's hard to know where to start.

Were you one of the ordinary people who looked at COVID regulations and rules and thought these make no sense at all? Did you look at people wearing two or three masks and rubber gloves to do their shopping and think that these people have lost their minds?

You weren't alone. Millions of us were thinking it was all insane and looking at the way people reacted and were told to react with complete bemusement. We saw the old couples separated by glass barriers in the nursing homes and thought it was stupid and cruel. We saw the "indoor-outdoor" plastic bubble extensions to restaurants in New York and thought it was mad. We saw the plastic screens (open at the sides) that were somehow supposed to block a virus in the air.

We thought that we had the right to decide whether we took a dangerous medical experiment or not.

We looked at people banging pots and pans for the National Health Service at set times in the UK as people who had gone crazy and didn't seem to know it.

But perhaps it wasn't COVID and all its madness that made you, the ordinary citizen, think that the Western world is getting madder and madder.

Perhaps it was the way everyone suddenly seemed to believe that the world is coming to an end, and we were all going to die because of climate change and that terrifying, horrific, previously never addressed genocidal crime of…cows farting.

Maybe you wondered why world leaders were suddenly listening to an autistic Swedish teenager who had skipped school? Maybe that seemed weird? Who was Greta? Where had she come from? Why the hell did anyone care about what she was saying? Why was the United Nations inviting her to speak to them?

Or maybe what really brought home to you how insane the mainstream had become was the running campaign of hatred against Donald Trump or the way a maddened and brainwashed middle class in Britain all started wrapping themselves in an EU flag and pretending that leaving the EU would reduce Britain to a Mad Max wasteland with cannibal gangs fighting over the last few dwindling resources?

Maybe ordinary parents—parents just like you, parents objecting to their kids being groomed and subjected to chemical and surgical gender reassignment—being labeled as domestic terrorists made you feel that everything was insane and upside down?

Perhaps you don't see why you should use imaginary pronouns or treat a man dressed as a woman as a woman based on the pure insistence on a delusion?

You might be an ordinary Jewish person in the West wondering how the hell we got back to the point where Jews are being chased across campuses and threatened with violence…by people claiming to be anti-fascists and anti-racists.

You might wonder whether experiments in geo-engineering to block out the sun are as insane as they seem on the surface and how serious institutions could contemplate schemes that look so much like the plot of a James Bond movie. Or why anyone would deliberately engineer viruses with an 80 percent or 100 percent fatality rate in humans.

The point is that on a whole host of separate issues—on borders and immigration, racial politics, gender, culture, war and which wars are necessary, parental rights and individual rights, and the planet itself—your experience as an ordinary citizen has been to see an increasingly vast gulf open up between your opinions and the opinions of the ruling class and their client professional servants (such as technocratic experts, hired scientists, academics and journalists).

And while this has happened, many of the basic things you thought everyone was in agreement on, like your right to step outside and walk around if you want to or to have a vote and see it respected, are gone.

You might look at our countries and our media and think not just that the world is going mad but also that its deliberate and malign. And the things they are doing are so crazy and so far removed from what you want or would vote for that these reactions can no longer be dismissed by them calling you names or labeling you as an extremist. You might realize that the entire Western world doesn't suddenly start praising a violent thug for his skin color or depicting dead kings of England as black without there being some kind of concerted effort behind that. You might recognize that Pride flags suddenly appearing on the side of police cars and buses also suggests a deliberate effort to push a certain agenda.

And you might look at how crazy it is that your joke or opinion to a friend on the internet gets policed but millions of people illegally entering your country do not. You might look at the growing anarchy on the streets with violent looters and rapists never being charged while your thoughts and speech are being subjected to ever greater control and realize that none of the people in charge are on your side at all.

You might question why they get to support terrorists like Hamas, and that's normal, while you aren't allowed to vote for the party of your choice, and that's considered normal too.

Because the end result of these contradictions, of seeing these things all around you getting worse and worse, is that you eventually realize that *they* are the extremists. Not you. Not ordinary people. The people in charge are the extremists. The media are the extremists. *The people you are told are more respectable and more moderate than you are the extremists.*

And somehow you have to survive what they are doing, what your political and media class want, and what institutions and transnational bodies like the UN and the World Economic Forum are putting in place.

Somehow you have to try and preserve your civil liberties, your individual rights, and your little patch of the world without being driven to despair and swamped beneath the tsunami of madness all these people who already have more money and more power than you do seem to have decided to inflict on you.

So, who are "they" exactly?

Well, that's where we get to talking about what Globalism is, and who Globalists are.

THE PATHOLOGY OF YOUR ENEMY

GLOBALISTS ARE OFTEN CLUSTER B PERSONALITIES

(Note: A version of this chapter first appeared as one of my Substack articles: "The Cluster B Revolution" on August 14, 2024).

*P*sychology Today describes Cluster B personality disorders as follows:

> There are four personality disorders within Cluster B. They include antisocial personality disorder, borderline personality disorder, histrionic personality disorder, and narcissistic personality disorder. Though the disorders can occur alone, symptoms and diagnoses can overlap, either within one cluster or across several.
>
> Antisocial personality disorder describes a pattern of behavior in which an individual regularly violates the physical or emotional rights of others; behaves recklessly, violently, or deceitfully; and lacks remorse for any harm caused to others

> Borderline personality disorder is a condition characterized by chronic mood instability, unstable behavior, difficulty maintaining personal relationships (often caused by an intense fear of abandonment), and frequent instances of self-harm or suicidal behavior.

People with histrionic personality disorder are self-centered, constantly seek attention, and may behave or dress in inappropriate or seductive ways. They are highly dramatic and may display extreme emotions in public,

> Narcissistic personality disorder, thought to affect anywhere from 1 to 6 percent of the population, is characterized by grandiosity; a need for excessive admiration; a lack of empathy; and manipulative, self-centered, or demanding behavior.

In the Edgar Allan Poe short story "The System of Doctor Tarr and Professor Fether" the narrator visits an insane asylum somewhere in France. The asylum is famed for a new method of dealing with the insane, which is called "the system of soothing." This system is noted for the humanity of its approach and its departure from the confinement of lunatics because of its concern that they should not be mistreated in any way. While kept under constant surveillance, the inmates of the asylum are free to roam where they please and do as they please. Their delusions are not challenged but accommodated. One of the staff explains the system's indulgence of the insane as the chief method of their cure:

"We contradicted no fancies which entered the brains of the mad. On the contrary, we not only indulged but encouraged them; and many of our most permanent cures have been thus effected.... We have had men, for example, who fancied themselves chickens. The cure was, to insist upon the thing as a fact—to accuse the patient of stupidity in not sufficiently perceiving it to be a fact—and thus to refuse him any other diet for a week than that which properly appertains to a chicken."

Can you sense where I am going with this? A system that purports to "be kind," but indulges insanity? Let us make the comparison explicit.

In the UK in 2023, there were widespread reports claiming that a pupil was identifying as a cat and being indulged by the school in doing so. A video was uploaded to TikTok from a year-eight class (generally comparable to the seventh grade in the US) in Rye, East Sussex, of a pupil discussion on gender and identity. While the video did not show any pupil claiming to be a cat, it did show a pupil asserting that gender is binary and claims to the contrary are crazy in the same way that calling yourself a cat or a cow because you "identified" with that is crazy.

Even debunking attempts by papers such as *The Guardian* were clear on the response from the teacher to what would once have been considered a common sense argument:

"A teacher is heard telling the student that their views were 'despicable,' threatening to report them to a senior colleague and saying: 'if you don't like it, you need to go to a different school.'"

In other words, while it could not be confirmed that a pupil was identifying as a cat, it was confirmed (even by those attempting to crush the story) that in a British school today saying that someone identifying as a cat is crazy was described as being "despicable" and effectively resulted in being bullied and threatened by a teacher for touching on these issues (in what could be described as a bluntly realist manner).

Meanwhile, the "debunking" attempt also had to admit that Katharine Birbalsingh of Michaela Community School, in the same area, was stating that she had heard of several cases where pupils were identifying as animals or as bizarre identities such as "a gay male hologram." Birbalsingh was interviewed by *The Telegraph* on these cases.

In Australia the year before this British "crazy cat" controversy, *The Herald Sun* reported that a schoolgirl was identifying as a cat in Melbourne, and again was being indulged by teachers to do so. A Google AI summary of these and similar cases (which may itself be suspect but is based on searching all available reports) says this:

"A teenage schoolgirl in Australia has identified as a cat and is allowed to exhibit feline behavior at her private school. The school's approach is to support the student as long as her behavior does not disrupt the learning environment.... The incident is part of a broader trend, with other schools in Australia and the US reporting similar cases of students identifying as animals, often referred to as "furries".... The school's statement emphasizes its commitment to supporting students with unique needs and identities, while ensuring a distraction-free learning environment."

Now we all know the limitations of AI, but the thing that rings true for me is the language given regarding the school's statement. That "commitment to supporting students with unique needs" line is identical to a countless number of policy documents and teaching guidelines I encountered when I was briefly in the profession twenty years ago. It reads as if they wrote it; it sounds like it's lifted from a real thing.

Oddly, the inhuman quality of the way modern pedagogy describes things becomes the strongest argument that an AI sentence was created by a human being (albeit a brainwashed one).

That immediate absurdist self-contradiction, the hilarious juxtaposition of allowing a pupil to behave like a cat while asserting that doing so will also ensure a "distraction-free learning environment" also seems very human, at least in terms of the delusional humans who now rule the world.

Primitive as AI is, it is learning fast, and it takes a real human being to talk so much like a humorless machine. AI is already a little bit better than that at pretending to be human. It's only woke teachers who speak such lengthy chunks of bland, professional insanity—or any equivalent state or corporate writer of real policy guidelines.

All of this is, of course, Poe's "system of soothing" in practice.

It is what the Western world did for real when it decided that insane asylums were cruel Victorian torture chambers and never anything better than that, or when it decided thanks to Michel Foucault, and similar

French thinkers, that definitions of insanity were simply the powerful demonizing and controlling the powerless.

For Foucault and his ilk, "insanity" did not refer to actual mental conditions that might need constraint but simply to a white patriarchal system of oppression where anyone who threatened the moral codes of the ruling class would be pathologized and removed from society. (To be fair, it's true that several totalitarian regimes have done this, most notably the Soviets who had a habit of deciding that dissidents were mentally ill, but the postmodern notion that *all* such judgments are merely brutal operations of power networks defending themselves is *itself* an example of irrational thinking and itself influenced by Marxist ideology.)

Here's the kind of sensible social advice great French minds like Foucault, perceiving insanity as merely a label of oppression, end up asserting (from Foucault's *Mental Illness and Psychology*):

"[Man] could and must experience himself negatively, through hate and aggression."

That's helpful, isn't it?

Poe's "soothing system" is, in fact, pretty close to the orthodoxy of modern approaches to mental illness and especially close to the curious modern phenomenon whereby having a mental illness becomes a matter of pride and a thing to be boasted about as a marker of courage. Dealing with issues privately is now described as inherently dangerous, while public concern about bizarre and anti-social behavior, which may be mental illness, is described as a "social stigma" (as if it's bizarre to be wary of people who are behaving erratically or acting irrationally).

"Ending the stigma of mental illness" has become *celebrating* mental illness, and some researchers begin to sound as if having traumatic experiences that inflict psychological damage is something we should encourage. Having a mental illness is a superpower that makes you more intelligent and a better human being and, importantly, more politically progressive. A 2021 study about stressful life events and their connection to depression in the *Journal of Affective Disorders* described the results in this fashion:

"We found that stressful life events were significantly associated with openness to experience; that participants with a history of depression exhibited higher levels of openness; and that openness to experience was related to overall intelligence."

Wow! So really horrible life experiences that lead to lifelong depression and anxiety disorders are actually great! By this logic, we should make sure that everyone suffers lots of horrible and negative experiences as often as possible…which might explain many of the policies "open-minded" liberals enact.

They are going to make our lives so shitty that we all have the depression superpower.

What is this openness to experience anyway, and is it really as good and intelligent as it's being described here? It could definitely mean openness to radical new social ideas, which, again, one side of politics will interpret as automatically a good thing but the other side of politics may spot as being loaded with risks and dangers.

But is it really the case that the most intelligent people are open to trying everything, or does that actually describe the recklessly stupid among us? I feel pretty good about the innate dumb conservatism that has prevented me from being open to very extreme sex fetishes or self-damaging acts like trying heroin and crack just to experience something new. I have a feeling these limits have helped me in life, rather than not.

And my natural instinct (now call me crazy for this) is to try to avoid really awful experiences if I can and to want my children to avoid those really awful experiences too.

According to the newly inverted moral orthodoxy *and* the way social capital is now gained by having a mental illness or mental health issues of one kind or another, this commonsense risk aversion is now more pathological than thinking you are a cat.

Remember Poe saying, "We contradicted no fancies which entered the brains of the mad. On the contrary, we not only indulged but encouraged them"? Remember "the cure was, to insist upon the thing as a fact—to accuse the patient of stupidity in not sufficiently perceiving it to be a fact"?

After his organization awarded a gold Olympic medal to a man for beating up a woman, International Olympic Committee President Thomas Bach said that there was no "scientifically solid method" for determining whether an athlete is a man or a woman.

Only, of course, there is. The scientifically solid method was applied by the International Boxing Association, which determined that Imane Khelif is a male with a rare condition, rather than a woman. Khelif was tested and found to have XY chromosomes. This finding matched photos of Khelif from Algeria dressed as a man and apparently living as a man, as well as matching the evidence of the senses when people without ideological brainwashing look at Imane Khelif.

Everything in objective reality and real science confirms that this athlete is a man. The conclusion reached by normal people using their eyes is the same as the conclusion reached by scientific tests to determine gender. And it's the same as the conclusion reached by some of the female boxers forced to compete against this man.

Only ideological indoctrination (perversely, an "openness to new experience," which is *delusional* experience) suggests that this athlete must be considered a woman.

And the more powerful institution, of course (the International Olympic Committee) is the one that decided to support the delusion and "insist upon the thing as a fact."

It's with so much insistence, indeed, that one of the world's foremost biologists can be forced to climb down from asserting basic biological facts. A person with XY chromosomes is a man. Richard Dawkins knew this and shared a meme stating it. Imane Khelif threatened legal action for "harassment." Dawkins deleted the social media post where he had expressed the *scientific truth* in the field that has been his particular area of expertise for decades.

So much for "respecting the science" on gender. It is the delusion that demands respect and is legally enforced today.

All this, though, is merely the tip of the iceberg. Inanities like pretending there's no "scientific" way to tell the difference between a man and a woman are just the most obvious peak of the insanity by which everything is conducted today. The genital mutilation of children for profit that calls itself the protection of their gender identity is particularly obscene and foul given the innocence of those being harmed, but its reflective of a process that occurs in Poe's story and that his narrator gradually comes to realize.

The "soothing system," the narrator finds, has been abandoned. Now, inmates are confined. Inmates are restricted. Inmates are punished.

The narrator is surprised by this change. But he's more surprised when he discovers the real reason for it: The lunatics who were being treated with the "soothing system" that had encouraged their delusions then violently and bloodily took over the asylum. The people he encountered as staff are the former inmates, still irreparably insane. The people he encountered as patients are the original staff members, after the revolutionary overthrow.

It's the short story that is the best ever expression of the phrase, "The inmates are running the asylum."

And it's the story of our entire culture too.

In 2007, Gallup conducted a series of more than four thousand interviews that found that Republicans had significantly better mental health than Democrats.

In 2013, BuzzFeed, the leftist media organization, tried to debunk this finding by commissioning an extensive mental health poll of their own. Unfortunately for them, their own leftist poll likewise confirmed that Democrats suffered mental illness notably more than Republicans in almost every category. Overall, their findings indicated that Democrats were twice as likely as Republicans to be mentally ill.

In 2020, yet another large-scale survey, this time with more than eight thousand respondents, also confirmed that those on the political left were significantly more likely to have been diagnosed with a mental illness.

In 2020, the Pew Research Center examined the same issue. Their findings were that a whopping 62 percent of people who described themselves as "very liberal" or "liberal" had also been told by a doctor that they have a mental health condition (as compared with just 26 percent of conservatives).

Studies and surveys consistently return the same results—mental health is getting worse, not better, under the "soothing system" of sympathy and encouragement, mental health is at its worst in those who vote for left-wing parties, mental health is worse for women than it is for men, and mental health issues are particularly associated with those who embrace very progressive or radical causes and those who claim to have unusual gender identities.

Even during COVID, the people who were most severely affected in terms of their mental health were the people *who most strongly supported the irrational measures that were supposed to protect them*. Media-led COVID scaremongering inflicted mental harm *particularly* on those who supported it. Democrat COVID fanatics victimized themselves (as well as everyone else).

When people on the Left are asked to describe their mental health, they consistently cite more mental health problems and more interaction with mental health services than people on the Right do. Despite the drawbacks of polling and surveys, these are not results that are being manipulated since they have been funded and conducted by both sides of the political aisle, each time reaching the same conclusions.

It is not something being ascribed to them by their political enemies. It is something they describe about themselves. In the most recent of these surveys (as of mid 2024), 38 percent of people who described themselves as Marxists also confirmed they had diagnosed mental health issues. The patterns are clear and repeat every time, regardless of who is doing or funding the research.

In a highly illuminating article penned in 2023, Christopher F. Rufo argued that modern events in the United States, in particular, could be understood by referencing Cluster B personality disorders. Rufo pointed out that the psychopathologies of Cluster B personality disorders (the narcissist, the borderline, the histrionic, and the antisocial) are now prevalent everywhere. That rather than being private issues dealt with in consultation with a psychiatrist, or shameful problems whose sufferers were "relegated to the fringes of society," these pathologies *are* our society today. They are especially prevalent in our social and financial elite, and they are shaping our institutions and our culture.

The lunatics have made the whole of society their asylum, and the rest of us are trapped in their delusional vision. That is the underlying explanation of why so many of these people cannot be reasoned with, why they move to more and more totalitarian responses and more and more censorship and authoritarian control, and why they are so blind to the flaws and crimes of the things they support. We are talking about *delusional people with power over rational people*, disgusted by any rational rejection of their delusional policies and lashing out in response whenever either their power or their sanity is questioned.

I once described, many years ago, dating one of these people and how her behavior pushed me away. I described a little of what it is like to date someone with a serious personality disorder (functionally hidden until you are in the intimacy of a relationship). My argument there was that if you look at how the Democrats have reacted to Trump and now to Elon Musk and if you look at how mainstream media applies a savage and delusional hatred to both men (which personality disorder sufferers elsewhere adopt as their own feelings), what you see is exactly what you would see from a spurned Cluster B partner whose behavior has caused the rift but who can never know themselves enough to blame themselves for it.

We are essentially being ruled by a Cluster B elite of narcissistic, hysteric, histrionic actors (Robert De Niro types) and their lower-level antisocial minions. These disorders are the standard psychological profile of those who are at the top of our system and of those most likely to support them, from the Antifa street thug to the white female journalist to the corporate suit to the Silicon Valley billionaire—and especially those delusional enough to suddenly decide that Kamala Harris is their mother goddess and Tim Walz their father.

What should one make of the kinds of people who post this on X:

> I said maybe
>
> You're gonna be the one that saves us
>
> And after all
>
> You're our Wonder Walz

Together with a picture of a beaming Walz being hugged by children? Or what should one make of the Cluster B who posted this on social media?

"Tim Walz is my dad; Kamala's my fun aunt who lives next door. They just found out I'm being bullied by the shittiest kid in my class, JD. When they try to talk to his dad, Don, it becomes clear he's the real problem. They go back to their car; Kamala pulls out her cop badge, Tim grabs his old baseball bat. They walk to Don's porch. As Tim reaches for the doorbell they look at each other and smile. This is going to be fun."

That last example, which managed to pack more disturbing delusion into five sentences than Poe got into his whole short story, was posted by Aaron Regunberg, a Democrat politician and a grown man of thirty-four (as of 2024), who is a lawyer and served as the member of the Rhode Island House of Representatives for the Fourth District between 2015 and 2019. And he fantasized about being a bullied little boy and having his party leaders be his imaginary family that engages in horror movie "fun," like killing the neighbors.

Their hatred of Trump or Musk or you is the hatred of the Cluster B ex with a kitchen knife in her hand screaming, "How *dare* you leave me!" People like Regunberg, or the thousands of other Democrat account holders who were upset that Trump survived an assassination attempt, prove my point far better than my words can. Reading them is both darkly hilarious and pretty chilling.

But that crazed voice, that Cluster B outpouring of delusion and hate, is also the voice in which pretty much every mainstream news article now speaks. Insane hate at Trump or Musk, insane instant love at Kamala and Walz. Just check out how many "Tim Walz is my dad" fantasies were being pressed by mainstream media as soon as he was selected as Kamala's VP running mate. *The Washington Post*, *The New York Times*, *Newsweek*, and *The Independent* all echoed Regunberg's delusion.

The shrill voice on the street screaming rage over Donald Trump's election in 2016, the angry imprecations of Democrat judges in 2024, and the style of thought and speech we hear from Globalists at all different levels of power and influence repeatedly suggest Cluster B personality disorders, especially the lack of empathy and narcissistic grandiosity personality traits.

Of course, this is not to say that everyone on the opposite side of politics from us is insane. It is to say that Globalist ideology especially appeals to, allows excuses for, and encourages disproportionate mental health issues. All of these issues may be especially prevalent among the most powerful and socially influential Globalists you can think of (whose wealth, influence, and social position protects them from the personal negative consequences from these Cluster B personality traits). These people, in turn, have a vested practical and psychological interest in normalizing their own traits in the rest of society.

The "me, me, me" histrionic screech is the truly authentic voice of Globalism, once the dishonest layers of alleged noble intentions are stripped away, and it sits there underneath the policy documents of the United Nations or the World Health Organization just as much as it sits in the minds of billionaire philanthropists, corporate executives, and the owners of Disney.

You do not need to keep wondering how the world became so crazy once you realize that the ideology being followed by the most powerful and being applied by them to the rest of us rewards people for delusions while punishing people for refusing to endorse delusions. Our society went insane because many of our leaders are, quite literally, insane and because some forms of insanity allow a person to function and prosper even while doing and thinking irrational things.

Ultimately, what Poe described in fiction has happened to us in reality and to the Western world as a whole:

"One fine morning the keepers found themselves pinioned hand and foot, and thrown into the cells, where they were attended, as if they were the lunatics, by the lunatics themselves, who has assumed the offices of the keepers."

We are not fighting a sane opponent. We are disputing the fate of the world with delusional lunatics acting out their "Daddy" fantasies.

Unfortunately, they have been far better than their more rational opponents in creating networks of power and influence, serving their exclusive interests.

WHAT IS GLOBALISM?

> World first and forever, nation never.
>
> —Abhijit Naskar, *Visvavatan: 100 Demilitarization Sonnets*

> The present window of opportunity, during which
> a truly peaceful and interdependent world order
> might be built, will not be open for too long.
>
> —David Rockefeller, speaking to the UN Business
> Council on September 14, 1994

Globalism is the dominant political ideology of the Western world today. It's a set of views and attitudes that nearly everyone shares in Western mainstream politics, media, and business, especially at the upper levels and in senior management and administrative positions. In *Rise of the New World Order: The Culling of Man* J. Michael Thomas Hays asserts that these words were also voiced by Rockefeller at the same time as the above quote "We are on the verge of a global transformation. All we need is the right major crisis and the nations will accept the New World Order." While unconfirmed, it is a telling example of the difference between a benign and a malign reading of Globalist intent. Mainstream media invariably accept the notion that Globalists have the very best wishes for the rest of mankind, while alternative media sources almost always take whatever benign hope Globalists express as the cover of much more sinister intentions.

Every time you read *any* mainstream magazine or journal or newspaper, you will be getting a Globalist perspective on whatever topic is being discussed. Every time you watch *any* mainstream news channel, you will be receiving Globalist opinions and prejudices often presented as factual news and objective analysis.

In many ways, the words "Globalist" and "mainstream" are synonymous, because Globalist ideology suffuses the Western world's mainstream now in the same way that Islam suffuses and dominates the Islamic world, or the way that Christianity used to suffuse every attitude and idea (and political approach) in the Western world. In some senses, especially when you think about the irrational nature of many of its attitudes and commandments and the fanaticism of its adherents for ideas and people that would not rationally inspire such devotion, it might be best understood as a religion that manifests through politics rather than as a purely political movement.

This is not, of course, how Globalists see themselves. Many of them are firm atheists or secularists, and one of their assumptions is that they are more rational and less religious than their opponents. Many Globalists are likely to have huge contempt and disrespect for Christianity without realizing that this is because Christianity provides a traditional moral framework they are seeking to destroy and replace (and which, in terms of the attitudes of the ruling and professional classes, they already have replaced). But this very dislike of Christianity and association of Christianity with ignorance and backwardness is a reflection of the fact that Globalism is in, some ways, simply a rival faith, a belief system in which automatic "truths" are held by means of magical thinking rather than rational analysis.

It is necessary to understand that Globalism is not just a political movement. Rather, it is a belief system that some adherents hold as an article of faith. It is a belief system you do not share and that is often directly opposed to your traditional beliefs, which it frequently views with contempt. Understanding that your Globalist media and political class are using all their power and influence to promote an alien and rival belief system allows you to comprehend the enormity of the gulf between your attitudes and theirs.

It works through politics, but it inspires fanaticism. Things that are assumed to be true are based on faith, rather than things that have been proved or can be proved. This is, ironically, especially true for those adherents of Globalism that are the *most* dismissive of religious faith and the most prone to thinking that "The Science" and rationalism is the foundation of their worldview.

As we saw during COVID, what Globalists believe in is *not* scientific inquiry, analysis, and research (they suppressed any part that reached different conclusions). They don't truly value or honor the scientific method. They don't reach rational conclusions based on evidence, and they don't allow a free speech environment in which *other* scientists and experts can dispute Globalist policies and responses, which only *claim* to have a scientific consensus. The very fact that *consensus* has become part of their mantra is, of course, a classic logical fallacy. It is their appeal to authority—which would have been the same basis on which many factually accurate but radically original scientific breakthroughs were disputed by prior "experts" who suppressed knowledge and discoveries—that did not suit the dominant cosmologies and moral systems of that period (which are always the worldviews of the ruling class).

In other words, the fact that a huge number of dissenting scientific experts were dismissed and silenced during COVID while baseless and inherently irrational approaches were adopted and mandated (instead of these things being fairly and properly assessed in an objective fashion), shows that Globalist views can be at their *least scientific* when they invoke "The Science" or use compliant and paid scientific professionals to press their case. What we are dealing with in those instances is *Scientism*, a *faith* in the pronouncements of anyone with the right degree and a lab coat *when expressing views already held by the ruling class that pays them.*

A typically Globalist take on "The Science" was expressed in a Twitter post by Eric Sorensen on November 30, 2022, which became a meme used by both sides of the COVID debate. Sorensen considered he had delivered a devastating blow towards anti-COVID policy commentators but really expressed a sort of confused, ignorant but all-encompassing love of being directed and ordered towards certain conclusions by anyone in authority:

"If you disagree with scientists about science, it's not really a disagreement. You're actually just incorrect. Science is not truth, it's the process of finding the truth. When science evolves, it didn't lie to you, it learned more."

Such expressions of total devotion to men in white coats, no matter what they happen to order or promote, is, of course, deeply irrational. It allows no such thing as civil liberty or a moral code to intrude on or limit Globalist scientists in any way. It ignores the difference between disputing a confirmed fact and disputing an alleged one, or a political policy in reaction to that fact. Most obviously of all, it ignores what it is saying itself—if science is not truth but a process of discovering truth, there should be no objection to anyone as part of that process looking at the evidence themselves or disputing the evidence where it seems to be debatable. In sum, it's simply an attempt to confer "absolute truth" on existing authorities, a step that always comes before punishing people who share any genuine *inconvenient truth*.

Globalist claims of *owning* the scientific consensus and being *purely rational* are, therefore, themselves aspects of their irrational nature and key elements of the faith-based nature of Globalism—its true nature is presented as a kind of creed we are all supposed to bow down to and accept rather than a thing really reflecting the evidence and objective reality.

A true respect for science would mean allowing dissenting scientists to speak and doing things like properly testing experimental gene therapy medicines before putting them in most human beings on the planet. It would not reduce itself to slogans like "Respect the Science," and it would not mandate things that are themselves irrational (like wearing masks that don't work or like obeying distancing rules that were simply made up with no scientific basis).

One of the very first things we must do in challenging Globalist attitudes is to know that they will *always* claim to be rational, be based in evidence and science, and represent moderate, standard, professional opinions supported by expertise and research studies. That's true of Globalist attitudes on social matters, gender, race, and everything from foreign policy to educational approaches to dietary choices and food policy. It's what we see when Globalist policies are advocated for in terms of the energy sources we use just as much as when Globalist policies are advocated for dealing with pandemics.

And in case after case, we can find that the Globalist position ultimately depends on *articles of faith* and pure assumptions rather than real, concrete, indisputable evidence. We find that the position and policy is reached *first* and the science and research *follows*, using enormous private or public (or public-private partnership) spending to *justify* the already decided upon position. All while contradictory evidence—no matter how expert, scientific, logical, or rational it is—is starved of funding or banned from public view. In many instances, we will see contradictory evidence ignored *after* it has proven some Globalist policy as disastrous or deeply irrational or harmful to the public (or all three).

So, the very first part of our resistance is in *never* accepting an argument by authority or an argument by alleged consensus (a version of the argument by popularity logical fallacy) as the basis on which a Globalist policy is accurate and should be followed. These are the views of the ruling class that are being imposed on us to benefit the ruling class. *Of course*, they can pay for technical support and research weighted to favor their position. *Of course*, they can find people in lab coats prepared to conduct dishonest or biased research supportive of their position. We are talking about the people who *already* have control of most institutions and most sources of funding.

Several areas of research now *only exist* because Globalist assumptions are dominant. The vast majority of experts and professionals are not going to admit that the branch of inquiry they work in is thoroughly corrupt or solely exists to produce specific results. It takes an unusual and brave climate researcher to say that his field is riddled with assumptions and errors based on false reasoning, bad computer modeling, and people paying his colleagues (and him) to reach predetermined conclusions. Few scientists will put their name to research that shows that all their professional friends and colleagues are in on a kind of moneymaking grift or even advance a paper they know they won't get funding for because it says or proves something uncomfortable.

With no conspiratorial intent, even, people do what their bosses want, and people produce what they are expected to produce to get paid, get fresh funding, and get promoted or praised.

Thousands of ordinary people lower down the line who are *just doing their job* can be persuaded to do increasingly terrible things if those things are described everywhere as normal, necessary, and rational, which is what we saw with ordinary doctors and nurses during COVID. Their senior colleagues and professional institutions were telling them a certain approach was necessary and vital. Their unions were largely doing the same and refusing to back those who had doubts. Their governments and employers were both demanding they follow a certain approach and paying them to do so. Their TV channels and the news they followed was praising them for that approach. It was made increasingly clear to them that if they advocated a different approach or questioned the approach followed by their clinic, hospital, or institution, they would then be fired.

So millions of trained doctors and nurses, those best positioned to have some professional awareness that the things that were being done were *not* necessary and normal—to be aware, for example, of *the difference between a vaccine and a gene therapy* or to be aware of the Hippocratic oath or of the normal timelines of safe and adequately tested research and development for a new vaccine—were the *least* likely to question these things. Their livelihood depended on *not* questioning these things. And so, they went ahead and were the people putting the needles in arms. Those who did question were those with *unusual degrees of courage* and critical thinking skills, rather than simply those with the right *professional degrees*.

This example might seem a long way from answering the question of what Globalism is or who is a Globalist. But it's vital as an illustration of some very important things.

Globalist attitudes don't just affect a small number of people. They affect everyone in the Western world and beyond. They are as global in their effects as in their ambitions. And Globalist attitudes and policies aren't just enforced by people who are themselves ideological Globalists. They are enforced and enacted by millions upon millions of non-Globalists who are just doing their jobs, just obeying the rules, just following the crowd. These are people who may have never even heard of Globalism and never have seen a connection between very different areas of politics and culture, which Globalists are shaping and radically impacting upon.

How many nurses would resist a policy if it meant losing their job? Not many. How many of those nurses would understand that the fact that their hospital enforced a particular approach to COVID has some connection to the fact that their hospital also has strict diversity and inclusion policies, a Pride poster in the canteen, and a diversity officer (or several)? Would they see those separate things as *all* being mandated from above and *all* representing Globalist views? No. And certainly not if that nurse then turned on mainstream news to understand the world and what was happening in it.

But in everything that nurse doesn't connect and maybe doesn't consider that much at all, everything that nurse was accepting as normal, and everything that nurse was obeying to keep her job, she would be following Globalist set boundaries, rules, procedures, and policies. She would be living a Globalist-mandated life, both professionally and personally, just to be a functioning and accepted member of society and just to earn a living and pay for a house.

This is what it means to live within a society shaped by a dominant ideology, even one that most ordinary people aren't worrying about, talking about, or that are aware and knowledgeable about. Especially when that ideology is both faith-based and extremely politically active. *Globalists are pushing Globalism into every single aspect of life, and they are doing it from the top of society down*. Globalism is an incredibly *active* force, and its agents have both massive profit motives and massive psychological and ideological triggers to keep pushing, keep enforcing, and keep spreading their ideology through everything. The average jihadist is no more determined about spreading his faith through whatever means necessary than the average Globalist is. Many other people, many non-Globalists, are people who have to go along with it to survive, while some can't even spot that it is happening *because it is already all around them.*

So, if it's active in so many different ways, if we are receiving Globalist direction and instruction on the food we eat, the science we believe, the gender and sexual politics we consider normal, the energy sources we use, and the whole culture, structure, and fundamental beliefs of our society, how are we to distinguish what Globalism itself is? How are we to recognize what the core of the ideology is separate to the various things it supports or pushes? Because without that core, we are just listing a whole series of things we don't like. What's the core of Globalism?

Well, a few very simple basics can define it, from which all the rest derives. And those basics are these:

1. Globalism is the political ideology and faith system of the ruling class in the Western world. Globalism is an ideology of the elites, and the professional classes to serve elite interests. As such, it is deeply distrustful of the ordinary citizen and the general public (who can't be trusted to provide the "right" votes for the "right" people).
2. Globalism believes that all the most important issues are best understood in a global context and best dealt with by globally active institutions.
3. Globalism sees purely national responses as inefficient and incapable of addressing the things that matter, as well as seeing nationalism as inherently evil and something to be moved beyond.
4. Because of the above, Globalism always transfers more and more power and resources to transnational bodies like the EU,

the United Nations, the International Monetary Fund, and similar bodies. It always advocates pooling resources internationally, sharing agreed aims and objectives, and following the same policies globally at the direction of transnational bodies. These measures both increase the power of the elite and lessen the power of the individual citizen and the general populace.

5. Globalism sees a single-world government, where every policy is aligned throughout the globe, as both inevitable and beneficial.
6. Globalism sees populism as a dangerous, extremist, and regressive force, which only opposes Globalist policies out of malice and ignorance or due to the demagoguery and "misinformation" of populist leaders.
7. Globalism is socially and culturally radical, supporting "progressive" leftist ideas on gender, sexuality, family, identity, race, and social morality as a cultural "new normal" on these issues. It is radically libertarian in terms of sexual kinks and even perversions that were previously taboo or widely considered disgusting or evil, adopting a bland and non-judgmental approach even towards taboos too extreme to actively promote (like child abuse).
8. At the same time, Globalism is severely repressive and authoritarian towards even still standard attitudes and traditional moralities that oppose or threaten it. It favors authoritarian measures against nationalism and populism, or even many general conservative attitudes, and it doesn't recognize traditional civil liberties and democratic boundaries on what can be imposed on its own civilians.
9. Globalist policies always serve the financial and social interests of the elite, and always negatively impact the finances and lives of the non-elite.
10. Globalist policies are both technocratic and heavily technologically based, requiring new technology or resulting in new and transhuman technological approaches with the abandonment of working, tested, and safe technologies that already exist.

These ten points are not the sum of Globalism but the core. If we look at other Globalist policies and attitudes, we can see that, in each case, they tend to be aspects of the above.

Take, as an example, the Globalist advocacy of climate change and its demand for a "net zero policy" that transitions the entire world economy away from oil, "greenhouse gases," and "fossil fuels" in favor of new energy sources like wind and solar power. This allegedly Green set of policies could easily have been placed on the list above. Globalists believe in man-made change, and Globalists support the radical policy of "net zero" to fundamentally transform the entire economic model and energy supply basis of the world.

But not everyone who believes in the man-made climate change theory is a Globalist in their other attitudes, necessarily. Again, there are lots of ordinary people who believe in it. It may even be true, partially or to a limited extent (climate temperature may, on average, have risen slightly since modern records began, and human activity may possibly have contributed to that).

But it's actually as a consequence of those other core Globalist principles above that ordinary people can go around assuming the case for man-made climate change is settled, and the proposed measures for dealing with that are normal ones. Because it was only when the ruling class took these ideas seriously that wider society did. A few years back, the Green movement was not supported by all businesses or by most ordinary voters either. A misanthropic Green idea of human beings as a cancer on the Earth polluting everything and destroying the planet was an *extreme* position. Now, every mainstream organization takes up the role of apocalyptic messenger of doom regarding climate and does so in a deeply religious fashion. You can't check the weather report without *every* variation (or even temperatures and conditions perfectly standard for the season and place) being linked to climate change. If it's wet, it is due to climate change; if it's dry, it is due to climate change. A storm is climate change and so is a period with no significant winds. Temperatures that twenty years ago were just "summer" are now backlit with the flames of hell on weather report maps.

All of this is irrational on the surface and not normal. It's not rational or normal to think that cow farts are going to kill off all life as we know it and turn the American Midwest into a dustbowl worse than the '30s or turn the leafy parts of Kent (also known as the "Garden of England") into the Sahara Desert within a few generations. These ideas are mad fear-mongering ones, directly equivalent to hellfire and brimstone sermons, because they are both ludicrously apocalyptic and because they are linked to our normal behavior and supposed moral failings.

You flushed that toilet too many times. You made too many cups of coffee or tea. You drove a diesel or gasoline car. Therefore, the planet is dying, and you are killing it. *Your normal everyday existence is an ecological and environmental crime, and you are guilty,* as is the level of modern comfort you expect or the populist politician or the nation-state that doesn't adopt radical, allegedly Green proposals immediately.

The core Globalist characteristics described above are actually responsible for the adoption of "net zero" by Western governments and for the normalization of even the craziest and most apocalyptic fantasies in society at large. The turning point—when environmentalist activists who were once considered fringe weirdos and tree huggers that ordinary people laughed at then became leading environmentalist politicians and when every school pressing apocalyptic climate change literature on five-year-olds—*came when the elite adopted these views.*

The Globalist core is in the whole "net zero" agenda—there's a *global* problem that can only be solved by *global* solutions (core points two and four). Almost everyone in the mainstream ruling class believes and presses this idea of man-made climate change and this solution of a radical energy supply shift to solve it (core point one). "Net zero" demands new technology and the abandonment of working and efficient technology (core point ten). Climate change science and the computer modeling that provides the only scientific "evidence" for man-made climate change being potentially disastrous comes primarily from a transnational organization (the

Intergovernmental Panel on Climate Change, a subsidiary of the United Nations), which accords with the Globalist nature of the United Nations and the Globalist assumption that transnational bodies are the arbiters of truth and policy (core point four).

So here is the summary. The elite have this crazy new religion, this ideology they fanatically believe in, which they are pushing on everyone else. But this religion is also a vast con. It is about increasing their power and wealth, and that's why they push it and love it. They can simultaneously claim to be stopping pandemics or saving the planet *and* force you all to pay for vast government projects, giving money to the Green or "health" companies and new technologies they own and invest in. They save Mother Earth…but you pay for it. They save Ukraine…but you pay for it. They save the LGBTQ+ community…but you pay for it. They save the migrants, dreamers, and refugees…but you pay for it. They support democracy all around the world…but your sons fight the wars, and their sons sit on the boards of Rebuild Iraq Corp or Rebuild Ukraine Corp as they make vast profits, just as their sons sat on the boards of Bomb Iraq Corp and Bomb the Russians Corp as *they* made vast profits too.

Every thing that you look at and say "but that doesn't make any sense," from the mask on your face to the rainbow painted on the police car to the foreign war you don't actually care about to the new medicine you don't want to take to the crack addict being encouraged to shit in your street is doing two things:

It's making money for Globalists somehow, and it's costing or harming you somehow.

And *every* thing that the "great and the good" in our society, and the institutions and organizations at both the national level and the transnational level that they control, are promoting, enforcing, and demanding is something that can be disguised as rational or scientific or as progress or as compassion or as doing good, but in reality is only ever about making them *feel* good, *appear* good, or *get more* of their way and more money and power concentrated in their hands.

That's Globalism. A kind of religion of the self-interest of the elite, masquerading as a set of things done for beneficial or rational reasons.

All of which reduce your rights and steal your money or waste the public funds and the public effort that could be going to the *real* duties of government and the *real* wishes of the general populace.

So, these are the next questions:

> *How do we reduce the power these Globalists hold over us, and how do we live and thrive and survive as, often, powerless people when we are being bombarded with all the policies and all the propaganda that Globalists can throw at us?*

TURN OFF YOUR TELEVISION

> Sometimes I look around my living room, and the most real thing in the room is the television. It's bright and vivid, and the rest of my life looks drab. So I turn the damn thing off. That does it every time. Get my life back.
>
> —Michael Crichton, *Airframe*

> I should go so far as to say that embedded in the surrealistic frame of a television news show is a theory of anticommunication, featuring a type of discourse that abandons logic, reason, sequence and rules of contradiction. In aesthetics, I believe the name given to this theory is Dadaism; in philosophy, nihilism; in psychiatry, schizophrenia.
>
> —Neil Postman, *Amusing Ourselves to Death: Public Discourse in the Age of Show Business*

The news media and the government are entwined in a vicious circle of mutual manipulation, mythmaking, and self-interest. Journalists need crises to dramatize news, and government officials need to appear to be responding to crises. Too often, the crises are not really crises but joint fabrications. The two institutions have become so ensnared in a symbiotic web of

> lies that the news media are unable to tell the public what is true and the government is unable to govern effectively.
>
> —Peter Vanderwicken, summarizing Paul H. Weaver's *News and the Culture of Lying: How Journalism Really Works* in "Why the News is Not the Truth"

In 2013, in his last film role before his death following a sudden heart attack in 2014, British actor and comedian Rik Mayall starred in a strange, low-budget movie called *One by One*. Cowritten and directed by Diane Jessie Miller, the film was an unusual choice for an actor who was normally cast in comedy roles playing frantic, slapstick losers or larger-than-life, charismatic, amoral opportunists and with a comedic style described as "energetic post-punk." A much bigger name in the UK than the US, Mayall had been a force on the alternative comedy scene of the 1980s. He was the handsome half of a long-lasting comedy partnership with Ade Edmondson and a regular scene-stealing guest star or leading man in British comedy series of the early eighties and onwards, including *The Young Ones* (1982–4), *The Comic Strip Presents* (1983–2012), *The New Statesman* (1987–1994), *Bottom* (1991–1995) and *Believe Nothing* (2002).

To give American readers some idea of the blunt, heavy-handed, and often adolescent satire where Mayall made his reputation, his most famous roles had names like Alan Beresford B'Stard (a fictional Conservative member of Parliament in *The New Statesman*), Lord Flashheart (a *Blackadder* guest role), and Richard "Richie" Richard in *Bottom* (opposite Ade Edmondson as Eddie Hitler). Unlike many of his contemporaries, he made little effort to establish himself as a household name in the US, although he did star in the moderately successful and cult classic anarchic children's film *Drop Dead Fred* (1991), as well as winning a Primetime Emmy for his role as Toad in the TVC London–produced *The Willows in Winter* (1996).

In Britain, Mayall had a big following and a cachet of cool rebelliousness thanks to both the frenetic energy of his performances, his good looks, and his occasional political comments (largely of a standard fake caring-leftist direction, but more from an anarchist than socialist perspective). In many ways, taking on a serious role in a small movie about a café worker discovering that the world is on the brink of an apocalypse or a planned wipeout of much of the planet's population was a surprising move, but clearly the movie appealed to his anarchist and antiestablishment leanings. The interesting thing about *One by One* is that it directly addresses, unusually early, a few points that have, depending on your viewpoint, become either repeated conspiracy theory fantasies or truly worrying facts about the modern Globalist elite.

The film revolves around the idea that the most powerful people on the planet want to wipe out much of humanity in order to secure for themselves a "sustainable future" with far fewer mouths to feed. This depopulation agenda is, of course, something that our real-world global elites have been accused of subscribing to in various degrees. Certainly, as Elon Musk has noted, the urgent problem for much of the world is not overpopulation but population decline, with birth rates falling throughout the developed world and causing real problems already in places as diverse as Italy and Japan. At the same time, many of the things that Globalists support seem to be designed to reduce birth rates still further (increasing access to abortion, encouraging gay and nonbinary lifestyles, social and economic policies that make raising a family prohibitively expensive, reduction of parental rights, and encouragement of trans "gender affirmation," which, in reality, sterilizes children all suggest a desire to reduce population).

Whatever your views on depopulation and the more apocalyptic fictional claims in *One by One*, the other key part of the movie is the one we need to concentrate on here. Because as well as describing a genocidal plot by a psychopathic elite, *One by One* deals extensively with the topic of the media and its dishonesty.

The central point of the movie is that the main character lives in a mediated reality where things happen of which she is utterly unaware, and Mayall's character exists to be a sort of narrator describing the true reality to her. Like the *Matrix* films, but in a much more low-key and low-budget manner, or like many of the novels of Philip K. Dick, the film explores the concept of living in a fake reality, a reality constructed by the malign to keep the majority of us passive, docile, and incapable of resisting the essential parasitism of the elite and their increasingly insane plans for the future.

People are kept ignorant and uninformed by a constant diet of "news" and entertainment that relates less and less to any shared objective reality and more and more to the social pacification of a majority who are intended to be harmed. In this fiction, TV, cable, the news, the entertainment industry, Hollywood, and the newspapers are all there to cover the truth and distract from the truth. They are all there as an opium of the masses (as Karl Marx described religion), a mass distraction (like Roman circuses and gladiatorial contests), or as a constant source of propaganda and direction that shapes opinion and renders resistance towards the elite and their plans as something most people don't even consider.

One by One ends with these words from Mayall's character:

> "Viewers, you don't know who the cameraman is. You don't know why you are being made to see these things. Neither do I. You're seeing me. I can't even see you. I may be dead by the time you watch this. That you possibly don't know who's the man who's making things he wants you to see. Destroy your television sets now. You must listen to no orders. That's all I can tell you for this point of the matter."

There's a chilling resonance between fiction and reality sometimes, as with an actor saying "I may be dead by the time you watch this" in the last major role he took before dying unexpectedly. And people sometimes look for connections that can't be proven or that are false. But it's interesting that a conspiracy theory developed about this too, with some asserting that Mayall's death was a suspicious one. Without wishing to support that theory at all, I think it's worth mentioning that it exists given the context of (1) what the film he starred in is about and (2) what the world we live in has become.

Because *One by One* is telling us at least one certain truth and that is that we *do* live in a mediated reality. That is as true in our shared real world as it is in the reflection of that world in the movie. All of us live in a world saturated by the media in all its forms, and all of us find our views and opinions shaped by television and similar modern technologies, even more so since we developed the mobile phone and "the cloud," the search engine, and the social media companies. Recent developments in AI only increase and extend this reliance on technology and this mediation of technology between us and reality.

And that technology, of course, *is* controlled. That technology largely works according to the instructions of a small number of people in a small number of companies. Even the governments that interact with the corporations that control the technology will themselves be entrusting decision-making powers to a small number of people.

A handful of billionaires own almost all the mainstream media there is. A handful of governmental bureaucrats staff watchdog bodies and media oversight committees that supposedly set the rules that media and social media organizations must follow—but these watchdog organizations can, of course, possess their *own* agenda, the agenda of a political party that created or staffs them or the agenda of a *shared administrative class* that is in almost every case a Globalist administrative one.

Here is Tim Schwab in his *Columbia Journalism Review* article, "Journalism's Gates keepers," from August 21, 2020, (the COVID pandemic year, when the same people he discusses were shaping the global pandemic response) talking about the influence of just one of those billionaires, Bill Gates:

> I recently examined nearly twenty thousand charitable grants the Gates Foundation had made through the end of June and found more than $250 million going toward journalism. Recipients included news

operations like the BBC, NBC, Al Jazeera, *ProPublica*, *National Journal*, *The Guardian*, Univision, *Medium*, the *Financial Times*, *The Atlantic*, the Texas Tribune, Gannett, *Washington Monthly*, *Le Monde*, and the Center for Investigative Reporting; charitable organizations affiliated with news outlets, like BBC Media Action and *The New York Times*' Neediest Cases Fund; media companies such as Participant, whose documentary *Waiting for "Superman"* supports Gates's agenda on charter schools; journalistic organizations such as the Pulitzer Center on Crisis Reporting, the National Press Foundation, and the International Center for Journalists; and a variety of other groups creating news content or working on journalism, such as the Leo Burnett Company, an ad agency that Gates commissioned to create a "news site" to promote the success of aid groups. In some cases, recipients say they distributed part of the funding as subgrants to other journalistic organizations—which makes it difficult to see the full picture of Gates's funding into the fourth estate.

Twenty thousand separate donations by 2020…to which thousands more have, no doubt, since been added. The Gates Foundation has funded journalism centers and teaching organizations, universities, individual journalists, state-media organizations like NPR, radio stations and networks, professional journals and magazines, and individual researchers. And this is standard. Absurdly, Schwab points out that Gates even funded a research paper on…the effect of philanthropic funding of journalism. No doubt that research reached the conclusion that the "philanthropic" funding of journalism is a good thing.

Other politically active Globalist billionaires, of course, are doing the same thing, pumping money into legacy media (film, television, TV news, radio, newspapers, cable channels, lifestyle magazines—everywhere) that they either directly own or that they can influence through professional bodies and institutions (including watchdogs) that they also fund. George Soros's Open Society Foundations do not just subvert and corrupt the US legal system by funding district attorneys who then enact Soros-approved policies—they, too, pump huge amounts of money into media outlets.

Jeff Bezos, of course, directly owns *The Washington Post*, but the legacy media newspaper is the smallest part of his media empire. The Amazon Prime network and the ability to fund gigantic entertainment ventures are far more significant, given the social programming, attitudes, and values shifting work that's put into almost all entertainment ventures today. Prime, as well as Disney and Netflix, use their own revenue and billionaire-owner funding, too, to engage in what are effectively mass propaganda exercises masquerading as entertainment. All of these will express the kinds of Globalist values (such as diversity, equity, and inclusion with environmental, social, and governmental attitudes, which are also mandated as corporate policy documents and ethics guidelines in the corporations' internal guidelines).

This is why so many entertainment companies are prepared to lose huge numbers of fans with direct progressive liberal messaging in established franchises. They are owned by a small number of Globalists who invest in and purchase these companies (just as they invest in and purchase news media) specifically to push the Globalist agenda. The investment banks like BlackRock demand Globalist attitudes from both news organizations and entertainment companies, but so do the handful of billionaires who own nearly every media company. On top of that, they keep Gates and other Globalist philanthropists at a clever distance, not directly owning an outlet but keeping them afloat with "charitable" donations.

Sometimes, of course, the established entertainment companies and their Globalist owners secure a win. Sometimes they manage to embed Globalist-favored attitudes and messages in an entertainment property and get away with it or even secure a huge hit, as they did with the feminist messaging in *Barbie* or the sympathetic treatment of Communism in *Oppenheimer*. A billion-dollar grossing movie that pushes a "girls can do anything/boys really suck" narrative is a social conditioning triumph for

Globalism as this is one of the social radical attitudes Globalists endorse. But as the "go woke go broke" slogan that has some truth describes, and as, for example, the disastrous collapse of most Disney-era Marvel and Star Wars spinoffs illustrates, the unsubtle use of established franchises for social attitude adjustment and conditioning (i.e., woke propaganda) tends to lose significant amounts of money. Crafting these entertainment properties in the first place is an expensive process, rendered worse when half the expected fan base fails to turn up or is, in fact, furious with the version of their beloved franchise that is being forced on them.

In the entertainment sphere, in some instances, we are talking about *very* established companies, companies working on a scale where even in a bad year they are generating huge amounts of revenue, but even so…even a Disney-level corporation can't afford too many movies that cost $400 million and only return half that or overall drops in revenue for streaming services or theme parks of 20 percent or more. The losses start to accumulate and prompt hostile takeover bids—as Disney recently experienced—or require a shift away from the most blatantly woke propagandizing. In quarter three alone in 2023, for instance, Disney lost $659 million on its streaming service. Overall revenue has declined every year with the single exception of a brief uprise following the COVID-caused decline of 2020. In 2023, Disney Plus lost four million subscribers. Big film flops like *Indiana Jones and the Dial of Destiny* (which lost at least $100 million) have been followed by *Star Wars*–series spinoff flops like *The Acolyte* (which garnered savage fan responses and was a hugely expensive series to make—costing roughly $22.5 million per episode with very little likelihood of ever earning that back).

All of the major Hollywood studios have seen stagnation, not just Disney. Independent analysis of expenditure suggested that for Universal, Disney, Warner, and Paramount in 2023, each studio spent over a billion dollars in the year to end up with losses ranging between $190 million (Warner) and $843 million (Universal). Multiple factors apply to these declines, and like giant corporations of any kind, these organizations can weather losses for some time. But going to war with fan bases because you want to push crude social programming messaging surely contributes to these financial losses. They can't even be explained as everyone decamping to cheaper streaming services and watching movies at home, since the streaming services are doing even worse.

Globalist messaging still doesn't sell and generally faces public resistance, which is as true in terms of entertainment media propaganda as it is in the popularity and approval ratings of Globalist politicians. The gap between the fans and the franchise is the same as the gap between the voters and the politicians. In both cases, large numbers of people know that they aren't receiving what they wanted or asked for, even if they don't know that they are subject to a vast project of social engineering.

Going back to news organizations and the TV, radio, and print that directly addresses political issues (without disguising what they promote as an entertaining fiction), the media here is (1) even more uniform and controlled and (2) even more expensive, failing, and in trouble. Most legacy media outlets, including some of the biggest names in print and TV, would go bust without continual infusions of cash from their owners or from "philanthropists" paying to see the kinds of stories they want to see dominating the news cycle.

In January 2024, "Jeff Bezos, other billionaire media owners losing 'a fortune' on struggling news outlets: Report," a Fox Business article by Lindsay Kornick, addressed the stark reality for the legacy media industry of which it is a part, noting that most if not all major news media outlets were losing significant sums:

> Despite massive purchases from billionaires like Jeff Bezos, many once-popular news outlets have reportedly lost big financially in recent years. The Amazon founder kicked off the trend in 2013 after he bought *The Washington Post* for $250 million. After him, in 2018, bioscientist Dr. Patrick Soon-Shiong bought the *Los Angeles Times* for $500 million, and Salesforce founder Marc Benioff bought *Time* Magazine for $190 million the same year.

In the past few years, however, all three publications have taken financial hits, according to a report from *The New York Times* headlined "Billionaires Wanted to Save the News Industry. They're Losing a Fortune."

The article goes on to describe that Bezos lost $100 million on *The Washington Post* in just 2023 (i.e., it's losing him almost half as much as it cost him to buy, every year). Less prestigious and strongly backed woke media outlets, especially those pushing Globalist attitudes to a younger demographic, have gone bust entirely, as the Vox Media organization did. Vox Media was forced to lay off 3 percent of its staff in 2022, followed by another 7 percent in 2023, as it struggled to keep going. Even Forbes had to undergo a similar process of reduction.

Legacy media and mainstream news has, of course, caught itself in a vicious circle. It hasn't worked out how to respond to the growth of alternative media except by sneers and insults or by pretending that alternative media doesn't exist. But the alternative media replacing it only exists because so many people have become aware, in recent years, of just how biased, just how controlled, just how like the maligned fake reality media as described in *One by One* all mainstream news is.

People, not conspiracy theorists or people who believe that depopulation genocide is coming, but ordinary people with normal fears about open borders, mass immigration, rising prices, inflation, energy and fuel costs, ordinary people who don't want a war with Russia or do want to be able to vote for Donald Trump, ordinary people who backed Brexit or who don't like the EU or who don't understand why luxury hotels are booked out for illegal migrants while ex-service personnel are homeless—all of these ordinary people, people like you, perhaps, have seen just how dishonest mainstream media is.

In the entertainment sphere, these ordinary people have seen Netflix pretending that a British king of the Middle Ages was black, disabled, and gay, and they know that is ridiculous and put there for a Globalist agenda. But in the politics sphere, in the real news (which becomes increasingly an oxymoron) they have seen how just wanting your nation to do well and your borders to be guarded is described as the return of Hitler. Wanting your nation to be great and successful (which surely should be an aim for any national politician) was described, by every news outlet, as far-right extremism.

Ordinary people might worry about Muslim terrorist atrocities and then be disgusted that these are downplayed or that they are called racist for worrying about them while Islam is described as a religion of peace. Ordinary people can see how biased and insane the mainstream media has become when these media people stand in front of giant flames and call that protest "mostly peaceful" or when the same media people then report a far smaller incident (literally a riot that lasted hours instead of months) as a deadly insurrection that was the worst thing to ever happen to America.

Ordinary people might snort in contempt when reading mainstream media articles describe an obvious man in a dress as a stunning and gorgeous woman and have the same contempt when the media pretends that individual states having authority over abortion legislation is the same as *The Handmaid's Tale*.

Ordinary people can see the media lying in real time, as they did when every media outlet (including Fox and other "right-wing" ones) pretended that free and fair elections are normally decided by massive, impossible vote spikes in one direction in the early hours of the morning.

When you constantly lie to people (for example by treating Russian collusion as real for years or by treating Hunter Biden's laptop as fake when it was real) those people start doing the first thing you need to do, too—they turn off.

Turn off your TV. Do it now. Rick Mayall in that fiction told you more truth than you will get from CNN, the BBC, MSNBC, PBS, or any mainstream news channel anywhere in the western world.

I stopped watching mainstream media years ago. I got tired of the lies and tired of the shamelessness of the lies. I urge you to do the same. If you pay a TV fee or subscription, stop paying it. Why do you want to fund people who are lying to you? If you pay a subscription to a Globalist entertainment network, stop paying it. If you use Google or a search engine that directs you only to Globalist-approved answers, stop using it and stop relying on it as your way to check and verify things. That, perhaps, is the most insidious control of all—not only that they pump out propaganda at all times, but that they direct you to where they want you to go for sources of information or for verifying news and facts.

The search engine is a tool of control. Of course it is. You are deferring the direction of your inquiry and the veracity of what you find to a machine that follows algorithms crafted by people who hate you. Think of the purple-haired programmers at Twitter before Elon Musk took over and where they would take your inquiries. Think of the fact that all the big social media companies in the US had "former" FBI and CIA personnel in senior staff positions, as well as regular communication with the FBI and the Biden administration (which has just been subject to a legal challenge that the Supreme Court refused to endorse—meaning that outsourced state censorship is allowed despite being unconstitutional).

But the biggest source of misinformation, distortion, bias, dishonesty, hypocrisy, lies, propaganda, and programming is the mainstream legacy media and mainstream news. These outlets construct a fake narrative again and again. They have been utterly loathsome and uniform in their loathsomeness on every topic for at least ten years. Turning off the news is the best thing you can do for your mental health. It's also the best thing you can do for your understanding of reality and for your perception of what matters, what is real, and what is true.

And it is something that an ordinary person can do that doesn't take power and influence over anyone except yourself. It's the immediate first step in reclaiming reality and recovering your mental freedom.

In 2011, a book was published by Elena Gorokhova called *A Mountain of Crumbs: A Memoir*. It was an account of living in the Soviet Union. In it was this quote:

"The rules are simple: they lie to us, we know they're lying, they know we know they're lying but they keep lying anyway, and we keep pretending to believe them."

This is the situation we are now in throughout the Western world, in what was once known as "the Free World." There is no truth on your TV. There are only lies. Perhaps the score of a sports contest is accurate. Perhaps the existence of a thing, like a war in Ukraine, is accurate. But all the rest are lies. The very few basic truths are there solely to form a few poles between which more lies can be strung.

Everything about the fact, the pole, will be a lie. You won't be told any details about this war or that war that you can trust. You will receive lies about the cause of the war and the start of the war. You will receive lies about who is to blame for the war and how to end the war. You will be told that terrorists are victims, as you are with the poor Palestinians, and that victims are genocidal maniacs, as you are with the "wicked" Israelis. You will be told that the war that is just is unjust, and the war that is unjust is just. You will be told that your sons must die while their sons profit.

And the conditions of your own nation will be lied about too. The things that destroy you, alienate you, ruin you, the things that make you a stranger in your own land, horrified by what you see…these things will be "our strength." The crime will be "our strength." The rapes will be "our strength." The deaths and the pain and the alienation will be "our strength."

Nothing but lies, but you must live in defiance of them. You must turn them off. You must curl your lip in scorn whenever you hear them. You must laugh at those who share them. This is what Globalism has done. It has taken every media source, every mediator, and filled them with lies to pour into your eyes and your mouth and your soul.

Yet you have the power to begin to resist. You can stop pretending to believe them. Millions of us have already started, and you are not alone.

You can turn the TV off.

LIVE NOT BY LIES

One man who stopped lying could bring down a tyranny.
—Aleksandr Solzhenitsyn, *The Gulag Archipelago, 1918–1956*

In the long run, the most disagreeable truth is a safer companion than the most pleasant falsehood.
—Theodore Roosevelt, address at Columbia Gardens, Montana, May 27, 1903

I cannot recall a time in my adult life when the mainstream media peddled such blatant lies on a daily basis. As an amateur historian, I am also unaware of any period in modern American history in which the so-called news media routinely and unapologetically perpetuated falsehoods on such a grand scale. Most Americans realize the mainstream media are biased. According to recent polls, Americans' trust in mass media has hit all-time lows.... So why has the mainstream media abandoned all pretenses of political neutrality in favor of pushing lies? Well, it could certainly have something to do with the fact that the vast majority of those in the mainstream media…hold leftist views.... As of 2014…just 7 percent of journalists self-identified as Republicans.

—Chris Talgo, "Mainstream Media's Incessant Lies Are Tearing America Apart," Townhall, April 27, 2021

A long time ago, during the Enlightenment, a very clever French polymath and philosopher started to think deeply about what was real. This was a man who studied optics and made important discoveries about how the human eye works. In the course of doing so, he realized that human beings experience the world through their senses and through perception, but that their senses can lie to them. In fact, in some ways, our senses are always lying to us.

Take the way we literally see the world. Not the metaphorical way we see things, like our attitudes, but the actual images. The human eye has a transparent front called a cornea. The cornea refracts light and accounts for about two-thirds of the eye's total optical power. It's a windshield for the rest of the eye, a protective layer. But the curvature of the cornea bends light entering the eye, creating an upside-down image in the retina. This is a basic and fundamental part of how we see things. The brain then processes this inverted image, flipping it over to create a view of the world the proper way up. It's thought that for the first few days of life a baby effectively sees everything upside down as the brain learns to adapt the image it is receiving to the external reality being perceived.

It takes time to recognize the inverted image as both normal and wrong and adapt to it.

Our sight of the world has to be processed and adapted by our brain in order to be accurate, and even our own eyes can mislead us. It's in this interaction between the organ of sight and the necessary processing of that information by the brain that things like visual magic tricks and visual illusions work.

Not only that, but the images our brain perceives are, in one sense, expanded from the information the eye gives us. In order to speed the process of perception, the eye delivers a certain amount of information, and the brain fills in the rest, like a painter who is given part of an image and then completes it. The edges of our vision are parts of the image the brain has just extrapolated from the rest.

When people started investigating how the eye worked, they gradually found these things out, but even during the Enlightenment, knowledge of these processes was not as refined as it is today.

Philosophically, though, it already prompted the questions that arise from realizing that our perception of objective reality is more complex than just our senses truthfully delivering everything that really is out there. There's a layer of interpretation, of the brain making assumptions, involved as well.

Science is grounded on the notion that there is an objective physical reality out there that our senses interact with honestly. One of the earliest principles of scientific investigation is that the scientist should conduct experiments to test his ideas, and these experiments are really just interacting with the world using his own perception, his own senses. Don't trust what someone else has said on this, dissect an eye yourself. Look at it. Investigate the eye with your eyes. Then you will understand it as a mechanism, and you can test your theories about it. Isaac Newton, who was also interested in optics, took this to an extreme. It's said that Newton stuck a needle in his own eye to investigate it more fully, to feel the shape of a living eye in operation. Apparently, he already knew enough to be able to do so without inflicting any serious damage on himself.

But for the other Enlightenment experimenter we introduced above, for the French philosopher René Descartes, understanding the mechanisms of human perception and the limits and nature of our sensory perception of the world leads to a radical doubt regarding the world itself. If our senses can lie, and in some ways everything we perceive is being interpreted by processes in our brain, can we be certain of anything out there at all? What do we really know? What can we be absolutely certain of? How much of reality is real?

For Descartes, the end of this series of questions was the idea that the only thing we can be certain of is ourselves. And not our senses, but our minds. If our minds are intimately involved in interpreting and filtering and "filling" in the world around us, the only thing we can be certain of, the only thing we can really know as a thing that exists and is real beyond any doubt, is that *we* exist—that *we* are real. Everything else is contingent on that. Everything is shaped by that. *We*, our minds, are the only solid ground, and the fact that we exist and think is the only certain fact, or at least the one on which every other fact is built.

Cogito, ergo sum. I think therefore I am.

I am the only thing I know to be absolutely real.

All this might seem a long way away from discussing the crazy world we live in today and what we should do about it. How do we react to Globalism and the fact that Globalism has seemingly made the mainstream into an awful lot of crazy ideas and dangerous policies? How do we survive it all and retain our own sanity in the face of it all?

Well, we do what Descartes did, and we realize that the entire *political world* we live in is something being constructed around us. It's not objective reality. It's often directly opposed to objective reality, and it is often and most definitely an *inversion* of true morality.

The political reality we inhabit is built by and for liars who seem to hate us. If we want to get back to reality, we have to flip that inverted morality back in line with objective morality, just like how the brain of a baby learns to flip the upside-down image on the retina and *see the world truly*.

So, what can we really trust? What is the really solid ground? It is our capacity to think, just like it was for Descartes. It is our existence as independent-thinking beings and the degree to which we can protect our thoughts from propaganda and deception that decides whether we will live by the truth or live by lies.

Trust yourself before you trust the news. Trust your ability to independently research a thing, like an early follower of the scientific method. Understand that sneering at your independent research and independent conclusions is something done by people who don't want thinking human beings in their society but would actually prefer us all to be unthinking receivers of authority, people incapable of independent thought.

The one person you can absolutely trust is you. The one resource that can never be taken away is your mind. So long as you think logically, you can spot lies. So long as you are confident enough to trust your own ability to think about the world and reach towards truth, you are more than a mere receiver and more than a thoughtless puppet. You are a real person.

Those who don't think will laugh at you for thinking, because independent thought is the greatest threat of all to authoritarian systems and to those who refuse to think for themselves.

But all of your independent thought is worthless unless it becomes a thing that informs your actions. It has to be a thing that is lived. It has to be the thing that guides and determines your actions more than any external pressure can.

What this means in a system of lies is that you have to refuse to live by those lies. And you have the power to do that. Nobody can take that away from you, although they can punish you for it. But if you decide to live by truth instead of lies, they cannot really stop you. Only you can decide to submit, and only you can decide to refuse to submit. All of that is in your power to decide.

During the height of the COVID madness I got a new job. I'm a working-class guy, and I have worked in a number of low-paid occupations. The longest I've worked anywhere was in a support role for the fire department that involved manual labor. I trained long before that as an academic, but my politics and background did not fit that career, and it was soon made obvious to me that I would never get an academic post, the thing I'd trained for. So, I always had to take whatever job was available.

During COVID, that included working as a picker and a packer, basically the lowliest grunt-level work, for Amazon. It was an illuminating experience in several ways, and possibly the least human experience of work I've ever had.

Pickers and packers at Amazon are basically organic cogs in a mostly machine system. They are integrated into a whole number of automated, computer-controlled systems that make Amazon efficient and that make Jeff Bezos obscenely wealthy. I've worked in similar-titled roles in other factories before. I've worked in lines of people doing non-repetitive tasks. When I did so twenty years earlier than the Amazon job, it was still very different. People stood next to each other and were allowed to chat as they worked. We were still picking things up and putting them in boxes, but it was a communal experience. There were laughs and jokes, and the job still got done. We were allowed to listen to a radio and choose the station. People who needed a toilet break just went and then came back. The monitoring that existed was human monitoring, with a supervisor or a boss looking at what you did but not in a constant or oppressive manner.

At Amazon, a picker or packer meets at a central point on one of the levels of a huge building. There he waits to be assigned a workstation. That's a coded number. He then goes to that coded number.

The workstation is a cage. It's a literal, physical cage, with metal sides and a little door. You shut yourself in. No other human being is close enough to look at, smile at, or talk to. There's no chatting as you work. There's no radio, unless it's elevator music chosen by the management. You can see people in the other cages, but you can't interact with them. Supervisors patrol around, checking on you all and making sure you are working constantly and quickly. But the main way of monitoring you is via your work screens. These count, constantly, how many tasks you have completed. They count any pauses. Toilet breaks are counted, with maybe a minute allowed for walking to and back from the toilet and a minute for being at the toilet. Go over three minutes with no activity counting on your monitor screen, and you get a visit from a supervisor. Any kind of reason to leave the cage should be completed within three minutes.

The whole system is automated and run by computers. Little robotic machines move tall frames with compartments. Empty ones are moved to the inner side of your cage, where there's a space facing the main factory floor. Except for when the machines break and need to be repaired, human beings don't go into that space. It's just machines moving around. When an empty frame reaches you, you fill it up according to codes that appear on your monitor. You bend and lift, you move item C5 to compartment C5, or similar, and you just keep doing that with no pause.

You probably have to be young and fit to do it very fast. The expected rate of doing it is very fast. People who are faster than anyone else get a little extra reward. These are announced like grand prizes at bingo or at a raffle, but nobody over thirty has much chance of winning them, and the prizes make an average bingo hall's cheap prizes look insanely generous.

I was unusually old in that job. Most people were twenty years younger than me. I was also unusually English. Most of the people working there were Eastern Europeans or other non-English immigrants. The ambitious ones spoke to each other about working like slaves for a few years but saving all the money and going back home to live like kings. The unambitious ones spoke about staying in England.

There were several canteens. The largest one had walls on which motivational slogans were written. These were chillingly stupid slogans, cribbed perhaps from management-theory texts or self-help manuals. It was dystopian. You could slip the line "Works Makes You Free" in there and nobody would notice a difference between that and the other slogans.

During COVID, of course, it was all even more dystopian than it was normally. Everyone was required to wear a mask. The canteen tables had plastic screens in the middle, the kind purchased by people that seemed to believe that air only flows in one direction. Social distancing was insisted on. In the entrance hall, a machine had been set up that worked by lasers and monitored the distances between people. It showed red circles and dots for the people moving in the crowd. If two dots got too close, the red circles flared angrily and an alarm sounded.

It was just like something you'd expect from a science fiction movie about a brutally controlled and oppressive society.

There was a COVID-testing station set up. Every employee was regularly called to attend and do a COVID test. Plastic gloves on. Testing kit open. Swab the nose. Seal the kit. Leave your DNA with us. This was considered normal.

I hated the COVID masks and the tests. I never wore a mask outside of work. I refused to wear them. I quickly realized that these measures made no sense. The masks were utterly stupid. Product specifications told us that. These things did nothing. I also found that they triggered asthma or panic attacks when I wore them. I could wear them for a little while and then would suddenly feel like I couldn't breathe at all. Supervisors kept finding me with the mask off and reprimanding me for it.

Everything about Amazon was horrible: the mechanization of everything, the machines counting everything, and the smiling-but-hectoring approach of the supervisors—the way even telling you off was treated as if they were doing you a kindness or as if you had some kind of disability they were concerned about out of pure kindness to you.

But it was a job.

When I finally quit, I can't describe the pleasure of throwing away my masks.

But I needed the money. You know how it is?

I'm not some leftist or millennial who thinks bosses can't tell me what to do or rules don't apply to me because I'm so precious and special. But in that job, at that time, I looked around and thought, this is mad. This is genuinely dystopian.

And I realized that the Amazon factory, the life of a picker or packer, was basically what Globalists want for society as a whole. A vast system mainly run by computers. Lots of people being constantly monitored and hectored. No community. No connection between any workers. Foreign-based, imported, cheap labor. Slogans everywhere. Brain-numbing slogans. Cages and duties. Small rewards for the most compliant. Dystopian behaviors and surveillance treated as normal. Complete control treated as kindness or opportunity. DNA harvesting as a normal part of the working day.

Amazon is its own social credit system. Its own China. It is what we are all supposed to plug into through our whole society now. It's the great promise of Globalism: some people making billions while the rest of us are sticking plastic straws coated in carcinogens up our noses just to get by—without even the sound of our own language for comfort.

In a collision of circumstances, the period I worked at Amazon was also the period of the theft of the 2020 US election. There were TV screens on in the canteens. They were always set to news channels, and you couldn't change them. So, I got to see these mainstream news channels lying constantly in my hour for lunch. Maybe it was innocent that the company with the slogans on the walls and the surveillance of its staff and the dystopian COVID measures was also pouring propaganda relentlessly into the air with no way to find another channel or a different view.

Maybe.

But also, it was my fault. I accepted all this. I went along with it.

I certainly didn't rip that lying fucking TV off the wall.

And I didn't tell Amazon to shove their low-paid slave labor until after I'd endured it for a good few months.

And that was on me. That was on me living a lie. My brain was interpreting all this fine. My brain was telling me what it really was. But my need for an income was telling my brain to shut up and bow down and pretend this weird fucked-up version of a job was normal.

That part was on me. Because we can always choose *our* actions. We may have to pay a price with uncertainty, poverty, or inconvenience, but *we* choose whether we live by lies. Us.

In Aleksandr Solzhenitsyn's great masterpieces *The Gulag Archipelago* and *One Day in the Life of Ivan Denisovich* he describes living in Soviet prison camps in Siberia. One of the most moving portions comes in *One Day in the Life of Ivan Denisovich* when he describes a man who refuses to live by lies even in the midst of torture and imprisonment. He describes a man who lives with truth and dignity and self-respect, no matter what:

> He was steadily eating his thin skilly [weak broth], but instead of almost dipping his head in the bowl like the rest of them, he carried his battered wooden spoon up high.... His face was worn thin, but it wasn't the weak face of a burnt-out invalid, it was like dark chiseled stone. You could tell from his big chapped and blackened hands that in all his years inside he'd never had a soft job.... But he refused to knuckle under: he didn't put his three hundred grams [of bread] on the dirty table, splashed all over, like the others, he put it on a rag he washed regularly.

Now this might seem like an absurdity to you, to go from my mild, still relatively comfortable, brief job at Amazon to this. People who think I am saying they are identical will laugh at this.

But I'm not saying they are the same. Or at least not in degree. Quite clearly people in Soviet Russia had it a lot worse than we have it today. Quite clearly, a Siberian prison camp is a lot worse than a factory in any Western nation today. But for the society as a whole and the jobs within it, it used to be that the West and Soviet Russia were fundamentally different *in kind*—as the West was fundamentally different from Communist China.

Because people in the West had real freedom, and because people in charge of the West did not want the majority of people to be modern slaves whose every action and thought is controlled.

Today, under Globalism, we don't have the KGB (Soviet secret police) or the Stasi (East German secret police). But how have the FBI been behaving lately? We don't have a *Gulag Archipelago*. But how many people have been arrested lately for thought crimes? Surely more than would be if we still had freedom? Hundreds of January 6 protestors were held for *years* without trial. Millions of us and all our Western governments apparently think that's normal.

The difference between Globalist-ruled Western nations today is a difference not of *kind* but of *degree*. OK, things generally aren't as extreme… yet. Look to places like Venezuela to see how extreme they can get and how fast, once the kind of ruler you have is the kind of person who built the Soviet system.

Both Marxism and Globalism attract a certain kind of person with some shared features. They attract people who have no moral code and no traditional values but who want to tear everything down, people who want a cultural revolution, people who imprison or attempt to imprison their chief political rivals, people who rig and steal elections, people who ban and censor and silence and mock independent thought.

The lesson of the Soviet Gulag is twofold. It tells us how bad things get under these types of leaders, and it tells us how the one thing we still control is our mind and whether it retains a sense of its own worth and dignity.

Our actions manifest whether we submit to or defy what surrounds us, sometimes in the smallest ways. Sometimes how you lift your spoon or how you eat your food can show so much more than what it seems to show.

What ways could you manifest your dignity and your defiance that you do not show? And isn't it better to show it *now*, before there are camps for people like you?

Back to another big capitalist corporation that says dystopian things that we now treat as normal but which only end up with people in camps. Remember when Coca-Cola just wanted to sell you a fizzy drink? When it was a company selling a drink, and nothing else? Not anymore. Here is an extract from Coca-Cola's "Better Together" global training materials. This is stuff that was being shared with thousands of employees. Like me accepting Amazon's bizarre and dehumanizing COVID practices, thousands of Coca-Cola employees have sat through insane Globalist drivel just to keep their jobs. A Coca-Cola whistleblower on February 19, 2021, shared this gem of pure hate and malice that featured as a standard and typical part of the "Better Together" material:

"To be less white is to: be less oppressive, be less arrogant, be less certain, be less defensive, be less ignorant, be more humble, listen, believe, break with apathy, break with white solidarity.... Try to be less white."

Try to be less white. Pure race hate. Sold as being "better together." And an impossible task. Escape your innate physical characteristics? But I thought blackface was racist?

But look at the other instructions there. Be humble. Listen and believe. In other words, be a receiver of instructions, rather than a thinker or an independent human being. Deny your own dignity and worth, and that of anyone like you. Accept instruction and punishment.

These are the terms by which we end up accepting anything. This is the kind of deal and the kind of thinking that puts *the wrong group* in death camps, eventually. That's no exaggeration. That's just how things like this progress when you set them rolling. The pebble becomes the avalanche.

The control of every action in a factory becomes the control of every action in society.

And that's where Globalists *want* to go. That's where all the crazy things they support, from "net zero" to race hate politics, go. They *all* demand complete submission and complete denial of your thoughts and your dignity. A friend of mine got a good government job. The first thing on the first day was a demand that he add his pronouns so they automatically appear on all his work emails. The head of human resources turned up and physically waited for him to do it, smiling all the while.

He complied. He hates that crap. But he likes having a good job.

But you control you. You can live not by lies but by truth, and choose to do it before the camps are built.

If a man can keep his dignity in a gulag, then you can do it when it risks just a job.

SPREADING THE TRUTH

Consider the case of the infamous Dreyfus Affair in late 19th-century France. Captain Alfred Dreyfus, a Jewish officer in the French army, was wrongfully accused of treason and sentenced to life imprisonment on Devil's Island.

The real traitor, Major Ferdinand Walsin Esterhazy, remained at large, protected by a web of lies and anti-Semitic sentiment. Yet, as the years rolled on, the truth began to emerge. The tireless efforts of Dreyfus' supporters, most notably the writer Emile Zola, coupled with the relentless march of time, eventually led to Dreyfus' exoneration.

Time, the great revealer, had discovered the truth. Time is a great equalizer, the ultimate arbiter. It cares not for the machinations of men, the plots of the powerful, or the schemes of the secretive. It is immune to bribery, impervious to threats, and indifferent to pleas. It is the silent witness to all deeds, the scribe that records the annals of reality. In the end, time discovers truth, for truth is the daughter of time.

—Aaron Gray, "10 'In Time, the Truth Will Come Out' Quotes You Will Dread," The Invisible Man website

Let's say that you know what is going on and you are aware of just how untrustworthy most of the sources of information around you have become.

You know that the mainstream media is owned by a handful of companies and pushes their Globalist agenda. You know that all the talking heads get instructions and repeat the same points. You know that organizations like the WHO and the EU, as well as national governments, are controlling what you are allowed to see, hear, and think. And you know that social media companies and search engines work alongside the intelligence services on a regular basis or take instructions from key members of an administration on who to silence and who to block and what information you are allowed to see.

What this puts you in is a radical position of doubt.

Now, that's an uncomfortable place to be. You need to be certain of at least some things.

So, you do your independent research. Knowing that many of the technological tools that, on the surface, make access to information so much easier today than it was in the past are controlled and biased, you adjust for that and try to confirm things from multiple sources or gradually rely more on other independent, seemingly uncontrolled voices in alternative media.

But as much as alternative media is flourishing, that can have problems too. Some of the outsider attitudes and theories actually are nuts, for a start, or malign, and you need to be able to apply some logic of your own to those sources.

Just because the government, transnational bodies, and the mainstream media are lying constantly, it doesn't mean that "it's the Jews" or "it's alien lizards" makes any sense. Just because you were massively lied to during COVID, it doesn't prove that the moon landings were faked.

I have lost track of the number of times I have agreed with people about the current elites, transnational bodies, or how crazy policies and crazy ideas are dominating the mainstream, only to then have to reject that basis when they tell me that every famous person in the world is a clone or that the "Khazarian Mafia" are pulling the strings.

You cannot believe anything just because it's mainstream and respectable. At the same time, you cannot believe everything just because it's alternative and edgy. In both cases you have to really think about it on a logical basis and see, for yourself, if it makes sense.

Everything in my personality and style of thinking that made me reject wearing masks and following little arrows on the floor (because I knew that the masks did not work and that a virus does not circulate in the air according to directional arrows) was the *same* logic and style of thinking that makes me realize that the idea that the world is secretly controlled by a dead Silk Road kingdom of the Middle Ages is *also* completely nuts.

It doesn't matter the source; always question the logic.

But there's a social cost to this. When powerful and malign figures *are* real and *do* influence what many people think, or even when a crazy idea becomes popular without too much behind-the-scenes manipulation, your logical and rational take on things is going to conflict with the opinions of people who are just functioning by what some other source tells them.

Your views are going to very quickly start conflicting not just with the news stances from propaganda sources but also with real people who believe those news sources, perhaps with friends, family, and relatives.

That can be very isolating and scary. That can be a social phenomenon, a social reality, that impacts on your courage and your ability to insist on the truth or to live by the truth. And it will be happening all the time in a society that has gradually moved into an unacknowledged level of tyranny, as the once democratic and free Western world most definitely has.

It's not just because you want to fight back and not just because the lies offend you and you love the truth. But it's just as a human being hearing lies from people you love—or you worrying deeply about the way the world is going and what you can do about it—is going to put you in a difficult position. You have to decide between buckling down, losing your dignity and self-respect to just get along under these new social rules…or trying to reconnect with people who are living by lies, trying to persuade them, and trying to share more reality with them.

Even putting it like this, of course, will lead to charges of arrogance or hypocrisy. Who are *you* to decide what is real and logical? Who are *you* to "question the science"? Who are *you* to make your friends and neighbors uncomfortable when you disagree with the established lies that everyone else is just accepting?

The answer is that you are a thinking human being, and part of the dignity of each individual life comes down to the fact that we can and should be free to form and assert our own political opinions. If those have just the same right of expression as another belief, assuming that neither is demanding atrocities or supporting obviously evil things, like torturing or raping children, then you live in a pretty free society.

If you aren't allowed to express your peacefully held views then you don't live in a free society.

The *second* answer is that, over time, we have found again and again that the enforced respectable view has been less rational, less logical, less beneficial and benign than the prescribed and alternative view was. Or just *not true*. The truth has been suppressed while lies have been tolerated and spread, all to serve narrow political, ideological, and financial interests, and we have seen this happening.

We know, for instance, that they finally had to admit that masks don't work for preventing viral spread and make no difference to the spread of a virus, or that a lab leak was the most likely origin, which they now admit having first described it as a crazy and dangerous conspiracy theory.

The usefulness of the COVID period is that it really did expose just how prone to dishonesty and "misinformation" the mainstream has become, how far the authorities and the respectable people will go in authoritarian directions, and how ordinary people can sometimes be much better judges (unpaid and generally neutral judges) of reality than paid experts are.

But you might still find that you are surrounded by people in your workplace, at home, or in social gatherings who don't know any of the things you bothered to research, who don't question (even years later) many of the lies supplied to them, and who still generally trust mainstream news sources, as well as policies and views on events controlled by Globalist opinion formers and authorities.

This has a social impact that matters. Human beings are social animals, and I can perfectly understand the instinct to avoid topics that set you at odds with people you otherwise like or force you to bite your tongue and say nothing when lies surround you. Keeping your friends and keeping your job are powerful ways of controlling what you are prepared to think and say. I get it. I understand that reluctance.

Unfortunately, curling up and rolling into a little protective ball isn't a very effective strategy, is it? Have you ever seen footage of this instinctual response when people are being physically attacked? It's an evolutionary strategy that makes some sense. Curl up your limbs to protect your major organs. Maybe with an animal or a lone attacker likely to get bored it makes sense and became an instinct for those reasons. But it's just about the worst thing to do when attacked by a gang of people who are determined to inflict serious harm on you. It makes you a vulnerable, static target. It gives them all the time they need to do as much damage as they want. Fighting back or running away are both better strategies than curling up into a ball.

The same rules apply to being bombarded with lies, to living in a society of lies that is an unacknowledged tyranny and that people are actively making worse. In that scenario, the scenario every citizen of the Western world is living through, these attacks don't go away if you submit. Or, at the very best, you get a slight pause before being hit again.

Think about one of these particular lines of attack. Let's take LGBTQ+ propaganda. Now that started, way, way back, perhaps as a legitimate cause. There was a time when gay people were unfairly treated. Being arrested just for being gay is an injustice. So, fine, insist on equal rights for gays.

Now ask yourself, when gays got equal rights, did it stop? When nobody any longer cared about whether someone was gay, did it stop? When gays had exactly the same rights as anyone else and had no legal and virtually no social differences at all in how they were treated, did it stop there?

Or did it keep expanding, keep demanding, keep forcing concessions and privileges and special treatment and special praise long past the point where equality had been gained? Did it expand from LGB to LGBT and then to LGBTQ+? Did it go from just "let me make my own adult sexual orientation choices with other adults" to "supply me with condoms for having sex in the public bathrooms at public expense" and "don't arrest me for public indecency" and "hey, I'm a pervert that's sexually attracted to children, and I'm going to join this ever growing identity parade and that's fine."

Of course it did. You know it did. And so do many equally disgusted gays as well.

These blows don't stop coming, these demands, this process that has less and less concern for the rights and lives of the majority and more and more concern for the most extreme minorities. And eventually, if you just curl up into a ball and accept it as part of the price of living under the "new normal," you find your local museum flying a flag that supports child abuse and telling you that it's normal, when it quite clearly isn't.

The process is the same in gender politics and in racial politics. Just go along with it, just repeat lies, just roll your eyes and shrug, and the next demand comes, the next blow, the next extension until any sane justification for it is as far removed from what's being demanded *now* as the values of Satan are removed from the values of Jesus.

If you don't start spreading the truth, you do start living by lies. If you don't insist on your rights, your values, and your dignity, these are taken away under the excuse, the name, of someone else's. Under Globalism, this whole process eventually allows everyone's basic and fundamental rights to exist solely at the dispensation of the Globalist elite, governments, and institutions rather than the things that the ordinary majority of the public consider fair and free. All your basic rights become theirs to grant or revoke, and they can do that in fundamentally unjust and uneven ways.

Do you have the right to think? To silently, internally, compose a thought of your choosing? Would the kind of society that denies you that right be a batshit crazy society, a society of mind reading cops and total thought control that only belongs in a science fiction dystopian novel?

Well, you already live in that society. In both the US and the UK, a Christian who stands near an abortion clinic can be arrested for standing near an abortion clinic and *thinking the wrong thoughts*. A prayer is a thought, an idea expressed to God. People have been arrested for *silent* prayer in the vicinity of an abortion clinic.

So perhaps it would be best not to be silent. You're going to get arrested anyway, eventually, for the wrong thoughts—or your children will. Better to speak out now. Better to share the truth now. Better to be *loud* before you are silenced. Better to realize the harm you enable for yourself and others by staying silent when you could still speak.

Measured against the acceptance of tyranny, is the discomfort of others really such a great price to pay? Is making somebody uncomfortable because of the *truth* a price you aren't prepared to pay? Surely letting that other person force you to agree with lies is a greater price to pay? Your expression of truth is, in fact, the price they—and you—should accept *to live as free human beings*. It really isn't so great a burden. It really is bizarre to accommodate those whom the truth offends and whom lies comfort all the time, constantly, and accompanied by the legal punishment of truth.

Freedom matters more than politeness.

The risk of tyranny is a far greater risk than the risk of offense.

Those whom the current tyranny does not offend, those who are, in particular, favored groups that the Globalist elite supports and prioritizes, tend to demand the removal of your free speech with yet another lie, with the insistence that their control of your speech is just basic decency, social etiquette, or being kind and considerate. It's not so hard, they say, they who are giving nothing and gaining everything. It's really not hard to *be nice*. All we are asking is that you consider other people's feelings.

Well, when it comes to freedom, my view is the opposite of that expressed by Arnold Schwarzenegger at the height of the COVID madness. While supporting COVID mandates and measures, Arnie said, in true Terminator style, "Fuck your freedom." He wasn't, of course, the first Austrian to think like that.

"Fuck your feelings" is a far healthier attitude. You can offend someone without physically harming them, imprisoning them, and forcing poisons into their bloodstream. Really, they are in control of their feelings, not you, or at least they should be. Your freedom matters more than their feelings, every single time. Of course, if you happen to be shouting in support of gas chambers, screaming obscenities at children, or grooming kids, those are different things that impact different social rules and different laws.

But if you are having a thought, offering a prayer, or saying that a vaccine that is harmful is harmful, if you are saying *anything* that is true and not a call to terrorism, torture, or serious harm, it is absolutely better to let you speak than to let someone silence you. And fuck politeness and authority when it tries to control you in those circumstances.

When free speech is already reduced, when tyrannical and authoritarian actions have already been normalized, when the mainstream guards insane and dangerous ideas and people attack the truth, you, as an individual, have a moral duty to speak out.

You have a moral duty to challenge lies. You are called to do so by whatever is moral in you. Your own dignity demands it, and your humanity demands it. You cannot let these lies control your society. In the long run, your safety and the safety of your family demand it. You are less if you submit and more if you do not.

The greater the cost demanded of you in lost friendships, lost opportunities, or lost jobs or advantages, the greater the reward to your soul, the greater the example of your actions, and the greater you become as a human being.

How could we ever value our job above our soul, our coin before our spirit, and our place in the society of lies above our identity as free and thinking human beings of whom certain types of submission should never be demanded?

So, we must speak the truth, both to those who are living by lies and to each other. Spoken to each other, we build community and connections among the free. We give each other the solace of knowing we are not alone, the strength of example, and the support of friendship. It is never wasted effort to express the truth.

Tactically, we face different choices with those living by lies or depending on Globalist media to tell them their opinions. If we love and care for these people, we should want to be truthful with them, even if we disagree. If they love and care for us, they will be able to hear the truth. We should never fear offending them because it is greater kindness to give them truth than to support their lies, just as it is kinder to deny an alcoholic a drink than to offer him one.

When it comes to strangers we argue and debate with, I tend to always try to respond to authorities, official bodies, and institutions when they lie to me. I don't expect my view to change them. But they should get some public pushback, no matter how determined they are to ignore it. When it is strangers or groups on social media, you know they will try to report and harass you. In those cases on social media, as a "keyboard warrior," it's best to comment and then block. The lie has been challenged, but you've limited the chance of an attack in response. Screw anyone who thinks this necessary and practical approach is cowardly.

Your main aim should be to live as a truthful person. To discover that truth through traditional morality and personal, consistent logic. And to be unafraid of offending others. All this is made easier if you build networks of like-minded people—if you gravitate to groups and platforms where these connections can be made without being censored and controlled. The more these friendships and connections translate from the virtual world to the real world, the better.

The powerful build their networks by purchasing people. You are likely to only be able to build your networks through friendship and decency, the very opposite of how they operate. But it is a start. It is a community of the free, and one of those with a handful of members is worth more than a whole organization of purchased and unthinking drones.

Community is vital. Every successful uprising or resistance of tyranny in the past has been built from the support of a community. Those acting alone, even in the expression of the most searing truths, are far more easily dismissed, punished, or disappeared. Community support is, of course, a huge advantage possessed by incoming groups like Muslims. Through clan structures, mosques, and patriarchal family networks that are very large, Muslims quickly dominate an area they settle, even without

Globalists in power more broadly favoring them and police forces fearing them. The atomized modern white community with smaller families, with broken homes, with few automatic networks of connection, and without a church or religious focal point aligned with their interests faces a struggle to compete even before we realize how much the white working class is deliberately sacrificed and betrayed by Globalist leaders.

So, building a community of the free makes a massive difference.

In order to really and seriously challenge the networks of malign power and the Globalist dominance of our society though, we probably need vast resources swinging to our side. We need billionaires and a stream of financial backing. The radical Left came to power first, and now via Globalism is in power everywhere in the West through both their "long march through the institutions" *and* their capture and seduction of the billionaire class.

But whatever we can do to share the truth between ourselves and outside our immediate social circles remains valuable. Create and join groups and organizations. Contact people who are telling the truth. Engage and organize.

No matter how powerless you are, you *can* live as an example, share the truth, and inspire others.

THE POWER OF YOUR POCKET

$1.4 billion. That's how much Bud Light lost in US beer sales last year after the controversy. The company lost over $27 billion in value following the controversy, and their US market share slashed by half since, largely fueled by US retailers reducing shelf space up to 7.5% for the brand.... Bud Light was launched into a culture war last year when the brand partnered with Dylan Mulvaney, a transgender influencer.... Alissa Heinerschied, then-vice president of marketing, said she wanted to change the "fratty" image of Bud Light to create a more inclusive reputation in an interview that sparked accusations the brand was abandoning its core customer base. The company was left in the middle of a political crisis.... Conservative celebrated a boycott against the company, resulting in a massive hit to the brand's reputation and sales in the US.

—Alicia Park, "Bud Light Boycott Effects Endure—
Brand Drops to Third," *Forbes*, July 23, 2024

In the 1950s, people in the Western world lived in traditional Western societies. It was the height of the Cold War. Majority opinion in the West, and government opinion too, was primarily anti-Communist. The Western intelligentsia who had supported Stalin had already been embarrassed by the news of Soviet oppression and atrocity, and although there were still middle-class families raised and being told that Uncle Joe was a very nice man and that capitalism was more evil than Communism, these were very much a small minority.

Most people in the West were firmly aligned with the West and against the Soviet Union, and they did not have to be coerced or forced into this position. Western anti-Communists did not need to invent negative stories about life behind the Iron Curtain. Those stories were real, and eagerly shared by those who had escaped.

First-generation immigrants who had escaped Communism, like Cuban exiles settling in Miami, were virulently anti-Communist, even more than their average white American counterparts.

Socially and culturally, America, the United Kingdom, Australia, New Zealand, Canada, and the whole of the Western world were still traditional and patriotic.

The nuclear family was praised in advertising and considered the aspirational norm. There was no widespread attempt to pretend that gender is fluid or determined by choice. The father was an expected part of childhood. Divorce rates across all communities were far, far lower than they are today, particularly in the US black community. Absentee fathers or mothers with children by multiple fathers were much rarer.

The Civil Rights Movement was there and building. In the US, racial politics were already extremely divisive, but black families were units where fathers were both present and sternly moral, where Christianity was respected and followed, where people would dress in their Sunday best to go to church, and where fathers or uncles who had bravely served in the armed forces during World War Two would not tolerate disrespect to the American flag. There were more people who listened to the Christian messages of Martin Luther King Jr. than to the more radical and hate-based groups, like the Black Panthers or the Nation of Islam.

The counter-cultural revolution had not happened yet. The explosion of "sexual freedom" of the 1960s had not happened yet (a sexual freedom that increased rather than decreased, by the way, the exploitation and mistreatment of women and that, years later, we would realize had been pressed by actual perverts and total liars such as Dr. Alfred Kinsey).

If groups were marginalized, they mainly wanted equal treatment, not special or better treatment, and they mainly followed the *same values* that society as a whole held up as valuable.

Outside America, without the history of slavery within the nation, without the divisions of the Civil War, and before mass immigration had reached its modern levels, most Western nations were far more ethnically and culturally homogeneous than they are today. Racial politics did not exist and was not a factor anywhere near as much as it factored in the US.

Instruction booklets given to every US serviceman in World War Two who came to the United Kingdom, issued by the US military authorities, described the differences between the two nations so that social errors and disagreements could be minimized. These included comments on the racial tolerance of the British, their lack of segregation, and the ease and familiarity with which they would interact with non-whites (all this a very far leap from the standard propaganda today, which was that Britain was virulently racist at that time).

Without huge immigrant and ethnically and racially diverse populations already being present, and without instructions in hate and hypocritical racism from things like critical race theory, in the UK, racial politics were far less of an issue and individual encounters were far more likely to be cordial, both between persons of the same race and between those of different races.

None of this is to pretend that the 1950s were perfect or that groups that formed parts of the US Civil Rights Movement were not mistreated previously. Arrivals from the Windrush generation to the UK did face racism in some quarters. Homosexuality was illegal in many Western statute books until after World War Two.

But the fact is that most people in the majority, then as now, were not wandering the streets looking for gays and blacks to attack, members of the KKK, or landlords putting up signs excluding certain races. Most people were living by Christian virtues, within existing laws, and most were concerned with simply getting a job, getting ahead, getting a house and a car and a family of their own, and having the occasional luxury or holiday to tell them that life was good, and the country was doing OK.

The most negative instances of that old pre-1960s social revolution society are concentrated in depictions that most people at the time would have known were extremes and not the common experience. It's not the only way to judge those times. In the US, the more common experience was of a postwar economic boom that really did seem to fulfil the promises of the American Dream and hold out the promise of plenty to many more people than were offered it in their parents' or grandparents' generations. Even ruined European nations were experiencing recovery and growth, aided by the US's Marshall Plan, but soon powered, too, by their own efforts. Near-bankrupt Britain, loaded with war debts, was still speaking in hopeful terms with fresh building projects and rewards like the creation of the National Health Service and the promise of universal, free healthcare (a disastrous and socialist promise that was a lie, but very tempting at the start and easily mistaken for an improvement).

But why all this talk of the 1950s when this chapter is called "The Power of Your Pocket"?

Well, two reasons.

First, for the US and, to a lesser extent, elsewhere, the 1950s show you what you should have in a society that genuinely is on your side and working for you, with leaders who haven't gone insane and aren't entirely malign.

Your taxes should be at a level that doesn't cripple you financially.

And at that level, they should still be able to buy you the basic promise of a decent life. If your leaders are anywhere near competent, the things the West had in the 1950s should not be impossible to achieve today.

You should be able to buy your own home and pay it off long before you die, get a reasonable or decent job, have a few holidays and luxuries, and see your children do a little bit better than you did. These are not unreasonable expectations.

You should be reasonably safe and protected in your own country, and your borders should be secure. Your streets should be free of litter and filth. You shouldn't have huge encampments of the homeless under bridges or in giant ghettoes in your cities or in every shop forefront in your small town. You should not have people publicly shitting in your street or bus station or subway station, and you should not have neighborhoods of gutted and ruined buildings, crack dens, and apartments where gangs terrorize people and shots are fired all night long. There should not be places where the police won't go, where kids can be killed while playing in the street, and where that sort of thing happens all the time.

And it's not difficult. It really is not difficult. It was not difficult to prevent all those places from emerging. If politicians and the people who fund them had just been less corrupt, less dishonest, and less insane, if they had done the small simple things well and avoided the big stupid things too, our countries could still be flourishing, could still be an example to the world of what hope and glory and a decent life looks like.

The power of your pocket comes with this reminder: you *paid* for a better world than this already. You did your bit. You paid your taxes. You obeyed the laws. If you had a kid, you stayed with them. You paid your own way and your child's way. You tried to raise them right. You tried to be decent yourself. Most of you avoided becoming gang members and drug addicts, and most of you worked. Most of you have never robbed or raped or taken a shit in the street.

Some of you gave your blood for your countries. Veterans, I salute you. And even if you never did, your father or your grandfather or your great-grandfather did.

Your family *paid* in blood for a better world than this.

And you and they paid in sweat and tears too, doing the right thinking and asking only the right thing from those above you.

And *they* renege on that deal. *They* destroyed it. THEY passed massive spending bill after massive spending bill. *They* loaded the country with gigantic debts. A trillion. A trillion more. A war. Another war. A pandemic they created. A vast wealth transfer into their pockets and the pockets of their friends.

You *paid*, and they *betrayed*.

Remember the power of your pocket in this sense. When they spend, it is *your* money, not theirs. There are no such things as public funds. There is only the money they have taken from your pocket and the money they borrow that you or your children have to pay back.

All this spending they did. How much of it improved your world? Did they use it to protect your borders so that there aren't people from Third World nations mugging you in alleys or blowing you up in terrorist attacks? No.

Did they spend that money, and you can look around the streets and see it? Is your neighborhood beautiful? No. Have they built any Hoover Dams lately where you can see where the money went? No. Is your infrastructure working and getting better, or is it declining and getting worse? Are there potholes in your road and on the roads you travel? Is there litter and filth everywhere? Do you have to wait months to see a doctor?

How does that work in a place like the UK? Universal "free" healthcare, is it? But it's not free, is it? I *paid* for it. My father *paid* for it. My children will *pay* for it. It's only free to the people who don't work or the people who come here from elsewhere and don't work. That's who gets it free. And you're giving so much of it to *them* that there's nothing left for those of us who did pay. We get giant waiting lists.

Where did all the money go?

It went into the pockets of people in the system. It pays for foreigners. It pays for strangers. It pays for nurses and doctors who vote for more of the same. And it pays for thousands and thousands of "public sector," gold-plated pension plans. And it pays for the politicians who pass that spending bill and sign that loan on their nation's behalf.

In the UK, we have just been told by our new Labour government that (1) there isn't enough money left to provide welfare assistance to the very elderly to help pay their fuel bills and prevent them from dying in the winter, and (2) we are giving an extra £11 billion in foreign aid.

You *paid*. They *betrayed*.

It is your money. It is always your money.

But what happened? What happened that let them do this sort of thing and built our vast debt, high taxes, and giant state? Why is it that in the 1950s we had growing economies, the US economically booming, and *normal* and decent values in our society?

How did we go from a world we recognized to one that hates us and works against us, using our money for things that destroy us? How did your power as a free person in a free society of decent families turn into drug-ravaged wastelands, urban blight, drive-by shootings, trans operations on kids, and invasions of people being given your money while you get nothing except more and more control of your thoughts and your speech?

How did the power of your wallet *and* your vote become so powerless when it should be the approval on which their power rests?

Money.

The short answer is money.

There is a lot of money in destroying a nation.

There is more money more immediately in destroying a nation than there is in making a nation great again.

They, the Globalists who have *zero* loyalty to you, your country, or any particular place or people, make small and regular profits if they do a good job. If they did the basic things right, there are contracts to be made and earned keeping everything working right, sure.

But the big money comes when everything is going to shit.

This is when you destroy an inner city you have ruled for fifty, sixty, or one hundred years and then demand a massive fresh input of money to save the place. Look at the squalor! Look at the deprivation! We need an "urban renewal fund" of $100 billion! Don't notice that we caused it all in the first place.

What changed is that the radical leftists seduced the money, gained control of the money, and then used the damage they had caused as the reason to claim even *more* money.

Radical left-wing terrorist groups like Weather Underground learned to seduce multimillionaire heiresses and the rich patrons who could bail them out or hire them lawyers. The lawyers got their big fees. The rich people got to distract from their own crimes and feel good about themselves at the same time. They got a cause! They got social justice!

Gradually, pumping money into insane radical causes becomes a great tax evasion, a way of purchasing power and influence, a way of avoiding monopoly rules and antitrust laws, or a way of getting social credit in your affluent circles of like-minded lunatics. It's a way of stealing from ordinary people and diverting their tax dollars or their hard-earned money to things the radical leftists want, the people they favor, and the causes that profit them even more.

They get to say they are saving the world, while they destroy your country or your city.

Now, you don't control public finances, they do. The people who hate you are hosing that money all over their pet projects and, in the short term, there is absolutely nothing you can do about it.

What can I do about Keir Starmer giving away another £11 billion? What can an ordinary American do about the next huge spending package in the US?

Well, you can pressure your representatives. You can back people who oppose the spending bill and criticize those who support it. You can get involved and try to get representatives who betrayed you primaried away. You can write angry letters.

I'm not saying any of that is worthless. All of that should be done. Engage as much as possible. Make yourself a pain in the ass. I had a friend who made a point of sending a letter of complaint, at least one, every week to his local member of Parliament. In one sense, it's petty. They just chuck them away and send a boilerplate automatic response. But say one thousand people did that every week in a single constituency. It gets to a certain level and it's much, much harder to ignore.

And the fact is that people engaging locally can get the worst representatives removed. A Liz Cheney can at least be forced out with enough pressure and then just has to spit venom as a panelist.

The attempt at least should be made.

But the power of your pocket, multiplied by other patriots, is still real. It can have an effect. Your lone letter isn't going to do it. So, send it anyway. Get others to send.

Bu more than that, since you aren't in control of what the corporations spend money on, what the government spends money on, or what public finances or private billionaire wealth supports, the power of your wallet becomes *more* important, not less.

You cannot yet tell them what to spend. But you can *show them* a cost to their choices. Your wallet is the only thing you control.

Can you afford to give *anything*, voluntarily, to the other side?

Can you afford to keep paying for a subscription to a charity, an organization, or a streaming service that goes woke?

Can you afford to willingly help companies that hate you, companies that fund LGBTQ+ propaganda, companies that fund race hate directed at you? Not really. There is so much money being stolen for them already that you cannot voluntarily add any more.

No matter how petty it might seem, and even if you see no immediate effect, you have to bother to research what that company supports and whether you give them your money.

We all saw the impact of the Dylan Mulvaney Bud Light disaster. Anheuser-Busch lost $27 billion in market value. Hundreds of workers at Bud Light were laid off, including some of the woke executives responsible for getting a trans activist to endorse their drink. These executives, in turn, endorsed trans activism themselves. Beer sales overall dropped 5 percent in the first nine months of 2023. Coors Light and Miller Lite sales spiked 18 percent and outsold Bud Light by 50 percent.

Woke corporations have billions to spare, of course. Anheuser-Busch controls a lot more than just Bud Light, and it's possible to stampede from a shunned product to a supposed "rival" that is actually controlled by the same group. But that's easily researched with a moment's effort. And despite their vast resources, none of these companies can afford too many hits like the one Bud Light took.

Boycotts do work. But they have to be immediate, and they have to be sustained.

In the first instance, a company will be forced into a pause, lose lots of money, and have to rethink their approach. Bud Light pretty quickly tried to backtrack. This is especially going to be the case when a huge backlash hits them by surprise.

The power of your pocket is real when multiplied. In order to make it multiplied, you have to act *as if it already is.* Go ahead and research and boycott and shop selectively. Let all your friends know which products and companies you trust and which ones you will not support. Starve Globalist institutions and woke companies of your money and intend to be a point of financial resistance. Join boycotts organized by others. Let the company know what you are doing and why.

Enough of us are pissed off. We need enough of us to act on it, and it really does not take long to control your shopping habits. If more people think and act like this, then we have already shown that we can cost them billions of dollars, force them to fire some of the guilty parties, and at least pretend to give a shit about our views and our willingness (or unwillingness) to purchase their products.

Sometimes you won't be able to persuade even your own family. But no significant boycott even begins without the first person starting it. Why not at least try for a series of Bud Light moments? *Your spending* and punishment of *their spending* go hand in hand. You won't control the second until you learn to control the first.

THE DIGITAL SAMIZDAT

Samizdat began appearing following Joseph Stalin's death in 1953, largely as a revolt against official restrictions on the freedom of expression of major dissident Soviet authors. After the ouster of Nikita S. Khrushchev in 1964, samizdat publications expanded their focus beyond freedom of expression to a critique of many aspects of official Soviet policies and activities, including ideologies, culture, law, economic policy, historiography, and treatment of religions and ethnic minorities. Because of the government's strict monopoly on presses, photocopiers, and other such devices, samizdat publications typically took the form of carbon copies of typewritten sheets and were passed by hand from reader to reader.

—"Samizdat," *Encyclopedia Britannica*

We will share with you the most up-to-date information daily. You can trust us as a source of that information. You can also trust the director-general of health and the Ministry of Health for their information. Do feel free to visit it anytime to clarify any rumor you may hear. COVID19.govt.nz. Otherwise, *dismiss anything else. We will continue to be your single source of truth.* We'll provide information frequently.

> We will share everything we can. Take everything *else* you see with a grain of salt. And so, I really ask people to focus.
>
> —(Italics added for emphasis), Jacinda Ardern, former prime minister of New Zealand, at the height of the COVID "scamdemic" in 2020

Totalitarian regimes always move towards the total control of information. They need to suppress news of their own crimes and sins and continually propagandize the alleged successes and positive qualities of the regime. As their behavior becomes more and more malign, corrupt, or criminal in the broadest sense, as their actions become more extreme and their misuses of power more obvious, the need to control information also increases.

They cannot let people see what they are, and even more, they cannot let people express what they are.

In the Soviet Union, this meant that the Communist authorities quickly developed a system of censorship designed to suppress any dissident voice, which worked hand in hand with a system of constant propaganda designed to present a constant, false image of life under Soviet rule. At its crudest, the propaganda presented the Soviet Union as an achieved utopia, as a perfect place of happy workers marching towards an ever more golden future. At the same time, repression worked by unacknowledged fear, by removals in the dead of the night, and by people being snatched from their homes and bundled towards interrogation cells.

Under a tyranny, it becomes a requirement to pretend that everything is normal and good, no matter how terrifying and abnormal it is. The people must smile by day, and those that smile the least tremble at night.

The propaganda branch of this essentially bureaucratic regime soon developed a stable of favored artists, writers, musicians and creatives who were rewarded for their efforts in casting the kindest light possible on Soviet life and Communist rule. Propaganda offices and government departments rewarded "agitprop," articles and novels that expressed Communist ideals. A writer submitting to this system could quickly gain a huge amount of support and endorsement. He would be promoted by the rest of the State's propaganda agency, and the possession of his works would be a mark of credit looked on approvingly by state agents, including the KGB. Essentially, he would be guaranteed a (literally) captive audience, status, and perks provided by the party for his presentation of their arguments and ideals.

This writer's efforts would be equally importantly in a system underwritten by a large and active secret police force, by arbitrary arrest and imprisonment, and by torture and murder by the State on an enormous scale. A writer in this system submits to the direction of an office of propaganda, produces exactly the kinds of text they want conferred a measure of protection to, and becomes a useful and sometimes favored literary pet of the Soviet regime.

Tyrannical systems understood the true meaning of "social credit." This was long before the Chinese Communist Party combined technological monitoring and surveillance with digital bank accounts in order to continually reward and punish citizens for their obedience or lack of it in an entirely automated fashion. And long before Globalists started proposing the same kind of social credit system for the West.

Writers who produced propaganda and obeyed the censors' instructions both got ahead socially and secured a kind of "KGB credit," whereby (like important party members generally) they had some protections from oppression that the average Soviet citizen was not provided. So long as, of course, they continued to toe the line and serve a useful purpose.

At the same time, every publication in the USSR was inspected by official censors. Any "private" correspondence was, of course, something the State was interested in and ready to intercept and examine, with strict consequences sure to follow if any proscribed thoughts and feelings were expressed in these communications. Any public text, whether a collection of poetry, a fictional novel, an autobiography, a biography, or a historical or scientific treatise, likewise passed through the censors' hands.

This meant that every publication you could obtain legally was censor-approved Soviet propaganda in one form or another. Anything dangerous to the regime or critical of its ideas was illegal, and possession or production of it could result in your imprisonment or death.

Despite this total control of information and the brutality of the regime, people still resisted. One of the ways they resisted was by the production of samizdat.

The samizdat were publications that were illegally and secretly produced and distributed. They had already been censored or banned, or they had never passed through the censorship and approval processes the system demanded. The term "samizdat" literally means "self-publishing." Dissidents were saying, "OK, you control all the publishing houses—we will publish this ourselves, free of your censorship, and without conforming to your propaganda."

Soviet control was so extensive that they even had lists of the typefaces used by every publisher so that dissident material could be instantly traced to its source. And when photocopy machines were invented, every use of a photocopier required official authorization, which was recorded and logged, so that any use of a photocopier to print copies of dissident or banned material could also be traced.

But the samizdat were made individually, often handwritten like some medieval manuscripts but also on hidden, privately owned typewriters. Multiple copies of a single text could be simultaneously made on carbon paper or tissue paper, which could be easily concealed and were cheap to produce. Covers were crude and blank, and the paper was of poor quality. The ink was often blurred. Yet, these aspects of the samizdat made them quicker and easier to both produce and conceal, and eventually, the home-produced look of these texts itself became a prized quality. A professionally produced work was a marker of inauthenticity and untrustworthiness, while a rough, home-produced look signaled courageous resistance and a willingness to share dangerous truths.

Via Samizdat copies, famous novels banned by the Soviet regime were distributed throughout the Soviet Union. Boris Pasternak's 1957 novel *Doctor Zhivago* was one of the earliest examples to receive this kind of copying and distribution. Solzhenitsyn's *One Day in the Life of Ivan*

Denisovich was similarly mass distributed this way. In other samizdat works, the equivalent of long-running magazines and periodicals were produced. Some were mainly poetry magazines, like Alexander Ginzburg's Moscow-based *Sintaksis*, or included poetry, like Vladimir Osipov's *Boomerang*. Under the brief Khrushchev Thaw of the mid-1950s, some of the Soviet restrictions were relaxed, but by the early 1960s, oppression had been fully resumed and these poetry editors were arrested. From 1965, following the show trial of writers Yuli Daniel and Andrei Sinyavsky, repression increased again.

The longest running and best-known samizdat (*A Chronicle of Current Events*, which ran for sixty-five issues between April 1968 to December 1982) was also the most directly political and the most embarrassing to the regime, since it essentially listed (in a surprisingly dry fashion that was nevertheless still damning) all the repression going on in the Soviet Union. Its regular features had stark headings such as "In Prisons and Camps" or "Arrests, Searches, Interrogations." Such accounts did the exact opposite of what the show trials were designed to do. While the show trial presented the repression as both just and to be feared, the samizdat account (stripped of every propaganda contrivance) showed the repression in its plain, ugly, squalid true form, as something unjust and to be defied.

How does this apply to modern circumstances and to the modern repression and control of information that occurs under Globalism? How does it apply to you?

The first way it applies is to show you the plain, ugly, squalid truth of what Globalist propaganda and Globalist censorship is. It is of exactly the same spirit and exactly the same methodology today as the Soviet system of propaganda and censorship was.

The modern mainstream media claim to be objective reporters of the facts. They claim to be custodians of the truth. But again, and again, we have seen that this is one of their greatest lies. The impartiality of the press—the freedom of the press—has become a grotesque lie. The reality is that they are as controlled and as politically directed as a publication like *Pravda*, the official Communist Party newspaper, was under Soviet rule.

We live within a system that still pretends to be democratic, accountable, and possessed of the qualities of a free society. We have allegedly differing political parties. We have newspapers that claim to be right-wing and newspapers that claim to be left-wing, with both claiming that they oppose each other and represent a free competition of ideas.

But on all the big questions, the mainstream media has a united, not a divided or competitive, voice. The same companies own both the "right-wing" paper and the "left-wing" paper. The Rupert Murdoch empire no longer really even pretends to be genuinely right-wing or even more outrageous than the populists, except at times in the *New York Post*. You can get a populist-sounding headline from the *NYP*, and they did try to publish the truth about the Hunter Biden laptop. But then Fox News went left, the Murdoch empire did a huge deal with Disney, the woke Murdoch children took over from their father, Fox and other parts of the supposed right-wing popular media organization went along with the 2020 steal, and News Corp-owned properties like *The Wall Street Journal* presented pure Globalist attitudes. The supposedly right-wing Murdoch empire includes the HarperCollins publishing house, which has published a string of critical race theory texts from "writers" and (even more laughably) "thinkers" such as Robin DiAngelo.

Fox News fired the late and much lamented Lou Dobbs (that rarest of all things today, an honest journalist) for being the only Fox anchor with the integrity to even discuss without instant dismissal the idea that the 2020 election was stolen. And later, of course, Fox news forced out Tucker Carlson when Carlson revised his opinion on 2020 and started speaking direct truth on other matters too.

During the recent UK election, *The Sun* newspaper, owned by Murdoch—which had once been pivotal in keeping out Labour governments—urged its readers to vote Labour, and did so when faced with an extremely socially radical, hard left, progressive Globalist Labour leadership.

The entire mainstream media, of course, pushed "Russian collusion" as a real thing, while ignoring the Chinese spread of influence and power through their purchase of Western politicians, including Biden and Justin Trudeau, and their purchase and funding of Western companies, universities, and organizations.

The complicity and uniformity of the mainstream media is absolute. Once "right-wing" outlets, like Britain's *Daily Mail*, now press LGBTQ+ and trans activism as if it were honest reporting. No mainstream media admitted that the 2020 election was stolen. None of them questioned perpetual war policies. All of them demanded COVID conformity and ran with every disgusting lie and every oppressive measure we saw in that period. All of them described normal patriotism as far right extremism. All of them gave credence to individuals and institutions with a firmly established track record of corruption and deceit. All of them used imaginary or false pronouns. All of them pushed for war with Russia and support for Ukraine.... All of them are Globalists.

There is no right-wing media. It is very difficult for a genuine patriot to get anything accepted by a publishing house. Populist voices, who are the modern dissidents of the Globalist Western world (just as the likes of Solzhenitsyn were the political dissidents suppressed by the Soviets), are kept off the radio airwaves, off the TV screens, and off the pages of newspapers and magazines. Populist figures up to the level of a serving president of the USA can be silenced and excluded on everything from social media to public broadcasts. When Trump was fighting the steal, Globalist broadcasters refused to air his full comments, and, of course, social media companies banned him. This was a serving president and a billionaire with a huge number of supporters. Everything done to him can be done much more easily to us.

Does it matter if the State directly censors and suppresses when it can outsource these actions to compliant and politically aligned social media companies and tech companies? When search engines like Google do the *same work*, via technology, at a far greater rate and almost invisibly, that the Soviet offices of censors once did?

All the time we are getting, from Globalist leaders, more and more of the kind of suppression, censorship, and thought control you *only* see in a tyranny defending itself, a tyranny as determined as the Soviet Union was to control all information because its own actions are repressive and vile.

We don't have a Gulag, Lubyanka building, or cellars where the KGB attach electrodes to genitals, that is true, but we do put people in prison for defying Globalist attitudes or publicly expressing populist ones. We do have CIA agents who use torture and CIA leaders, like the Trump-hating John Brennan, who support the use of torture. We do have, in the West, FBI agents who will shoot you dead on your doorstep in response to social media posts you have made. In Britain, we have just had the police arrest a man for an opinion on Facebook, and we do have an obviously unjust two-tier policing system where rampaging gangs of hundreds of Muslims terrorizing city centers face no arrest—are offered protection in fact—while police and the government promise to hunt down every white protestor and lock them up.

As Elon Musk tweeted to Globalist puppet and fresh British Prime Minister Keir Starmer, "Is this Britain, or the Soviet Union?"

Under Globalist rule, the comparison is not just understandable, it is necessary. It is the truth, and increasingly, it is not in the least bit exaggerated either. Of course, we haven't had the mass murders of Communism, thankfully. (Although you might well be able to count COVID vaccine excess deaths or things like fentanyl deaths in the US, which come from Globalist policies, as somewhat equivalent to Soviet famines.) But we have acquired virtually everything else, this time backed by a technological agency of control neither the Soviets nor the Nazis could dream of possessing.

Many of us still live in relative affluence and comfort and do so as long as we consider that to be the same thing as being free, so long as we do not speak the truth on the ways we are no longer free, we will be left alone. And harm that comes to us will just be from some favored other ethnic or religious group (that won't be harmed) rather than from a government goon kicking our heads in or a "boot stamping on a human face—forever," as George Orwell put it.

Does it make us *still free* if they outsource violence to Antifa, Black Lives Matter (BLM), or Muslim gangs, just as they outsource censorship to Facebook or Google?

But the fact that we live in a world more saturated with media and more driven and expressed via technology does offer us a solution that was not available to those resisting the censorship and propaganda complex of the Soviet Union.

Just as modern technology makes it easier to steal or block our money when we protest (through banks, as was done to Canadian truckers and their families), just as modern technology and the Globalist control of it means that a president can be turned off for telling the truth, so too does the same technology provide much greater opportunities for resistance.

And here we must take a moment to thank God for the existence of Elon Musk.

What Elon Musk did in acquiring Twitter was break the total wall of control Globalists had over all social media and all mainstream legacy media. Twitter was a woke playground where blue-haired progressives got to censor and control the speech and thoughts of everyone else, just like the whole public sphere in the Western world today. But behind that, it was also a company founded by CIA investments and working hand in glove with the US deep state and the intelligence agencies.

Because many of these new technologies—search engines, social media, the internet, and even companies like Google and Twitter (now X)—behind the scenes had been built with the assistance of DARPA grants, US military developed technology, and US state involvement and direction. It wasn't just a tech revolution emerging out of nowhere from the work of a spontaneous genius or two. It was also the consequence of huge military budgets and tech development budgets being incredibly excited by the idea of instant analysis of public opinion, instant vehicles allowing the transmission of messages to millions of users, and new means of monitoring and then shaping public attitudes. Psyops specialists helped create these platforms in order to use them rather than these platforms just springing into existence and then being suborned by the State.

And these entities, plus aligned billionaires they had created or who did genuinely independently reach similar conclusions, controlled it all. People like Mark Zuckerberg were ideologically aligned with them, so much so that he pumped hundreds of millions of dollars of his own money into fixing the 2020 election. People like Jack Dempsey would either be ideologically aligned or willing to do whatever they were instructed to do. People who resisted in the least would be threatened with the breakup of their new empires, with monopolies and antitrust cases against them.

Musk broke through all of that and has given us the same technological edge the other side has. We have a virtual space infinitely more powerful than a samizdat publication. We can sit at a keyboard, each and every one of us, and potentially reach millions of people through this technology. Even a lowly independent writer such as myself, with no prior assets or contacts, with no nepotistic or corrupt support, can gradually build a small and dedicated following of people who want to hear what I have to say. Anyone can, and many have been far, far more successful at it than me.

While new technology allows the outsourcing of some of the actions of a tyranny and promises a techno-feudal nightmare of future existence if full social credit systems are imposed according to Globalist aims and desires, the same advances allow us to produce the alternative media resisting it all and produce a digital flurry of samizdat far more widespread than the paper version was that resisted Soviet censorship.

Musk is being hit with all manner of attacks for his stance. And he's not a perfect human being whom I agree with on all things. For one, like many of these billionaires, he's tied up in military contracts still. Secondarily, he has a technophile's attitude to transhumanism when it comes to the interface of man and machine. He's developing man-machine interfaces that have all sorts of dangers to them.

But even with that said, his support for free speech has been genuine. And it's vital. The X platform has become the best place to get real news, instantly, free of the propaganda and censorship of all the other outlets. The platform still bans accounts, sometimes unjustly, but it doesn't do so as a constant, ruthless, totally partisan elimination of everything critical of

Globalism. It doesn't do so in a two-tier fashion, as the courts and police of the Western world, as well as the governments, now do.

On many key issues, Musk is on our side. Instead of arguing for abortion, euthanasia, fast-track death panels, and depopulation agendas as rival billionaires like Bill Gates do, he argues that the birth rate of the Western world is a cause for concern by being too low. He is literally on the side of humanity in the sense that he wants more human beings to exist.

Instead of a fantasy of the planet's death, he worries about the death of the species and acknowledges huge problems like declining fertility rates in women and sperm rates in men, declining IQs in Western populations, and the sheer danger of woke and Globalist ideas that dehumanize us or tend to, at the most basic level, be very poor survival strategies.

He does seem to be genuinely committed to a social model of free choice, fair elections, and basic civil rights in ways his critics are not. And at the same time, he's committed to the right of people to protect their culture, identity, borders and region from mass immigration and social breakdown. There's a sense of understanding of where populism is coming from.

With X, Rumble, and Truth Social, we have three platforms with a generally good record so far, and with Musk, we have a billionaire who may prove as significant to the saving of the West as Donald Trump is. We have the opportunity to use these networks to resist tyranny, build our own voices and alliances, and escape the fascistic alliance of state and corporations that is the rest of the media world.

With Substack, which has so far been pretty good in not imposing on the writers who use it (although there are woke executives in place and recently an attempt at more censorious control), we have a means of sharing articles and immediately getting those supplied to every paid and unpaid subscriber to our accounts. This, by itself, is more than any Soviet dissident writer had at his disposal for resisting that tyranny.

The more Musk commits himself to truth and embarrasses Globalist leaders, the more pressure will be applied to him, with concerted efforts to destroy him and X and to break up his business holdings. He's already become a hate figure for the woke and a constant target in legacy media, which tells us that he is doing everything right at the moment.

But we should think about how few people those paper manuscripts in the Soviet Union could actually reach and yet how great an impact they still had. People made those laboriously by hand and built networks of trusted friends and allies to pass them onto. People who wrote them were arrested and imprisoned. But the words still spread. The defiance still spread.

We have at our fingertips the ability to reach hundreds, thousands, millions. If a post goes viral, we have provided a digital samizdat that undermines the entire censorship and propaganda network that is costing our enemies an awful lot of money to keep running. Not all of us will be Tucker Carlson or Paul Joseph Watson or even a less alternative figure like Douglas Murray speaking decent amounts of truth and reaching a lot of ears.

But there are cracks in the wall of propaganda. There are routes out of the censorship. There is news that is actually true. And you can both use and be a part of alternative media, which is your only home until the mainstream is forced to tell the truth again.

Everyone who wishes to access large numbers of people or merely to access the truth for themselves and get news sources that aren't pushing Globalist lies, has to engage with alternative media and be on platforms like X. They have to support a figure like Musk despite some areas of difference, just as he supports in a very real way our freedom of speech and our freedom of thought. We cannot reject him because of his machine-man interface efforts, and unlike Globalists engaged in vaccine development or geo-engineering, I think he at least accepts our right to question the technology he is advancing.

The digital samizdat is waiting for your involvement. Get to it.

LIFE UNDER GLOBALIST RULE

Letters obtained by The Denver Gazette from the law firm representing CBZ Management—whose apartment complex in Aurora was shut down over what the city described as safety issues last month—show officials were fully aware weeks ago of accusations that a Venezuelan gang had "forcibly taken control" of the property.

In a June 28 letter to Colorado Attorney General Phil Weiser, the law firm wrote that CBZ Management had been informed that "Aurora Multi-Family Projects have been forcibly taken control of by gang(s) that have immigrated here from Venezuela." Based in Brooklyn, CBZ Management operates rental apartments in New York and Colorado with 11 properties in Denver, Aurora, Colorado Springs and Pueblo.

Aurora officials initially dismissed the company's claims publicly, calling them "diversionary tactics" and "alternative narratives." The issue, the city insisted, was the numerous violations of the local government's code. Officials have since walked those claims back.

—Nicole C. Brambila, "Attorneys' letters warned Colorado officials of Venezuelan gang control at Aurora apartments," *The Denver Gazette*, September 3, 2024

> The same judges who sentence rioters to time behind bars prescribe sunshine and an outdoor lifestyle to other criminals. This month, for example, Judge Mark Bury sentenced three men to over two years in prison each for violent disorder at a riot against immigration. Yet just a few weeks ago, Judge Bury advised Simon Pritchett, who possessed several hundred indecent images of children, to "get out more" because "what you have been doing over an 18-month period is downloading and retaining indecent images of children and extreme pornography images." Rather than sentence Pritchett to prison, Bury suggested that he "get some fresh air and meet people." After all, Pritchett lived in a coastal town.
>
> —Abigail Anthony, "In Britain, Two-Tier Policing and a Two-Tier Judiciary," *National Review*, August 18, 2024

Some readers might still be unsure on what all this is about. Is it really true that there is a ruling political and media class whose attitudes and ideology is fundamentally opposed to the best interests of ordinary people? Is it really true that the legacy and mainstream media exists solely to lie to us?

Maybe "net zero" is just a necessary change from an old technology that is harming the planet?

Maybe there are lots of kids who are gender confused with good reason and what people like me call perverse activism is just about being kinder and more compassionate to those kids?

And maybe this idea that "the Globalists" are pushing a whole range of disastrous things is a little paranoid or a right-wing conspiracy theory?

I'm suggesting that you should become more politically aware and politically active and that Globalism is deeply harmful to you and your children. I'm saying you need to carefully think about the companies you are supporting when you shop for anything and treat the news from most well-known news sources and channels as lies.

It's a reasonably fair question to ask whether people like me are just angry outsiders, raging at the fact that our brand of politics and our type of ideas are not socially dominant, that society has moved away from us and is going in directions we don't like, and that this is all there is to the perspective I'm sharing here.

Maybe he's just an angry old white guy out of tune with the world and too racist and ignorant to get with the program? Maybe he's annoyed at things getting better, at people treating ethnic minorities or gender and sexual identity minorities with a bit more compassion?

Obviously, I don't think that is the case. But the best way of expressing that truth and justifying everything I am saying is not by simply declaring myself a reliable and decent sort of guy. I'm not Jacinda Ardern, and I don't claim to be your only source of truth. I think it's much fairer to look at consequences. *It's by looking at what Globalism actually delivers.*

Because the truth is that under both parties of the official Left and parties of the official Right, we have been living under Globalist-progressive rule for some time now.

The idea that man-made climate change is real and dangerous has been the dominant climate orthodoxy for thirty years or more.

The black and gay civil rights movements are much older than that, going back to the 1950s and 1960s, and these form the alleged basis and inspiration for the modern expansions of them into affirmative action, public support for groups like BLM, or institutional accommodation of critical race theory and organizations like Stonewall.

Similarly, feminism has been around for a long time now and departments of women's studies or gender studies in universities have been around for much of my lifetime.

So, we could ask ourselves what is really new about all this? What is really threatening about it?

Transnational bodies like the European Court of Human Rights, the EU (first as the European Economic Community), the UN, the World Health Organization, and the IMF have largely all been part of the fabric of the normal bureaucratic infrastructure of the Western world, straddling multiple nations, since just after the end of World War Two. This was the system set up, supposedly, to prevent another Nazi Germany, as NATO was set up to prevent Soviet aggression in Europe and now, quite naturally, defends against the Russian conquest of other nations.

All of this globalization—trade across the whole globe and the whole globe becoming more interdependent and served by the same official bodies regardless of borders—was supposed to be a good thing. China would be drawn into the wider world and gradually enticed away from repressive measures. A China welcomed into the international fold and made part of the world economy would naturally, over time, become more like us, more democratic, more free, and more capitalist (in a good way).

And a West that engaged abroad more would also do it, this time, in a kinder and better way than it had under imperialism. It would provide vaccines and healthcare to the Third World, as the Gates Foundation has done. It would save smaller nations from the aggression of larger nations, with the US and Western allies acting as global policemen doing it all out of altruism, without a thought of their own interests. The UN would help prevent wars, the EU would prevent war in Europe, and NATO would deter aggression and prevent war, too.

The international order was one of trade and peace, and the Soviet Union was eventually defeated. Globalism meant that Western freedom, democracy, and values would spread everywhere, and everyone would grow connected to each other in ways that ensured peace and plenty for all.

Immigrant communities were a very good thing, filling roles and jobs that we didn't want to do, and adding youthful vigor to an aging Western population. We needed them for the National Health Service in the UK and the US needed them because, after all, everyone is an immigrant at some stage.

All these idealistic hopes and dreams of a "better world" are the ways that Globalism sells itself. It will be a world with less racial division and more racial equality. It will see fewer wars and fewer crimes. It's about being polite and being kind. It's a world with empathy. A world concerned about the most vulnerable. A world that is less polluting and more sustainable. A world with a better human rights record. A world where everyone is valued.

That is still the image of Globalism presented by Globalists themselves and, of course, presented within the school textbooks they write or the promotional advertising they scatter throughout society.

You have been living under the rule of these idealists for some time. Tell me, *does it feel like the world you live in has gotten better?*

Has critical race theory, Race Relations Acts in the UK, sixty years of affirmative action in the US, trillions of dollars of race-based spending, diversity officers in every company, and race-awareness training courses as part of the standard requirements of every business *made life for the majority of black or white people significantly better?* More importantly, are black cities and areas in the US, after all these decades of advocacy, activism, and spending on their behalf, the safest cities in America, the cleanest, the least affected by drugs and crime and gangs and violence?

Is Chicago world renowned as one of the safest, nicest, and most affluent cities on the planet, or is its reputation a little different to that?

How about the US school system? After the scale of investment there, after a move to a high tax, high spend, and deeply progressive model of education, the US school system must be the envy of the world, right?

What's that? School districts with massive investments returned not a single student capable of basic math and literacy? The Common Core program that was a disaster? A collapse down international educational ranking tables?

But surely there are successes elsewhere under Globalist policy and Globalist rule?

Quite clearly there must have been a lot of new wars under the only *non-Globalist* leader of the US or the UK in the last thirty years? All the wars must have started under Donald Trump, right? I mean he's a dangerous, reckless, stupid guy who ignores the clever, brilliant, strategic minds of all those think tanks and foreign policy units, right?

What's that? His period saw the Abraham Accords, North Korea negotiating with the US, and China and Russia contained, and when he was ousted we got the Afghanistan withdrawal disaster, the Russian invasion of Ukraine, the West prolonging that war when there could have been peace, the whole world closer to a nuclear conflict, and Hamas committing mass genocide in Israel?

Does that sound like *things got better* to you?

But those Globalists at least know how to run an economy, don't they? How are your food bills doing? Your energy bills? What kind of people drove the world economy off a cliff in 2008 and then drove the world economy off a cliff *again* with totally unnecessary COVID lockdowns in 2020? In most Western countries, Globalists were in charge of both of those disasters, and Globalists were in charge of the entire fiat banking system and the explosion of debt and spending by Western governments in recent decades. Every head of every Western national bank and pretty much every *other* bank (including many that have gone bust in recent years) was a Globalist following Globalist economic principles.

The ONLY major Western leaders during COVID who weren't Globalists were Donald Trump and Viktor Orban in Hungary, and Trump was crucified in the Globalist media for even *suggesting* that lockdowns weren't needed or should be ended rapidly.

If you are an ordinary person, a low- or even middle-income person, *you have already been severely harmed* by Globalist economic positions. You've endured a cost-of-living crisis and an inflation crisis, after a banking liquidity crisis, and periods of sustained economic stagnation. Right now, as I write this (September 2024), we are seeing a stock market crash (particularly in or coming from Japan). During COVID in 2020, billionaires gained $3.9 trillion, while workers and the middle class *lost* $3.7 trillion, as reported in TRTWorld in "Viral inequality: Billionaires gained $3.9tn, workers lost $3.7tn in 2020."

Globalism can be very good for some of us. Particularly when it's very bad for *most* of us.

If you are a British pensioner being told that your country cannot afford £1.2 billion for your Winter Fuel Payment but *can* afford £11.6

billion to "tackle climate change" in foreign nations...is Globalism working for you or against you? Your life is being made worse, quite clearly.

The current US generation is the first US generation since World War Two to see its life expectancy *and* its economic prospects decline, to see a negative shift in which they are likely to die younger than their parents and struggle more than their parents financially too.

IQ rates are declining. Fertility rates are declining. Excess deaths have risen significantly. Crime rates have laughably been reduced by reclassifying crimes or not recording crimes, when in real terms by the old systems of measurement...they too have risen.

There are more cancers. There are more heart attacks. There are mysterious sudden deaths.

Anxiety rates have risen. Suicide rates have risen. Race-based assaults have risen. The current generation in the US and the UK is the most suicidal, depressed, and mentally disturbed generation of the modern era.

That's strange, isn't it? All this *gender affirmation*? All those school counselors? All those policy documents on compassion, kindness, empathy, inclusion, diversity, and equity...and the kids are unhappier than they were before and more likely to kill themselves? Wait, wait...the *gender-affirmed* ones are forty times more likely to kill themselves than the others?

For most people, life is harder, shorter, more dangerous, and more unpleasant, and the societies they live in are more divided, more crime ridden, more dispiriting than they were a generation or two generations ago.

It's almost as if every noble ideal expressed by Globalism was expressed by a policy that was actually extraordinarily destructive.

Judge them by the consequences—not by the virtue they signal or the lies they sugarcoat every disaster with. Judge them by the simple impact of what they do and whether it works and whether it makes things better for ordinary people.

In the effort to be fair in the writing of this book (far fairer than Globalists ever are), I decided to research things from their perspective too: to read the critical race theorists, read the arguments for mass immigration, and read the UN policy documents on the Sustainable Development Goals.

And if you take them strictly at their word, if you mindlessly ignore every possible negative consequence, then yes, some of the aims read as things you would support, just as some of the labels they apply to their initiatives sound like good things before you analyze or look at what they actually involve.

Like social justice. Who wants *social injustice*? Who wants to say, "I oppose justice"? The aim is deliberately cast in irrefutably noble language, language you might be embarrassed to oppose. But *what does it actually involve?* Well, then, you see that the label is not an honest one because it involves deliberate, racially applied injustice. It involves giving one race perks and advantages, while telling the other races that they are born with perks and advantages they don't actually possess. It means stopping deserving Asian Americans and whites going to college so that more places are available for black people with lower SAT scores.

You don't have to take my word for it that Globalist-progressive policies are founded on lies, enact injustices, and create disasters—that they make life worse for most of us. You can use your own eyes when you see Jews being chased across a US college campus, a campus where everyone claims to be kind, empathetic, and anti-racist. Or you could go and read Thomas Sowell, who will provide you with a lot more detail and evidence than I do (but fundamentally say the same things).

Or you can just look at your food bills today compared to four years ago.

Life under Globalist rule is worse than life before Globalism, and it's getting increasingly worse all the time, so much so that we are dying sooner, dying in larger numbers, and dying poorer than our parents did.

And these people demand more and more power over everything (your choices, your diet, your health, your bodily autonomy, your thoughts, your speech, and your private accounts) and more and more tell us that criticizing them, disagreeing with them, or voting for people other than them are now criminal offenses.

You are economically worse off under their rule, and you have less freedom too.

That's the real face of Globalism. Forget the idealistic promises of a kinder nation. Look at the reality, the consequence—like a 300 percent rise in rapes in certain neighborhoods of New York. Forget being told that they are saving you from a pandemic—look at the number of excess deaths following an experimental gene altering "vaccine." Forget being told you are heartless towards the poor women and children fleeing warzones—look at the fighting-age men crossing the US Southern border or filling the dinghies landing in England. Forget the "Be Kind" slogans-and remember that these people will place whole populations under house arrest and curfews, just like Communist China did.

In the interests of being fair, I looked around for something other than the policy documents, for a text explaining to me why so many people in the middle classes think that Globalism is a good thing. Why were a large number of people in the UK passionate Remainers? Why do middling affluent Americans still vote for the economically disastrous Democratic Party?

Psychologically, there's an awful lot to go into there because we are essentially dealing with people who have been indoctrinated and brainwashed and who now invest their own identity and sense of self in a patently ludicrous set of beliefs. But these are beliefs that tell them they are better than you or me: kinder, smarter, more evolved, and more enlightened. And they love feeling that and believing that.

At the upper levels, of course, every Globalist is a crook who is personally benefiting enormously from the damage they do to others or to their nation. Asset-stripping (profiting from ruthlessly selling off and gutting national infrastructure in ways that harm the nation) is very profitable to those doing it—diverting public spending is too. But more than the greed, corruption, and psychological sense of self-regard it allows them, how do Globalists justify all the disasters their policies enact?

The short answer is that they don't. They don't see these things. *They claim the negatives don't exist.*

They are capable of ignoring millions of deaths, just as earlier supporters of Communism were unconcerned by the 100 million deaths in the name of that ideology.

So, they can definitely ignore your rising bills and your lowered life expectancy.

The best summation of the attitudes of an enthusiastic Globalist I could find was in a little book called *A Beginner's Guide to Globalism*, written by Celia Engelbrecht. It actually encapsulates Globalist thinking and the kind of person who is a Globalist better than anything else I've seen precisely because it is intended as a brief introduction rather than an exhaustive treatise.

The author claims to be some kind of entrepreneur or business executive. The whole thing reads almost like a satirical spoof of the overly eager, unknowingly vapid business hustler, offering a motivational talk built entirely on self-satisfaction. It's almost touchingly stupid, painfully upbeat, and as chillingly awful as the management-theory version of a Zumba dance class conducted by a very keen, purple-haired instructor of indeterminate gender.

What's interesting about it is that it is, on the surface, a business text, an explanation of how to network and advance in a global business environment. But it's really much more like a cross between a little book of prayer (for people who think Christianity is *The Handmaid's Tale*) and a self-help book by a self-elected guru.

It's full of happy, positive, excited talk about saving the world and building a utopia, and hilariously, it links all of these moments to business examples where people called names like Adrian or Augusto manage a Zoom conference call between investors in Japan, Switzerland, and Brazil all at once.

For the author, Globalism is the opportunity to develop an app with somebody in Germany, allegedly to make crop rotation easier for a farmer in Zimbabwe. Profit and philanthropy are entwined, just like Saint Bill Gates.

The sheer absurdity of it all doesn't register. The bemusement of the Zimbabwean farmer or the fact that he doesn't want an app because his government has already killed him doesn't register.

There's lots of talk about avoiding cultural offense and how different cultures might have different rules, but the thinking is essentially that everyone, no matter where they live, wants to develop an app for Zimbabwean farmers. Or buy one. Or have a synergy brainstorming session about potential business Finnish Congolese-fusion opportunities with this bizarre First World overly familiar creep.

And this genuinely is how the middle-level Globalist views the world. *Things like the nature of Islam don't intrude any more than things like ordinary people wanting you to fix the potholes in their road before you develop apps for Africa intrude.* The whole world is not so much a global village as a vast Zoom conference call, where everyone from every nation is just a moderately successful, unknowingly dim-witted guy who wants to develop apps for Africa and go to his Zumba class feeling like he's saved the entire planet.

In the UK today, as I write, Muslim gangs have just run amok, kicking in heads and carrying swords, while the media rant about the imaginary far-right threat and the government tells us that if we share the truth we will go to jail. That's the reality of living under Globalism, while the view presented by the Zumba-class entrepreneur is just a sort of semi-religious utopian dream of what Globalism is.

And that's why your reactions and actions matter, even while you are perhaps politically homeless and powerless. A Globalist government is never on your side.

Part of surviving that is becoming a lot more independent yourself, by acquiring personal skills and disconnecting yourself from the State, police, and all the other institutions that don't care about you at all. You can't keep relying on people who hate you.

Living under Globalism is always going to hurt your interests, so trying to live outside of that system as much as you possibly can becomes a matter of survival, as well as a proof and protection of your integrity.

The aim must be self-sufficiency in as many areas of your life as possible, with independent thinking and freedom from propaganda being just the first step taken along that path. It must be self-help in the real sense, like the self-publishing of the samizdat, rather than in the bullshit sense of the kind of books "Mr. Zumba Class" would read.

YOUR GUNS

THE SECOND AMENDMENT AND SELF-DEFENSE ON GLOBALIST STREETS

A foundation of American democracy is the natural law principle that every human possesses certain inalienable rights. Inherent in this is the right to self-defense—that is, to forcibly resist infringements on inalienable rights. The right of the people to keep and bear arms, enshrined in the Constitution's Second Amendment, is centered not on hunting or sport shooting but on this natural right of self-defense. It gives 'teeth' to the promises of liberty, ensuring that attempts to reduce our natural rights to mere dead letters may be met with meaningful resistance.

—*The Essential Second Amendment*, The Heritage Foundation

> If you wanted or if you think you need to have weapons to take on the government, you need F-15s and maybe some nuclear weapons.

—Joe Biden, "Remarks by President Biden and Attorney General Garland on Gun Crime Prevention Strategy," The White House Transcript, June 23, 2021

There is, of course, a startling cultural difference between the United States and most Western European nations, particularly the United Kingdom. That difference is the Second Amendment of the Constitution of the United States of America. It is the right to bear arms, the frequency of gun ownership, and the huge number of Americans who are familiar with firearms and own firearms.

The Founding Fathers of America considered the right to bear arms vital to the preservation of American freedom and a means of protecting the people from an over-mighty government. Self-formed militias were, of course, vital to the creation of the nation, and Washington's army could not have been formed and could not have resisted the professional soldiery of the greatest empire on Earth without the populace already being familiar with and possessing arms of their own.

Guns and gun ownership are part of the unique identity of America. They feature in the stories of citizen militia crouching behind hedgerows to snipe at red-coated adversaries. They are integral to the expansion of the new nation into the Indian territories of the West, which had been treaty protected under British rule. They are part and parcel of both the romantic vision and the sometimes more squalid reality of the Wild West. America is the nation that coined the term "gunslinger." It's the nation where huge parts of its cultural mythos are based on a good man with a gun defeating an evil man with a gun and, of course, large numbers of that evil man's hired killers.

From the Westerns to *Dirty Harry*, from Clint Eastwood to Bruce Willis, from John Dillinger to John Rambo, American men have been offered a template of manliness in fiction and reality which is always and strongly connected to guns. Of course, real-life examples (Billy the Kid, Dillinger, Prohibition-era gangsters, real criminals, and real FBI agents alike) blur into their fictional counterparts or into mythologized versions of themselves in a constant retelling of stories in which the gun is the only actor to star in every single version.

"The Home of Freedom" has always also been "the Land of the Gun," the land seized by their gun, tamed by the gun, and created and built because of the gun. And the possession of freedom and the possession of a gun has, for many Americans both in the past and today, been inextricably linked and what the Second Amendment is fundamentally about—what the Second Amendment enshrines and preserves.

Today, about a third (32 percent) of Americans say they own a gun but a larger group (44 percent) say they live in a household with guns. The percentage of Americans owning guns has held relatively steady since the 1970s, with anti-gun campaigns and extremely emotive arguments following incidents like school shootings doing little to impact on the (at the least) third of Americans who do want to own a weapon.

Illegal and unregistered gun ownership is, of course, something much harder to estimate but undoubtedly vastly even higher than the best estimates, which are taken solely from registered weapons. Criminal possession of firearms is, of course, common in gangs and among hardened US criminals (the quixotic gun-shy gangbanger would likely not last very long, even more so than the counterparts who are armed).

Those who do own guns tend to own more than one. The Small Arms Survey (2020) estimates that there are roughly 393 million privately owned firearms in the US, with a startling 120 guns for every one hundred Americans.

The latest 2023 figures show 82 million gun owners in the US. That's out of 345 million people (remember a large number of the overall population will be children). To repeat, 82 million people are armed. That's even more than the number of people who voted for Joe Biden and that figure included the dead, the imaginary, and people in asylums. The US has 40 percent of the civilian-owned guns in the entire world.

By contrast, the UK has just 3.3 civilian-owned firearms per one hundred citizens. There are 204,901 registered gun owners aged between fifty to sixty-four, who are 36 percent of all certificate holders. If the same rate of ownership covers other age categories then that would very roughly work out at between 800,000 and 1.5 million gun owners (one-eightieth of US levels, although of course closer than that when adjusted for relative population levels).

In most cases, it's the rural population of the UK who own firearms, with shotguns being the most common firearms owned. In other words, gun ownership in the UK is dominated by the relatively small percentage of people who work the land, such as farmers, groundskeepers, and the like. These gun owners are a distinct minority much smaller than the third of Americans owning guns, and gun ownership in the UK is heavily restricted by the Firearms Act of 1968. All licenses are determined by the police and subject to criminal records checks, mental health assessments, and the provision of "a good reason" to own a firearm. UK guidance insists that "Firearms are dangerous weapons, and the State has a duty to protect the public from their misuse."

Even illegal gun ownership is likely to be significantly lower in the UK than it is in the US. Stabbings and acid attacks partly become significant due to the general lack of firearms or difficulty obtaining firearms, and most gang violence-related deaths in the UK have been from knives and other melee weapons. Guns have been featured in attacks, but at far lower rates. There was a spate of gun incidents in Nottingham a decade or more ago, representing an unusual peak that caused national comment.

The UK has had mass stabbing incidents and one or two mass shootings, but it's nothing like the number of such incidents as they occur in the US. (It should be pointed out here that, devastating as they are, the frequency of things like school shootings is often exaggerated in the media while an ongoing toll of gun crimes that are gang related or from things like home invasions or domestic crime are downplayed. The majority of gun deaths even in the US are *not* from lone psychopath mass shootings but rather from suicides, domestic murders, and gang violence.)

The public perception of gun ownership in the UK (and UK ideas about gun ownership in the US) tends to much more broadly reflect the attitudes held by US opponents of gun ownership and be based on much of the same emotive reasoning that ignores where the majority of gun deaths occur. Europeans often have a sneering superiority when talking about US gun ownership, with the assumption—particularly from our ruling classes, media, and ordinary citizens who only follow mainstream news—being that average American families are constantly dodging bullets at the school drop-off and are just not sophisticated enough to dislike that experience. (A little arrogance flows in the other direction too, with many gun-owning Americans sneering that the British, for example, are sheep who gave up their right to defend themselves.)

Bu what's the importance of all this in relation to Globalism and living in Globalist-run countries?

Well, the significance for you and how you protect yourself is twofold.

First, you have to consider whether guns or weapons protect you from your increasingly authoritarian government. Globalist-led governments across Europe and in the US, Canada, and Australia have shown that they *will* take away your basic civil rights. They will place you under house arrest, curfew, and lockdown when you've committed no crime. They will prevent you from assembling in churches, weddings, and funerals, let alone in political protests (current Democrat vice president pick Tim Walz set up snitching hotlines so that people could report transgressors of COVID rules).

They *are* prepared to talk about forcibly holding you down and injecting you with an experiment you don't want to take. They are prepared to break the Nuremberg Code on medical consent and coercion. And they are all introducing more and more draconian measures regarding free speech and the right to protest or dissent politically. The director of public prosecutions in the UK has just reminded people that they could be arrested for sharing (accurate and truthful) footage of riots online.

Globalist governments function by what has been termed "anarcho-tyranny." They create anarchy on the streets as they mass release genuine violent criminals (as George Soros–funded district attorneys do in the US or as the new UK government did in response to alleged prison overcrowding) and as they decriminalize or refuse to prosecute crime and anti-social behavior from favored groups (for example, asylum seekers, migrants, and ethnic minorities). They create two-tier justice systems that excuse their own crimes while inventing crimes to be charged against political opponents. And they turn police agencies into partisan actors, enforcing not the rule of law equally to all but the arbitrary power and unjust whims of one particular party.

Under Globalist rule, the streets become more dangerous, violent offenders are emboldened, dangerous people are imported over open borders, and lawlessness that harms ordinary citizens thrives. That's the anarchy.

At the same time, your thoughts and words are more heavily and unjustly policed, your political choices and associations are potentially criminalized, and more and more aspects of your life are subject to rules, restrictions, fines, and potential imprisonment if you defy the instructions given to you by the Globalist elite. That's the tyranny.

In the US, mothers who pray publicly and peacefully (for a daughter murdered by the police) can be arrested, as Ashli Babbitt's mother was. Or in a different example, a grandmother who protested at an abortion clinic can be arrested, charged, and imprisoned by a smirking Democrat judge who taunts her family about her beliefs as they beg for clemency and justice (Judge Kollar-Kotelly's comments to seventy-five-year-old Paulette Harlow and her husband John Harlow). Or another can be sent to prison for wandering around the Capitol Building having harmed nobody, offered no violence to anyone, and committed no property damage—while people from the other side of politics, who burned down federal buildings, were never arrested or charged.

In Canada, another grandmother peacefully protesting can be charged by officers on horseback, knocked under a horse's hooves, and ridden over because emergency legislation that was supposed to only apply for wars and major disasters was applied to people (once again, let's emphasize this, *peacefully*) rejecting COVID mandates.

In France, Macron put snipers on the rooftops of Paris and tanks on the streets against "yellow vest" protestors, but Arab or Muslim riots go ignored and multiple areas of Muslim settlements in France, where these criminals get to do as they please, are no-go areas for the French police.

In Britain, we are simultaneously arresting people for what are, effectively, *mean tweets*, while ignoring armies of Muslims (gatherings that have one hundred, three hundred, and even seven hundred people at a time) marching through town centers looking for whites to attack.

This is anarcho-tyranny in action, and it means that you can no longer expect the police to protect you. You can't even expect, when you have a Globalist government and media, that the police will try to arrest people who attack you or to stop them. They could just as easily arrest you for defending yourself from assault or for you saying something they didn't agree with. Just the other day, during our recent Southport riots, a woman offered the police tea and refreshments on her street. But she told them at the same time that immigration has ruined her neighborhood over the last sixteen years…so they arrested her, and she spent the night in the cells.

The police, under Globalism, will be your enemy. They will help and assist the immigrants imported to replace you, and they will let them commit crimes. They will police your thoughts rather than protect your streets. They won't be there when you are scared and need protection. They won't catch your rapist (see the rates for how many rapes lead to a successful prosecution). But they will crack your skull open if you shout hurtful words about mass immigration. They will say they don't have the resources to investigate a burglary or home invasion. But three of them will turn up to investigate your Facebook post.

And this is because they are following the new rules laid down by their Globalist senior officers. These are people who have been promoted into senior roles after years of political and ideological loyalty and box-ticking identity rather than for policing experience and actual competence.

So, you are forced to think about self-defense but also to negotiate those laws that are designed to leave you defenseless in increasingly dangerous societies.

If you can legally obtain a firearm, train yourself in its use, visit a range, learn to shoot, learn to use that weapon safely, and follow safe procedures for its storage, then it is now increasingly sensible to do these things. And it will grow more sensible the more your Globalist government holds open your borders to millions of fighting-age men from the most dangerous and violent and culturally backwards regions of the world.

The laughing condescension of the "liberal" on gun ownership, whether British, European, or American, is an active suppression of your ability to defend yourself and your loved ones from the consequences of the kinds of policies and attitudes they vote for and enact when in power. They don't care if you and yours are hurt or defenseless. They expect you to prefer to be beaten, raped, or murdered than to want to own a firearm and defend yourself.

The arguments against gun ownership are now outdated ones, laughably naive in the face of savage hordes being invited into your country. The only people who can afford that disdain for firearms are people who can afford private security (which is armed) or who are wealthy enough to live exclusively in places the violence will probably never reach.

Obviously, it remains far easier to obtain and learn the use of firearms in the US than in places like the UK. And that is a significant advantage US citizens have when protecting themselves from violent criminals. US gun advocates and lovers of the Second Amendment are right on that, and Europeans are wrong. Trusting others to protect you only works in a cohesive, well-ordered (usually homogeneous) society that is *culturally* safe. It works in Japan, for example, or it worked in Britain fifty years ago before mass immigration.

In a Globalist-run world or nation, all such trust is misplaced. You can't rely on the authorities to make your country a safe and well-ordered place. You can rely on them to do the opposite.

Even without firearms, it is now sensible to look more closely towards protecting yourselves. If you can, move to a safer area. Get out of the worst places; get away from the Democrat-run cities or the Labour-run inner cities of Britain. But learn to protect yourself too. Learn some form of self-defense. Try to keep fit. (I say this as a person who knows he has often failed in that regard and could do a lot better.) You could have a whole life without ever needing those skills of physical defense. You could be lucky like that. But the first time you face a dangerous situation and need those skills is the time where they could save your life.

Just like owning a firearm could, too.

One final point to make, and this is one that will be harder for Americans to hear. This is about how effective your right to bear arms is in terms of protecting your freedom from an over-mighty government and the abuses of tyranny.

It's only as effective as the willingness you have to use those firearms, and even then, it won't be effective as an individual. It is only effective at all in terms of a citizen militia (which is why militias are so demonized and the Democrats want to portray them all as domestic terrorists).

One of the most chilling authoritarian things that Biden let slip during his period as "zombie president" came with his comment mocking the Second Amendment and those who support it:

"Right now, you can't go out and buy an automatic weapon. You can't go out and buy a cannon. And for those brave, right-wing Americans who say it's all about keeping America, keeping America independent and safe—if you want to fight against a country, you need an F-15, something a little bit more than a gun.

"No, I'm not joking. Think about this. Think about the rationale we use, that's used to provide this, and who are they shooting at? They're shooting at these guys behind me [referring to the police]."

Those mocked gun owners and right-wingers were quick to point out that in several places, at least abroad, the vast resources of the US military had indeed been defeated by people armed with just guns, people who did not possess F-15s. And that's true.

But it also missed the real points. The real points here are that Biden is actually right in terms of the difference between what a Globalist leader can apply to you and what you can apply to a Globalist leader. The State has the monopoly of power and the monopoly of the armed forces even in a nation where lots of citizens are armed.

Individually, the possession of arms does not protect you from the government, from the State, as it becomes more tyrannical. Even if you have an arsenal of weaponry, the government has more than you. So, you hate the government, and you own firearms. That doesn't make you a person empowered to resist. It makes you a target to be crushed.

The State can send fifty or one hundred FBI agents to your door. It can send SWAT teams to your door. It can murder you on your doorstep. It can shoot your dog and your wife and your son, and it will. All your possession of arms has done, on the individual level, is give them an excuse to kill you. You don't have the power to resist as an individual. No stockpile, legal or illegal, really changes that.

If the US government wants to kill you, it can. Your gun collection doesn't change that.

And if we look at tyrannical actions by Globalists and compare them between a country with high gun ownership and a country with low gun ownership, there is no difference.

Compare the UK and the US.

I've lost track of the number of American friends who have commented about the terrible situation in Britain. They warned each other that if they aren't careful America is going that way too or boasted about the Second Amendment and offered versions of "if they tried that here, see what they would get."

These comments seem unaware of the fact that the Globalist march of tyranny has been very successful in the US, just as successful as it has been in the UK. The US has had a stolen election. Did the possession of arms prevent that? The US has had thousands of people arrested on partisan political grounds. It has had protestors held for years without trial. It has had protestors tortured in prison. It has had the government telling social media companies who can speak in public. It has had a relentless expansion of the surveillance, monitoring, and control of ordinary people.

The US has seen a presidential candidate illegally spied on, then spied on *while* president. It has seen rogue security and deep state intelligence operatives breaking every law imaginable. It has had the FBI creating terrorist plots to kidnap politicians. It has had multiple state-sanctioned murders of unarmed people or murders of individuals on their own property.

How much of all this did gun ownership prevent?

The answer is *none* of it. The answer is that the US is already a Globalist-run tyranny, just like the UK, France, Canada, or Australia.

Your possession of a gun can protect you from a home invader. It can protect you from a school shooter. It can defend you and your family in your car, your home, or the street outside from criminals who want to attack you, as Kyle Rittenhouse defended himself from Antifa attackers.

But it has not stopped Globalist crimes, crimes by the ruling class and the progressive elite, crimes that turn your country into a tyranny stage by stage. It has not stopped the Democratic Party from committing crimes and getting away with it or creating crimes and charging people with those crimes.

The only time your possession of arms matters in terms of tyranny is when there is already a civil war or when hundreds of thousands of you are prepared to use those guns against the State and its agents.

Americans have not made that choice. The truth is that the brave right-wingers are naturally decent and law-abiding people who don't want a civil war. They, like the people of Britain, have peacefully accepted an awful lot that their ancestors would not have accepted.

They live and continue to live under burdens the Founding Fathers would have been astonished and revolted by, under terms the Revolutionary War-generation would have considered intolerable. And this has crept up on them by degrees over generations of the expansion of the State and the corruption of the deep state.

So, a gun is not automatic freedom and justice. A gun-owning society is not automatically protected from the revocation of freedom and the triumph of injustice.

It is only as free as the amount of injustice it finds intolerable. It is only free when it acts to secure freedom (peacefully or violently). Arms only repel tyranny under civil war conditions, when a large number of people use them. Under normal conditions, they do not protect the individual from the State, and they do not prevent the society becoming a tyranny. But they *are* useful in terms of individual protection from smaller-scale attackers in an increasingly dangerous society.

Mutually assured destruction between nuclear powers acts as a deterrent, but the Globalist is not deterred by gun ownership. Of course, he wants to remove it, but he's already got away with a huge amount because the people he is oppressing are mainly people who want to be left alone, want clean and safe streets, or want decent schools rather than being people who want civil war.

IS IT WORTH VOTING?

If you are bored and disgusted by politics and don't bother to vote, you are in effect voting for the entrenched Establishments of the two major parties, who please rest assured are not dumb, and who are keenly aware that it is in their interests to keep you disgusted and bored and cynical and to give you every possible reason to stay at home doing one-hitters and watching MTV Spring Break on Primary Day. By all means stay home if you want, but don't bullshit yourself that you're not voting. In reality, there is *no such thing as not voting*: you either vote by voting, or you vote by staying home and tacitly doubling the value of some Diehard's vote.

—David Foster Wallace, *Up, Simba!*

I don't vote. Two reasons I don't vote: first of all, its meaningless. This country was bought and sold and paid for a long time ago. The shit they shuffle around every four years doesn't mean a fucking thing. And secondly, I don't vote 'cause I believe if you vote, you have no right to complain. People like to twist that around, I know; they say, they say, "Well if you don't vote, you have no right to complain." But where's the logic in that? If you vote, and you elect dishonest, incompetent people, and they get into office and screw everything up, well.... You caused the problem. You voted them in. You have no right to complain. I, on the other hand, *who did not vote*, who, in fact, did not even leave the house on election-day, am in no way responsible for what these people have done, and have every *right* to complain as loud as I want about the mess *you* created that I had nothing to do with.

—George Carlin, *Back in Town* comedy special

If things were still normal and the Western world was what it used to be, you would have peaceful, easy options for removing a government you don't agree with. If the majority of people did not support that government or its policies, it would, at the next election, be removed from power and the *policies the majority of people prefer* would be tried instead.

You would have regular elections. Those elections would be free and fair. There would be no significant electoral fraud. There would be no rigging of the vote. The parties at these elections would present manifestos with different policies, and the approaches of these parties would differ on important issues allowing voters a genuine choice.

Nobody would be able to *purchase parts of the electoral process*. Nobody would be able to selectively silence millions of people on key topics. Nobody would be able to spy on a political candidate for partisan reasons and get away with it.

The West would still be the Free World, and it would be able to honestly tell places like Russia, China, Africa, and South America that this is how you run genuinely accountable and democratic systems where ordinary people have rights that can't be violated and votes that can't be cheated.

Sounds good, doesn't it? We had that, and it was taken away.

We were the Free World, and it was taken away.

Largely, we had elections we could trust and choices between different political approaches. And that, too, was taken away.

We had free and fair elections. An independent, nonpolitical judiciary. An independent, objective, and unbiased media that would hold any party in power to account. Political parties that represented genuinely different ideas, so that everyone could feel that they had some political representation even if their party didn't win. A police force that was politically neutral. A civil service or administrative state that was politically neutral. Some sense that the people in power were themselves following the law and had limits on how they behave and what they can do to the rest of us. These were the standard features of a liberal democracy, and by and large most Western nations, until recently, possessed them.

Sounds good, doesn't it? It sounds like a system that people fought and died to obtain, a system that took centuries to emerge. It sounds like a system that stood as the apex of human civilizational effort, at the very end of a long, long history of the enfranchisement of ordinary people, and as the application of restraint and civilized rules to the behavior of powerful people.

It is the thing that the entire history of the Western world flowed towards, and it was, despite horrors and reverses and frailties along the way, despite corruption and chicanery and attempts to halt its surging tide, despite the occasional traitor or would be tyrant, and despite rich men wanting solely their way or scribes and journalists printing half-truths and lies, even despite the grim rise of foul regimes and ideologies in the early twentieth century…it was magnificent. Beautiful. Glorious.

Or as Donald Trump might say, great.

Or as we once knew it to be, *free*.

Anyone who still thinks the Western world is being run this way is a blind fool.

Globalists love to talk about democracy. They absolutely love the word. They like to say that they are saving democracy at home, and they like to say they are spreading and saving democracy abroad.

You could paint the word "democracy" on the bombs they drop.

They love the word, and they mean the opposite. One of the most telling little phrases of the period between 2016–2024 when it comes to the difference between the things Globalists say and the things Globalists actually mean is the two word phrase, "our democracy."

Lots of Democrats who hate Trump love saying, "our democracy." Lots of Republicans who hate Trump use the same phrase: "Our Democracy is under threat!" they thunder.

What they mean is the exact opposite. *It is democracy that threatens Globalists and the style of tyrannical, autocratic, and unaccountable government they actually want.*

The thing that is so worrying about the people, for Globalist elites, is that the people are an unwashed, uneducated, and uncontrolled mass who might, heaven forbid, vote the wrong way. They might elect a Donald Trump or a Nigel Farage. Can you imagine? They might pick a policy that Globalists don't want.

The Globalist fear of the common man, of Populism, is that the views of ordinary people might shatter the cozy consensus of the ruling class. The Globalist political consensus is that the views of rich people with blue ties and rich people with red ties and rich people from the same schools and country clubs and golf clubs and tennis clubs must not be challenged. Wealthy Globalists who lunch together, socialize together, and think exactly the same way about everything cannot allow ideas and policies to bubble up from the "flyover states," nor can they accept ideas which rudely intrude from the rural counties, or which come shambling into the affairs of the nation still smeared with the disgusting grease and grime of real work and real life.

Can you imagine? That's real democracy, and they hate it. They find it deplorable.

The operative word in "our democracy," the word that really counts, isn't "democracy" at all. It's "*our*." The thing that matters is their *possession* of the system, their control of the game.

So, they "fortify" the election results, as the famous *Time* magazine article put it. They rig the votes. They steal the elections now. They twist the law and abuse their total control of the mainstream media to cover it all up. They commit massive electoral fraud. They love postal voting, which makes that fraud a lot easier. They hate ID and proven citizenship-based voting in person, which makes that fraud much harder.

Ever wondered why the same people who want ID for *everything* and are really strongly in favor of digital ID systems and monitoring every citizen as much as possible, the people who are fine with ID for purchases, mortgages, and every time you move five feet or take a shit or interact with any branch of officialdom—these people *oppose* using IDs when voting? That's a curious contradiction, isn't it?

The other forms of ID increase their control over you, so they like them. ID for voting reduces their ability to steal an election, so they don't like it. With non-ID voting and not in-person voting, they can fill in the ballots themselves, and they have more control over you, not less. So suddenly their usual love of ID requirements flips around.

They flipped in a similar way, as it happens, on electronic vote tabulation and vote tallying machines, like those provided by Dominion. When Democrats wouldn't have been in control of these machines, they pointed out all the truthful things about them—they can be hacked, they can be programmed to give false and weighted tallies, they aren't reliable, and they make fraud easier. As soon as they or people allegedly on the other side who are working with them (like Republicans who want Trump to lose) have control of those machines, well then, those machines are 100 percent safe and secure and questioning them becomes a criminal offense or a thing that Dominion or similar companies can sue you for questioning.

The integrity and reliability of the machines did not change. Who would have control of them and be able to program them changed.

Electoral fraud follows the old "Machine politics" of Chicago and is now completely routine and very important to the determination of US elections. It requires a fairly large, but not ridiculously large, number of ground-level operatives, like mules harvesting votes and ferrying them to drop boxes or like people ready to board up windows, push out election observers, run fake ballots through machines, and the rest of it.

But it actually requires more operatives at the other end, the *reporting* end. You also need to ensure that nobody in mainstream media is a real investigative journalist and impartial and objective enough to report the fraud. You need them *all* to say "nothing to see here" or "tinfoil hat conspiracy theory." There are thousands of them, and they were all on the payroll and said what they needed to say.

Even letting people speak who were questioning it at all became a firing offense, as the fate of Lou Dobbs illustrated. Even allowing one side to speak became a thing that had you reaching a settlement handing over vast sums of money, as Fox and Rupert Murdoch discovered.

When questioning a suspicious election becomes a crime, that suspicion is confirmed, not denied. Any election that can't be questioned is an election that should be questioned.

People who say, "Ridiculous, you'd need thousands of people to pull off a conspiracy like this" seem to be completely unaware that thousands of people are *routinely* purchased, if you have enough money. They're completely unaware that the entire media can be directed to speak with an identical voice and ignore fraud and corruption.

When elections were rigged in places like Venezuela or Zimbabwe, nobody in the West said, "Of course, they can't be rigged. It would take thousands of people." Everyone understood that Robert Mugabe *had* thousands of people prepared to do that stuff.

And so do Globalist leaders in the West. These people were openly purchased as election workers and Democrat election observers.

The year 2020 established a precedent in the West that you could really blatantly and openly steal an election now. You could do it so obviously that it involved stopping the vote for hours while people were cheating and then extending the vote for days while votes were manufactured and pumped into the places that changed the overall result. You could do all this and get away with it. You could have filmed evidence of this fraud and have it ignored. You could change the rules (without any legal basis for that) as you go along and have that ignored too. You could have eyewitness accounts and signed affidavits of hundreds and thousands of people who were prepared to go to jail if their declarations were false saying, "I saw it being stolen" and that didn't matter.

You could have absurd vote spikes that are statistically impossible, and people seeing a vote result flipped as they watched, and that didn't matter because you already owned the media and the Supreme Court was *terrified* of intervening.

People who say it should be forgotten now have no understanding of how precedent works, not just legally but psychologically. This was a big moment.

It told Globalists that they could get away with anything. They could steal a US election and oust a president they didn't like and none of *them* would ever go to jail for that. And it told *us* that the reason that election was stolen that way was because Trump was genuinely different to the rest of them.

The elections only require massive fraud and being rigged when one of the candidates isn't owned and controlled and isn't a Globalist. When it's an illusory choice between two Globalists, they don't have to go that effort.

That's why the "uniparty" approach is favored over electoral fraud, when they can win that way. It's less obvious; it's less dangerous; it's less expensive. It's easier and cheaper just to purchase the politicians you need from both parties—or control them some other way (blackmail, etc.).

Quite frequently, you don't need the huge fraud when the competition between parties is *itself* a fraud. People are getting the same policies anyway. One government goes, and the next government does all the same things. No populist idea ever gets in, and no Globalist idea ever gets kicked out.

If you look at something like the Tony Blair years versus the David Cameron years in Britain, you find absolutely no difference in the type of people in charge and the policies that people got from the government in power. Any Blair minister could have seamlessly settled in a Cameron government and vice versa. Blair was not in the Labour Party in any real sense and Cameron was not in the Conservative Party in any real sense. Both were and are archetypal Globalists.

So, the game is rigged, and if you are an ordinary person who wants a smaller state, lower taxes, fewer wars, normal attitudes on gender and race, your kids taught rather than indoctrinated, your civil liberties respected rather than removed, and your energy policies cheap, efficient, and reliable, then you aren't getting what you want out of a vote.

If you oppose or don't want any Globalist policy or action and if you find all the woke stuff crazy, all the climate change stuff hysterical, and all the race stuff hypocritical, divisive, and racist towards you, where are you going to go?

You're going to go to new parties, because all the established ones are owned and crooked and keep betraying you. You'll go to the populist alternatives like the Alternative for Germany party, the Reform UK party, or Prime Minister Giorgia Meloni's Brothers of Italy party. You'll only keep with a main established party if they have a movement like MAGA and a leader like Trump.

But is it worth voting at all?

After all, if we think, if we *know* that the game is rigged, why keep playing?

Well, most people aren't quite ready to tip up the board and scatter all the pieces yet. Most people remain desperately desirous of some peaceful solution. We don't want to riot or burn things down. We aren't those sorts of people. Most of you just want to be left alone and have some basic freedoms and not have propaganda you don't agree with shoved down your throat.

And as rigged and corrupt as it all is, we did get Trump elected in 2016, we did get Brexit voted for in 2016, and we did get Meloni elected in 2022. Argentina is coming out of its socialist nightmare thanks to Javier Milei, elected in 2023. The Alternative for Germany party has made significant gains in Germany. Viktor Orban is still dominant in Hungary. Geert Wilders has the largest party in Holland (but won't be the next prime minister when Mark Rutte steps down).

It is possible for very large electoral surges for populism to overcome attempts to rig the vote. Although, even if they get into office, any sensible person will face the running sabotage and effectively treason from Globalists, including within their government and groups like the intelligence and security agencies or the permanent administrative state, as their term continues (as Trump did).

At the moment, it is, just barely, still worth voting on the hopes of that kind of surge. But it's with the realistic expectation that our side doesn't just have to win—we have to win by a margin that is so large that it becomes embarrassing to repeat the events of 2020.

And yes, relying on the embarrassment of the shameless is something of a fool's errand. There are no discernible limits to how much Globalists will rig, cheat, steal, and lie.

Until you are personally prepared to engage in a sort of ongoing resistance of activism, direct action, mass protest, mass strike, or even a 1776-level response, until very large numbers are prepared to do that and basically mount the kind of never-stopping protest and uprising you get in actual revolutions that change entire systems, it does not cost you anything to keep voting.

Nobody can really expect to vote their way out of tyranny. But you have a partial chance in a partial tyranny. It's up to you to estimate how fully along that path your nation has gone, although for me, I'd say all of the Western world is much further down it than I ever thought possible in my lifetime.

Faced with the reality of votes being manipulated or ignored, with the absence of choice when every main party wants or does the same thing, and with the same Globalist policies being delivered regardless of election results, many people are becoming disillusioned enough to voluntarily disengage from the political process entirely. In the 1980s, this attitude of disillusionment could sometimes still be portrayed in an amused fashion that was surprisingly free of bitterness, as for example in the "none of the above" scene in the film *Brewster's Millions* (the Richard Pryor version). But today, we have had another forty years of many people being ignored and left behind.

In the UK, elections always used to receive 70 percent-and-higher turnouts. In the 2024 UK election, turnout was at least 20 percent lower than that, and the trend is further downward. But does refusing to vote have more impact than voting for a small or outsider party? Low turnout and lack of mandate does not seem to be a thing that any Globalist fears, whereas voting against them still is. If the 40 percent of people who did not vote in the UK had voted for the Reform party, that would have represented a significantly higher number of people the system would need to cheat to put in place its Globalist-chosen administration.

Perversely, Globalist calls to outright ban parties like the Alternative for Germany and Globalist efforts to imprison (or murder) Donald Trump do suggest that there is still some benefit to voting, even though huge amounts of corruption and fraud are now being applied at all times.

But every vote is pointless without concerted efforts to reduce the fraud and reduce the Globalist manipulation of the results (including the media's false reporting). If you don't acknowledge and look to prevent the cheating, you become another compliant servant of the emerging tyranny.

JULIAN ASSANGE AND HACKING THE SYSTEM

Secrets impose a cost, usually on the victim or their loved ones. To properly understand their wound they need to understand what happened, and why.... It's understandable the US doesn't want to start discussing all this in public again. But it also helps illustrate a truism that we too readily forget: that governments keep secrets for the wrong reasons—usually to conceal from their own citizens that rules have been broken. But at the same time it goes out of its way to punish as severely as it can any individual like [Chelsea] Manning or [Julian] Assange—*pour encourager les autres*. That, so far, hasn't worked: Think of all the whistleblowers who have followed in Assange's wake—[Edward] Snowden, Antoine Deltour (LuxLeaks), Maria Efimova (Malta), Reality Winner (NSA), Frances Haugen (Facebook), Hervé Falciani (HSBC), Rudolf Elmer (Julius Baer), the still anonymous Panama Papers leaker, Xavier Justo (1MDB), Howard Wilkinson (Danske Bank), nearly all of whom have through their bravery helped launch investigations and/or changes in policy, despite great peril to themselves and the journalists who report their stories.

—Jeremy Wagstaff, "Yes, we should care about Julian Assange," Medium, February 23, 2024

On June 26, 2024, a plane touched down in Australia, and a man returned to his nation of birth having been incarcerated in Belmarsh Prison in London from April 2019 to June 2024. Before that, the same man was confined to the Ecuadorian embassy in London, having claimed political asylum there from June 2012 to April 11, 2019.

He was a man who was wanted by the Swedish authorities who had issued a European arrest warrant for him in 2010, in relation to claims of rape (with all charges and the investigation finally dropped by Swedish authorities in 2019). He was also wanted by US authorities for releasing sensitive military information. The US authorities indicted him for conspiring to commit computer intrusion and for violating the Espionage Act of 1917. British authorities found him guilty of breaching the Bail Act and sentenced him to fifty weeks in prison for that offense. The US government attempted to arrange his extradition to face charges there, but these efforts were battled through the British courts.

In June 2024, this man agreed to a plea deal with US prosecutors. In return for pleading guilty to one Espionage Act–charge of conspiring to obtain and release classified US national defense documents, the US agreed to treat the charge as having been addressed by time already served. It was this agreement that allowed the world's most famous fugitive to return home.

The man in question, of course, was Julian Assange, founder of WikiLeaks, a non-profit media organization that specializes in leaked documents and whistleblower cases. WikiLeaks published a series of leaks from Chelsea Manning, a former US Army intelligence analyst, which included footage of a US airstrike in Baghdad, US military logs from the Afghanistan and Iraq wars, and US diplomatic cables. It was these releases that precipitated the US' and UK's pursuit of Assange.

Some of the work done by WikiLeaks was mainstream enough to result in collaborations with legacy media, such as a report on political killings in Kenya that appeared in the UK's newspaper, *The Sunday Times*. Other releases included embarrassing financial details and investments from high-profile individuals, such as the Julius Baer bank leak, which led to an eventually dropped prosecution. WikiLeaks was also consistently quick to share embarrassing files and information already discovered by others, as they did with the Panama Papers (financial details consisting of 11.5 million leaked documents published from April 2016, which included information on more than 214,000 offshore entities).

It's clear, though, that as embarrassing as some of the financial information being leaked could be, *the real threat posed by Assange and WikiLeaks was as a depository and clearing house*, as well as a sanctuary and ally for any and all whistleblowers emerging from business or government globally with a story to tell about damaged powerful interests or the reputation and standing of Western governments.

The Manning information showed the willingness of Assange and WikiLeaks to include national security information and classified military information in the kind of materials they were prepared to openly reveal, share, and discuss. It was a step significantly in advance of what most legacy media outfits were prepared to do (especially as mainstream media gradually evolved out of 1960s idealism on investigative journalism and more towards being the cultural and news mouthpieces of predetermined, sanctioned, and owned positions supportive of Globalist aims and policies).

In a period where the news is being more owned, controlled, and unified than ever before, an organization like WikiLeaks represents a profound threat in the same way that citizen-journalism or alternative media does, but one which also has immediate security implications and draws the attention of the Secret Service too.

As an ordinary and largely powerless citizen, my attitude to figures like Assange or whistleblowers like Manning and Edward Snowden (a US National Security Agency contractor and former CIA operative who, in 2013, leaked classified documents that revealed the existence of global surveillance programs run by the NSA and the "Five Eyes" intelligence agencies in cooperation with telecommunications companies and European governments) has radically altered in recent years.

Back when I was a Conservative, fairly trusting towards the institutions and authorities in charge, my patriotism naturally inclined me, like many others, to see people who released national military secrets as traitors. I saw the likes of Assange, Manning, and Snowden as people who endangered the lives of real patriots. These three were people who might assist foreign powers or terrorist organizations due to the kind of information they released.

To an extent, some of that attitude remains. The blanket release of tens or hundreds of thousands of documents risks some of that information genuinely being the kind of stuff that is perfectly legitimate for a still accountable and still democratic nation to want to remain secret. The names and private addresses of undercover agents active abroad, for instance, would be genuinely sensitive information, with obvious potentially disastrous consequences. *Operational details* of ongoing security actions or technological data on advanced weapons systems or security systems are, I think, data that most ordinary people can understand should usually be, to some extent, secret.

The problem with this trusting attitude comes when the authorities, and especially the national security agencies themselves, prove that they aren't trustworthy. The problem comes when (and sometimes based on information that is only ever released by whistleblowers, leaks, or computer hacking and only ever shared by people like Assange) the information you have seen shows your "defenders" and "protectors" (the alphabet agencies that are supposed to be protecting you from foreign regimes and defending your freedom too) *are themselves corrupt or treasonous in their behavior*.

What do you think of people like Assange, Manning, and Snowden when you realize that a vast continual surveillance operation exists that isn't tracking foreign agents or terrorist threats but is prepared to classify concerned parents as "domestic terrorists" for speaking against pornographic or trans activist literature at a school board meeting? What do you think of the NSA when you realize *they are spying on you when you haven't broken any existing laws,* and when you find out that they are often more concerned with monitoring Trump-supporting Americans than actual Chinese agents active in America?

For the traditional, ordinary patriot in 2024, our attitudes have undergone a huge shift based on the increasingly insane, ideological, and tyrannical actions of a whole host of institutions we used to support.

It's hard to trust a police force that kneels to BLM and cracks your head open for waving your national flag or voicing concern about mass immigration.

It's hard to trust intelligence agencies that work to remove a legitimately elected president and spy on him but have done seemingly nothing to prevent the spread of Chinese influence and Chinese spy networks.

It's hard to see something like fifty or so intelligence agency experts signing their names to a partisan political lie, which many of them, like John Brennan of the CIA, absolutely, categorically knew to be a lie when they spread it, endorsed it, and signed their names to it.

And it becomes stupid to think of these experts, agencies, and individuals as sharing the same patriotism as yourself, for you to see them as being the best defenders of your nation available, or of being the sources you trust most when they work against you and against your interests on purely political party lines.

When the security agencies shifts from being an outward-facing force protecting you essentially from foreign threats to being an inward-facing force protecting a chosen hierarchy from your legitimate criticism and concerns, when they shift from protecting you with your consent to oppressing you against your wishes, these institutions have become parts of a Globalist regime you do not support and should not accept.

And if you discover that more and more of what they are doing seems both corrupt and malign, then, of course, you need to revise your attitude towards whistleblowers, hackers, and people sharing previously classified information.

If you think differently about John Brennan and his type, if you no longer trust them, then you must also think differently about Julian Assange and his type and trust them more than you did before. The two things are inevitably linked, since the whistleblowers release the information the security agencies want hidden.

In many cases, they want that information hidden and under wraps because it was doing good or because brave and decent servants of the nation would be endangered by its release. In many cases, *they want that information hidden because it reveals a catalog of crimes which they have committed*. Or because it reveals a totally malign, ideologically driven set of priorities and obsessions that are themselves inimical to the freedom, safety, and concerns of the average patriotic citizen.

No ordinary person wants the lives of their military personnel unnecessarily endangered. They don't even want that to apply to the lives of the police or the FBI. But they want all of the security agencies, police personnel, and surveillance and monitoring that is actually necessary *to be focused on our actual enemies and not on our own people, to be focused on foreign threats and not peaceful citizens.*

They can understand tracking and stopping Islamic terrorists. They don't buy the lies that the biggest threat to the American, British, or Australian people is "the far right" or that voting for Trump is a threat to democracy but taking money from Chinese companies linked to the Chinese Communist Party and the Chinese military is perfectly fine.

The crimes and misinformation of *both* Globalist politicians and the deep state or the alphabet agencies have now been exposed to the extent that there is far more patriotism in listening to an Assange than there is in wanting him imprisoned.

Without the kinds of leaks he facilitated, if we had relied solely on the mainstream media for news, much of the most important news of recent years would be completely unknown to us (as it is to those who still insist on only trusting mainstream news sources).

One of the tools at your disposal, still, is to independently critically assess the information that a whistleblower releases, ask yourself whether it is something you and others should know, and whether it is something that, after learning about it, you would wish to change.

If you can walk around with your head up your ass trusting mainstream media entirely and thinking that the CIA are beyond reproach, the FBI aren't in the least bit politicized, the wars we fight are all based on rational strategic interests and for the good of our nation, and that if anything really bad is going on, those brave guys at the NSA or those truthful guys at The *New York Times* will sort it all out for us, then I salute your mental and physical gymnastics.

A position of complete trust today is, after all, something that takes a lot of moral and mental dexterity to attain. You have to twist yourself out of the way of every opposing fact and every already revealed sin.

For me, the whistleblowers are worth defending, and they are revealing things that might help me, restrain my government, or inform my friends. The government and the mainstream media are doing nothing but lie to me—they are attempting to lie in such a way that my rights and freedoms are being taken away, and my nation is changed beyond all recognition, perhaps irrevocably.

The relationship between the State and the individual is a negotiated relationship dependent on trust. Like any of our normal interactions, such as our personal interactions with neighbors, family, and friends, we must be able to trust that, broadly speaking, our government sees the world similarly to us, has our best interests at heart, and can mostly be trusted in what they say and do.

We cannot expect them to hate and attack us but still offer them our trust and support.

We cannot hear nothing but lies and believe the next word is true.

One of the most interesting things about the information released by whistleblowers and organizations like WikiLeaks, about the kind of information Julian Assange was sharing, is that *it is almost never the case that even those who wanted him imprisoned ever said that he was lying. They never asserted it, let alone proved that the information was false.*

Quite the contrary. If the censors and imprisoners had any justification for their actions at all, it could only be based on the information being true.

Imaginary classified information is not a threat. Only real classified information is a threat.

What this means then, what we should recognize when judging all this, is that even for its detractors and the people intent on shutting it down, WikiLeaks has a record of veracity no mainstream news organization can match.

It is considered a danger by the authorities because it tells the truth.

Whereas mainstream media is a danger to us because it never tells the truth.

If you want the truth—if you think an adult in a democracy or a modern, supposedly liberal nation-state (in the classical liberal sense) is primarily allowed both the right to know the truth and the right to speak it to others, then it is clear which side is more aligned with your interests today.

Just as it is clear that the people moving towards the criminalization of all dissent are not serving the interests of the average citizen when doing so.

THE CENSORSHIP-INDUSTRIAL COMPLEX AND YOUR FREE SPEECH

In his 1961 farewell address, President Dwight Eisenhower warned of "the acquisition of unwarranted influence…by the military-industrial complex." Eisenhower feared that the size and power of the "complex," or cluster, of government contractors and the Department of Defense would "endanger our liberties or democratic processes". How? Through "domination of the nation's scholars by Federal employment, project allocations, and the power of money." He feared public policy would 'become the captive of a scientific-technological elite." Eisenhower's fears were well-founded. Today, American taxpayers are unwittingly financing the growth and power of a censorship-industrial complex run by America's scientific and technological elite, which endangers our liberties and democracy.

I am grateful for this opportunity to offer this testimony and sound the alarm over the shocking and disturbing emergence of state-sponsored censorship in the United States of America.

The Twitter Files, state attorneys general lawsuits, and investigative reporters have revealed a large and growing network of government agencies, academic institutions, and nongovernmental organizations that are actively censoring American citizens, often without their knowledge, on a range of issues, including on the origins of COVID, COVID vaccines, emails relating to Hunter Biden's business dealings, climate change, renewable energy, fossil fuels, and many other issues.

—Michael Shellenberger, *The Censorship Industrial Complex: US Government Support for Domestic Censorship and Disinformation Campaigns 2016-2022*, testimony to The House Select Committee on the Weaponization of the Federal Government, March 9, 2023

With whistleblowers and organizations like WikiLeaks, with individuals like Edward Snowden, Julian Assange, or Chelsea Manning, what is being suppressed is truthful information that is embarrassing to the authorities and to the governments of the USA and aligned nations.

Some of that will be sensitive military information, and we can differ on how much of that it is legitimate for a government to want to remain confidential, even if we, on the whole, favor transparency and free speech.

But that's not the only information that is suppressed.

When intelligence agencies and surveillance, security, and police agencies become politicized, and when only certain types of Globalist policy are allowed and the security agencies and the courts are trying to rig the system so that people who would pursue different policies can't get into power, then inevitably it is not just operational military information or genuine state secrets that would be damaging to release and are covered up, lied about, and banned from the public sphere.

It is *everything* that might make you vote the "wrong" way, think the "wrong" way, and criticize the Globalist agenda in any way.

It is anything that opposes the Globalist agenda, *no matter how truthful that thing is*, and no matter how widespread and commonplace that opinion is. Indeed the neologism "malinformation" has been coined specifically for information that is known to be true but that the authorities insist must be suppressed. People who are supportive of this new pervasive censorship approach bandy around the terms "disinformation," "misinformation," and "malinformation" with the seeming total assurance that they have the right to decide for all of us what is true or even what truths we are *permitted* to access.

The central problem for Globalists is this: they believe a whole set of things that most people don't believe, they profit from a whole set of things that impoverish everyone else, and they want a radically different social model that very few other people actually want.

And they have inherited democratic systems with elections and once high standards of free speech, allowing people to criticize their governments and the policies of the powerful.

In these circumstances, if elections are not rigged or interfered with, if the public have a free press that is honest and discusses key topics without favoring one side more than the other, and if the people could then also freely discuss things among themselves and reach their own informed conclusions because they have free speech…Globalist policies would die.

In a genuine democracy, Globalist policies are unpopular and therefore could not become the standard policies of democratically elected governments.

And there are obvious reasons why, honestly discussed, every major Globalist policy is unpopular. Let's take two seemingly unrelated examples:

Are most people fanatical climate activists who think the world is going to be destroyed in ten years unless we move our entire economy away from cheap and reliable energy sources…or are they people in the main who want cheap and reliable energy?

Look at how ordinary people trying to get to work respond to activist groups blocking the road, ask them what they think of such groups, or see what share of the vote Green parties get—and you can see that the majority, despite years of propaganda on the man-made climate change theory, are not convinced by Globalist policy on the planet and the climate.

Nobody has ever got anyone to vote in a majority for the "net zero" policy. Globalists just demand that policy and start instituting it through unelected transnational bodies and conferences. Then governments enacting the measures demand it without ever asking the people if they support those policies.

Any honest person would have to admit that still, despite hundreds of millions of dollars' worth of propaganda (if not trillions) over the last thirty years, the radical climate policy is still not the thing that would be done if the public had a real say.

Or how about the whole "woke" issue and the attitudes to, say, race and gender, which Globalists support?

Are the majority of people social radicals who think that white people are born inherently evil and need to apologize for that and that school children need lessons on how evil whiteness is and how things like objectivity, meritocracy, and logic are all white inventions, which are racist?

Of course, this is not an understanding of what opposing racism means for most ordinary people and the majority of the population.

But this is, again, the understanding of the ruling class and the political and media elite. It is the understanding of race and racism taught in our universities and now in our schools too. That's been the critical race theory consensus among the US elite for decades, and most universities in the US make accepting this nonsense mandatory for staff to work at the institution, for pupils to receive classes in this thinking, and for research based at that institution to be allowed to go ahead and receive funding.

For years, too, this sick, hypocritically racist set of beliefs has been taught in US schools, against the wishes of the majority of US parents (of all races). In the UK, the current (elected 2024) Labour government plans lessons on the evils of whiteness for all pupils, starting in primary schools.

Did even the tiny percentage of people who voted for the Labour party want such lessons? Do the majority of people in the UK already think that white children are born possessed of racial advantages, racial guilts, and racial crimes that others don't have or aren't guilty of?

No. The majority see such automatic hatred and discrimination aimed at white people as no different to aiming these things at non-white people, and they are right.

But the ideology that white people must be taught to oppose whiteness is the Globalist attitude, the attitude of the people in power, and that is what is enforced now.

It would not, if honestly discussed, win any vote, anywhere.

So, the problem for Globalists is that they have adopted ideas and policies only a minority of fanatics want. These are damaging, divisive, and ruinous ideas that would not win a fair vote and have not persuaded a true majority of voters.

What do you do if you want things that the people don't want as a government or as a ruling class?

Well, you lie about the things you want, you propagandize them, and you sell and promote them constantly through your complete control of mainstream media.

And what do you do if the majority *still* don't want the things you want? If they start distrusting the media you control and going to alternative media instead? If they start abandoning voting altogether out of disgust with the parties you control, or if they start forming new parties that do listen and will offer real difference?

Well, then you start censorship. Then you start saying you will ban those voices of dissent, remove them from social media platforms, and silence the most successful critics of your unpopular Globalist policies and the most honest exposers of your most frequent Globalist lies.

Then you move from going after a Julian Assange or an Edward Snowden to going after everybody who shares the information they have released.

Then you delete millions of posts, hire fact-checkers to police millions of accounts, exclude anything that hints of dissent, and you instigate new laws designed to limit the expression of even peaceful disagreement with Globalist policies.

Or you go after platform operators and owners who allow free speech and non-Globalist comment, like Elon Musk or the CEOs of Rumble or Telegram. You follow the advice of Robert Reich, as shared in his *Guardian* article called "Elon Musk is out of control. Here is how to rein him in" on August 30, 2024:

"Regulators around the world should threaten Musk with arrest if he doesn't stop disseminating lies and hate on X. Global regulators may be on the way to doing this, as evidenced by the 24 August arrest in France of Pavel Durov, who founded the online communication tool Telegram, which French authorities have found complicit in hate crimes and disinformation. Like Musk, Durov has styled himself a free speech absolutist.... Musk's free speech rights under the [f]irst [a]mendment don't take precedence over the public interest."

Who defines the existence of hate? Why, Globalists like Robert Reich of course! Who defines "the public interest"? Why, Globalists like Robert Reich of course! What is his proof that Elon Musk is spreading "hate" and "disinformation"? It's this:

"Musk owns X, formerly known as Twitter. He publicly endorsed Donald Trump last month."

This is, in Reich's world, sufficient to qualify for an arrest. Hilariously, he accused Musk of "backing Trump and other authoritarians around the world," apparently oblivious to the fact that he is himself publishing op-eds calling for people who vote differently to himself to be arrested for it.

But Reich is not alone in this stunning self-blindness. It's the standard Globalist position, and it is informing the law-making and legislative creativity of every Globalist government as they justify to themselves a now sacred mission to silence all dissent.

The more you lie about everything, the more you have to censor everything too. The more distant, remote, and unrepresentative your views and attitudes become from those of the ordinary majority, the more you have to label normal views and attitudes as misinformation, disinformation, and malinformation (ideas you *know* are true but don't want people hearing), the more you destroy free speech and impose censorship.

This process is everywhere now and increasing in severity.

We are long past the point where the only people needing to worry about persecution and imprisonment were the people releasing highly sensitive military data.

There are people still going around thinking that they live in free and democratic nations that don't behave like tyrannies behave. There are people who think the news reports the truth, the press is unbiased or that there is some equal distribution of bias, the whistleblowers are traitors, and if you haven't done anything wrong, the police and the courts can't be used against you.

These people are painfully deluded and living now by a touchingly anachronistic view of the Western world.

It's a view, as a patriot and a lover of Western civilization, I wish was still true. But under Globalism, it isn't.

You do not have free speech.

You might have the "Universal Declaration of Human Rights" that includes free political association and free speech as principles and is one of the supposed founding documents of the UN—but today your government will imprison you for Facebook posts and the UN will reprimand it after hundreds of people have been imprisoned for hurtful words and mean tweets, for not policing your thoughts and words hard enough.

The UN will call you racist unless you lock up more white people for politically incorrect opinions on mass immigration. That's what the UN has just done to the UK—one of the most Globalist, most censorious, and most thought-policing Western nations there are.

Because no matter how Globalist a government becomes, no matter how much it restricts its majority white population and actively persecutes them…the UN will demand more.

As I write and as mentioned above, France has arrested the founder and CEO of Telegram because Telegram allows free speech on its platform. This is an outright tyrannical move, rather akin to arresting and imprisoning Alexander Graham Bell because somebody using a telephone said something you don't like.

The EU recently wrote to Elon Musk, threatening him for planning an interview with a former president and current presidential candidate.

The purpose of these moves, along with the arrest of hundreds of people in the UK for opinions on social media, is to chill and scare everyone else from saying similar things or from questioning any Globalist or government policies. Interestingly, UK judges cited as criminal and vile comments they deemed to be spreading "anti-authoritarian" rhetoric and views. Strong condemnation of the police, the courts, the judiciary and ruling political parties was seen as hateful and criminal.

That casting of anti-authoritarian commentary as being criminal is a version of what is criminal that, of course, encompasses *any* criticism of the institutions and government of the day and which makes perfectly peaceful dissent just as impossible or criminal as violent dissent or actual revolution would be.

Targeting Musk or Pavel Durov is intended to bring the platforms they control *back within the censorship-industrial complex, back under Globalist control*, silencing the accounts and blocking the opinions that Globalist security agencies tell them to block and silence. These are *not* the accounts of people linked to real terrorism or real incitement to violence, but those of people simply causing embarrassment to or critiquing Globalist policies.

Even Mark Zuckerberg, so much himself a Globalist that he poured over $400 million of his money into controlling parts of the election process in 2020 to get Biden "elected," ended up shocked by the censorship-industrial complex he was part of and the threats it issued to him and to Facebook/Meta in order to make the platform hostile to Republicans.

On August 26, 2024, Zuckerberg wrote to Jim Jordan (chairman of the Committee on the Judiciary) stating this:

> There's a lot of talk right now around how the U.S. government interacts with companies like Meta, and I want to be clear about our position. Our platforms are for everyone—we're about promoting speech and helping people connect in a safe and secure way. As part of this, we regularly hear from governments around the world and others with various concerns around public discourse and public safety.
>
> In 2021, senior officials from the Biden Administration, including the White House, repeatedly pressured our

teams for months to censor certain COVID-19 content, including humor and satire, and expressed a lot of frustration with our teams when we didn't agree. Ultimately, it was our decision whether or not to take content down, and we own our decisions, including COVID-19-related changes we made to our enforcement in the wake of this pressure. I believe the government pressure was wrong, and I regret that we were not more outspoken about it. I also think we made some choices that, with the benefit of hindsight and new information, we wouldn't make today. Like I said to our teams at the time, I feel strongly that we should not compromise our content standards due to pressure from any Administration in either direction—and we're ready to push back if something like this happens again.

In a separate situation, the FBI warned us about a potential Russian disinformation operation about the Biden family and Burisma in the lead up to the 2020 election. That fall, when we saw a *New York Post* story reporting on corruption allegations involving then-Democratic presidential nominee Joe Biden's family, we sent that story to fact-checkers for review and temporarily demoted it while waiting for a reply. It's since been made clear that the reporting was not Russian disinformation, and in retrospect, we shouldn't have demoted the story. We've changed our policies and processes to make sure this doesn't happen again.

In other words, even a fellow Globalist now cites two major instances of a Globalist government censoring true information on important topics affecting millions of people and forcing, via threats, that social media platform towards a platform policy to remove the ability of ordinary people to receive, share, and discuss the truth.

Zuckerberg's letter makes it clear that this was a politically directed action straight from the Biden administration and therefore an instance of that administration ignoring the First Amendment of the US Constitution. *It was a direct attack on the free speech of the American people by a serving US government.*

Zuckerberg also makes it clear that this was not false information being restricted. It was both truthful information *and* content that was satirical and humorous.

The Biden administration did not just censor the truth during COVID. They even made jokes verboten. And this was relating to political and medical information that could not be more important. Massive restrictions of civil liberties were being enacted. Every US citizen was being impacted one way or another.

Every citizen had a Nuremberg Code–derived right to truthful information on the COVID policies. These were policies related to an experimental treatment, and such policies require informed consent. How many would have supported social distancing if they knew that it was just made up with no scientific basis, as Dr. Fauci later admitted? How many would have taken the experimental mRNA gene therapies if they were accurately labeled as such instead of the definition of vaccines being changed? How many people would have taken them without being inaccurately told they were safe and effective?

The Globalist Biden administration censored all debate on these things, working through the social media companies they forced to obey through the threat of removing the protections an online platform has against being sued for content shared by others.

With the second case Zuckerberg cited, the FBI, a supposedly neutral and non-partisan police agency, forced his company to share and promote a lie that undoubtedly affected the 2020 election. This lie—that the Hunter Biden laptop was Russian disinformation—was also shared and supported by the CIA, with fifty-one then current and former intelligence agency leaders signing their name to the lie in a public letter.

That is electoral interference by the CIA, as well as a similar level of corruption (which we are now sadly used to) by the FBI. The combined effect of the censorship Meta and Facebook were strong-armed into applying, together with the lie being promoted, was to rig the 2020 US election via federal agency electoral interference against one candidate, the sitting US president of the time.

Analysts have since suggested that the Hunter laptop story alone, if shared and acknowledged as true on social media platforms and by mainstream media outlets at the time, was enough to swing the result of the election the other way (even if you are still obtuse or dishonest enough to deny all the electoral fraud).

Now, think what this means for you, as the ordinary citizen.

It means that the intelligence agencies of the US have already taken away your free speech regardless of its constitutional protection. And it means that your elections have been manipulated by the intelligence and police agencies, some of whom are actually tasked with preventing such interference.

It means that social media companies were directed to censor the truth and spread lies, leaving you unable to trust any official labeling of what is or isn't true. And it leaves you certainly unable any longer to believe that the rules on all this are fair ones solely designed to limit harmful or violent extremism or protect people from, say, lies spread by a foreign power.

Instead, Globalist powers were being protected from truths spread by *you*.

So, we come to what you can do about this, beyond disengaging altogether and feeling a growing hatred towards the Globalist authorities who have been both censoring the truth you need to hear and filling every medium with lies instead.

Most particularly, we are beyond the point where you must just be skeptical about the mainstream media line or the words of your government.

And we are also beyond the point where your greatest risk is that a social media post will be deleted or that your social media account will be closed.

We are now at the point where telling the truth can get you fired from your place of employment, lose your license if you are doctor or a lawyer, or even result in a jail sentence if you are an ordinary person who has never been involved in a legal issue before.

The UK government has arrested more people for "hate speech" and political content online than are arrested for political content that Putin disapproves of in Russia. From memory, there is something like a five-to-one ratio applied to the eagerness of both nations to arrest people for opinions online that the authorities don't like.

Many of those swept up in the Southport riots' wave of arrests had no previous criminal convictions and no previous arrests to their names, rather like many of those arrested and imprisoned over January 6 in the US.

In these circumstances, we have a moral and pragmatic response that differ from each other. Our moral response must surely be an extremely and justifiably angered one, a feeling that it is horrific to see former free nations take away our basic rights and the fundamental right of free speech. Morally, we should want to speak out all the more, and we should be inspired to oppose Globalist tyranny (let us be honest, this whole process is a tyrannical one) as much as possible.

Pragmatically, though, it is also the case that many of us would rather not be arrested.

In this context, a flight response of no longer talking about or engaging in politics at all is commonplace and very understandable. It is partly that which is responsible for so many people staying quiet when they hear complete lies expressed in any public sphere, but especially in the workplace. It is that which sees people who don't believe in any of it sitting silently through mandatory lectures on the evils of whiteness or the wonders of diversity, equity, and inclusion in work-based training.

People want to keep their jobs, and they want to stay out of prison. *So, they end up going along with it all, while hating it all.*

Personally, I have decided to continue to speak, even though Globalists have now extended what counts as criminal speech into many ideas and opinions I consider accurate and normal ones.

This is a moral judgment everyone must make for themselves, and I do not condemn anyone who decides to no longer sharing their true thoughts. We all have families to think of, too, and how their lives are affected.

I think, though, that we can be cautious, we can protect ourselves a little, while still challenging what is happening. We can do obvious things like avoiding any statement that a biased official, a partisan "Karen," or a personal enemy would view as a direct call to violence or harm. We can be moral enough ourselves to never mean such harm but have a metaphorical or figurative use of it in our language be taken as a literal call to violence we never intended. That's a frequent way, in fact, that tyrannies work—by treating the metaphorical or satirical as the literal and punishing it as such.

We can be aware of our language to the extent of not phrasing it in ways a malign interpreter would pretend is a call to violence. That, at least, makes it a bit more difficult for Globalist authorities to justify our persecution.

I say this in the context of the UK having imprisoned a man for a bad taste online joke (his dog giving a Nazi salute)—or of US mainstream Globalist media and the Democratic Party taking the words "peacefully assemble" and "go home peacefully" to be incitement to violent insurrection.

You get some protection from speaking wisely and with a consciousness that the maligned will take everything literally if it helps them silence you.

But really now, you need to start from the assumption that the police, the courts, and the law will be against you simply because these things are controlled by Globalists who have now determined to silence and criminalize any opposition they happen to notice.

Be aware of what they have done to their powerful opponents, how much legal warfare and trouble they can unleash on a former president, for instance, and expect the same level of fairness and justice (i.e., none) to apply to the interactions you yourself have with a Globalist-run state.

Wisdom is in expecting injustice now, since this is the only way Globalists can impose policies most people don't want.

But to be courageous is to still oppose it regardless and know the necessity of that opposition, the intense necessity of still being prepared to hear the truth, share the truth, and speak the truth. The worse things get, the more important that courage becomes—from everyone.

It is the irony of an emergent tyranny that the less rights you have to speak your mind, the more important it is that you do so, in one form or another. For, if some of us, if many of us, do not accept the risk of still speaking out, then all of us accept the reality of a new paradigm in which all our old rights are *gone forever*.

MANAGING YOUR INTERACTIONS TO PROTECT YOURSELF

THE POLICE, MAINSTREAM MEDIA, AND SOCIAL MEDIA

> Transparency International observers remarked, for example, that corruption is an important element of populist rhetoric. Populist leaders tend to use public outrage for corrupt behaviour to punish political adversaries. Populist movements present themselves as an anti-corruption force drawing on the idea that corrupt elites work against the interests of the people. In many cases, such movements are not accompanied by an actual anti-corruption strategy and even facilitate new forms of corruption.
>
> —United Nations Office on Drugs and Crime, *Module 10: Citizen Participation in Anti-Corruption Efforts*, University Module Series on Anti-Corruption

The UNODC quote given above is a beautiful encapsulation of the situation we face as ordinary citizens in a corrupt system.

In a functioning system or a democratic one, there are established and trustworthy institutions to appeal to. We can be whistleblowers and receive some protection. Or we can expose crime and corruption as citizen journalists, as activists, or simply as concerned people raising our voice, and legitimate authorities will respond to that on a fair basis.

If our accusations are truthful, they are heeded. If they are false, they aren't. But there is somebody in a position of authority already that we can take this information to. If we know a politician is corrupt, we can give our evidence to the police or to a journalist who will report it. If we know a journalist is lying, we can ring up his employer and complain. There are police complaints bodies, and there are media regulators.

But what do you do when the regulators are corrupt? What do you do when you see something political and crazy in your kid's school, report that, and then the school governors call the police on you for voicing an opinion? What do you do when you can take evidence to the police of "grooming gangs," like the ones in the UK, and they threaten you with arrest for hate crimes and racism?

Look at that UNODC quote. It comes while claiming to represent part of a broad effort to increase citizen engagement in politics and to empower citizens to expose corruption. It's supposed to be an anti-corruption measure.

But what its actually doing is spreading propaganda that any genuine attempts at addressing corruption are merely populist rhetoric, lies, tricks, and disinformation. You can be sure that if you took any evidence of UN corruption to this body, the UN would dismiss you as a manipulative populist.

In other words, the corrupt police find themselves innocent and then criminalize any real demand for anti-corruption measures as populism-telling lies. Who watches the watchmen in this scenario? The answer: other Globalists, leaving the rest of us having to ask some consiglieri to process our criticism of the Mafia family he works for.

This was, of course, essentially what happened to the mass of people who saw and experienced US electoral fraud in 2020 when they tried to report it.

F*ck the Planet

One of the first things you have to realize when your country and your institutions are being run by Globalists is that (1) you are not in any way in control of what the authorities do, and (2) all the traditional limits on what the authorities do will be ignored.

You have become a "nation of one."

It doesn't matter how law-abiding you have previously been. It doesn't matter if you are a person of good character. It doesn't matter if your statute book, your Constitution, your common law, or your traditions provide you with all sorts of established protections from tyranny.

Globalist institutions and individuals do not care and won't be functioning by those things or within what you once understood as the limits of the law.

For them, the law is not a thing that applies equally to all. It is a thing that is a weapon, or a power, to be seized and used against the enemies of Globalism.

This is what they have done with January Sixers, Donald Trump, and former members of the Trump administration like Peter Navarro or Steve Bannon.

There isn't this set of laws that spring into action whenever anyone breaks them. There is power over the Department of Justice, over the New York courts, and over their equivalents in the UK, Australia, or Canada, which can be wielded and will be wielded selectively.

Every scintilla of power, of official authority, to tax, investigate, surveil, detain, charge, arrest, and imprison will be used ideologically and politically to crush dissent and reward compliance (or reward favored groups). None of it will be used as originally intended or as the framers of these laws (especially going back to their origins) expected them to be used.

In these circumstances, you only control *you*.

Globalist institutions have no accountability, and Globalist agents accept no moral or traditional limits.

In this, they are exactly the same as any other totalitarians in history.

Now think about where this leaves you as an individual. You are dealing with hostile institutions and hostile authorities.

How you manage what you are doing is your only way of mitigating what they do. As just an ordinary person, you can't stop them from applying the law unfairly, arresting you, or being unjust towards you.

If you organize in large groups, create or join new political parties, support populist alternatives, and engage in mass strike action or similar very large-scale protest, you have some chance of moving towards another direction. But that all takes time and is part of the process of getting non-Globalists back in charge where the powers of government can be used for the people instead of against the people.

That's not an immediate thing, and in the meantime, your police, courts, judiciary, media, and government and nongovernmental institutions are all working against you and opposed to your basic freedoms. They are all working by Globalist assumptions and ideologies now, which include a Cultural Marxist interpretation of race and history and a ruthless willingness to deny your free speech and right to political representation.

So, you have to *moderate your behavior to protect yourself* as much as possible and navigate a decision-making process that allows you to keep resisting and retain as much freedom as you can when freedom is no longer your automatic right.

It's probably best to describe how to interact with Globalist-run entities one by one, at least in a few broad categories.

The Police

Sir Robert Peel came up with the principles of policing in the 1800s. These boil down to preventing crime, winning the support of the local community and enforcing the law impartially. At a time when public confidence in the police's ability to prevent crime and disorder has fallen to its lowest-ever recorded level, police chiefs would be wise to rediscover the Peelian principles. Sadly, right now, their embrace of identity politics has led to a form of two-tier policing. So we see those expressing anti-Semitic hate on pro-Palestine marches get a ticking off [reprimand] at worst, while gender-critical feminists risk a knock on the door and a possible charge for stating biological realities. We see officers who rarely turn up to the scene of a burglary continue to make fools of themselves at Pride marches."

—Paul Chapel, "Take it from a copper—two-tier policing is real," *spiked*, January 26, 2024

In a traditional, functioning liberal democracy, the police are, by and large, *politically neutral*. They will police different groups the same way, applying the same laws. Leadership will come with experience and proven results, with senior officers having risen through the ranks over long periods of time.

For such police forces, particularly the British police force when it had a good reputation, the key to policing was that policing was *by consent*. The police, often locally based, were regionally organized and raised in the community they were policing and not strangers enforcing dictatorial edicts. They were locals with an organic connection to the people. Especially when old fashioned "beat" policing was in existence, foot patrols and local origins combined to make the police known, recognized, and respected familiar figures in the community who were recognized for providing assistance, as well as enforcing rules.

This is what "to protect and serve" means or used to mean. The police might drop a drunk off at his own home instead of to a police cell. They would give directions to strangers or break up fights without any bias or favoritism towards a particular group.

The processes by which this changed were long and varied and not the key topic of this book. Suffice to say that the process of *disconnecting the police from the people* ran alongside their growing politicization and indebtedness to one side of politics. Replacing foot patrols with cops circulating by car and a system of established local knowledge with anonymous police reliant on central HQ to tell them who they were dealing with was just as big a step in the corruption of the police as ideologically brainwashed university graduates being drafted straight into senior positions or cops of a certain skin color being more rapidly promoted.

In a Globalist-run nation, there has already been a process going on for many years where *senior officers are politically and ideologically selected*—and more than just by being affiliated with a party platform and elected as is the case in many instances in the US.

Today, to enter the police force, you must match Globalist-selection criteria, which have replaced practical old considerations like physical fitness or height. The intake of recruits will be adjusted to favor certain groups, and the advertising and selection criteria will often specify that white male recruits are no longer wanted. Once in, diversity, equity, and inclusion (DEI) practices and the assistance of race- and religion-specific interest groups (like race-based police associations and unions) will offer additional support to these individuals. They will be more rapidly promoted than anyone else, based on innate characteristics and ideological conformity rather than competence and results.

White officers who wish to advance quickly will have to have some other characteristic that ticks the appropriate boxes, like being female and lesbian. And if unfortunate enough to be white, male, and heterosexual, they will have to compensate for that by being even more progressive, woke, and ideologically driven towards unequal and unjust policing than anyone else.

By the time a Globalist government is in power, they already have police chiefs and police officers in place who share their ideological agenda and who are very willing to apply the law unevenly and in a two-tier manner based on which groups are seen as a threat to Globalism and which groups aren't.

Ironically then, for the Trump voter of any color, or for the white British voter who supports free speech and opposes mass immigration, the lessons to be learned regarding the police are the same ones that blacks in the US have been taught for generations (sometimes accurately, oftentimes inaccurately). These can be summarized as follows:

- Never assume the police are on your side.
- Never expect the law to be applied evenly and justly.

- Minimize your interactions with the police.
- If you can, keep them out of your home without violence, do so.
- Lawyer up as quickly as possible, preferably before something happens.
- Get badge numbers and specific identities.
- If you can record what's happening, do so.
- Don't speak to them unless you absolutely must.
- Be polite.
- Avoid them if possible.
- Obey instructions promptly if interaction is unavoidable.
- Assume they are looking for an excuse to hurt or arrest you.

The behavior of the police *will* be unjust now and in every country with a Globalist government. They *will* treat a white working-class protest differently to a black protest or a Muslim protest. They *will* be using far more aggressive tactics of kettling and charges against any protest they deem populist or right wing. They *will* be *absent when favored groups commit crimes and present in large numbers ready for trouble when populists, patriots, or the white working class gather in groups (no matter how peaceful)*.

They are not your friends, your protectors, or your servants. They are people who obey Globalist orders and specialize in the application of force. They are people who are prepared to dance like an idiot at a Pride festival, smile and take selfies next to a Hamas flag, and charge at you and crack your skull open because you are waving an England flag or wearing a MAGA cap.

In Canada, the Royal Canadian Mounted Police launched a cavalry charge against a disabled grandmother in a disability scooter. The full force of the Emergencies Act was used and violent police conduct applied against peaceful crowds who had done terrifying things like setting up bouncy castles. Legislation that was supposed to be about preventing the violent mobs that were sponsored by powers you were at war with was instead used against Canadian families, women, and crowds with children there because they peacefully protested against a Globalist vaccine mandate.

None of those powers or cavalry charges came against groups burning down Catholic churches or pulling down statues.

The police have picked a political side, and it isn't yours. Act with a full understanding of what that means. The police are, sadly, now the enemy of any group that Globalists wish to point them at and the accomplices of any crime that Globalists themselves commit or that comes from a group they favor.

Don't expect fairness or justice in any of this.

The Mainstream Media

> If I were a father and had a daughter who was seduced, I should not despair over her; I would continue to hope for her salvation. But if I had a son who became a journalist and continued to be one for five years, I would give him up.
>
> —Uncertain origin (attributed to Soren Kierkegaard)

We have already spoken about understanding that the mainstream media are all corrupt and have become pathological liars who spread propaganda constantly while also concealing or demonizing the truth and burying stories that expose their Globalist paymasters. Hopefully everyone reading this far (and more people besides that) already know how much of a moral duty, as well as a political one, it has become to be highly skeptical about everything in the news and everything that Western media is asserting.

Your interaction with the media *should shift from passive consumption to active avoidance*—or automatic distrust.

But we don't necessarily interact with the media just as consumers, sitting at home watching a TV screen.

If we are a public figure or a political candidate already, if we get into some legal trouble personally or as witnesses, if we are at an event that is "newsworthy," or even sit in a TV studio audience, we may interact with the mainstream media as interviewees and as people being asked questions by them.

How does an ordinary person handle this, and should we even do it?

Some individuals have made it very clear that they no longer see any point in talking to the mainstream media. When Dominic Cummings was Boris Johnson's chief political adviser, his reaction to mainstream journalists was often bluntly dismissive. There is footage showing him and a few other figures simply telling mainstream reporters that there is no point in talking to them because they are disgusting liars. Such a response can be a very effective one, but not so much if it is given in anger.

Saul Alinsky advised in *Rules for Radicals* that constant mockery was one of the strongest tools anyone has. It's a tool the radical left have deployed so successfully for so long that once normal positions and attitudes are never argued against by their side but simply laughed at immediately and without any intervening necessity of thought.

As soon as you take a position seriously enough to debate it, you are also conceding something to it. And with the media, if you answer their questions, you are accepting their right to ask and almost implying that they have a legitimacy equal to your own.

Given the malice and dishonesty of the media, that's almost being far too respectful towards them.

That said, stonewalling silence isn't a strong position either. The media can quickly present that as cowardice or lack of accountability, especially if you are a candidate or someone who would normally be expected to talk to them. Even someone the media is working for, covering for, and wants elected (like Kamala Harris) will generate criticism by avoiding interviews altogether.

Look at those instances where citizen journalists have managed to accost leading Globalists and pose real questions to them. There are several examples of these, some quite lengthy, where World Economic Forum figures or attendees at Davos have been pursued by citizen journalists or people working for alternative media outlets like Rebel Media. Those who trudge along saying nothing at all while these questions are fired at them do not come across as persuasive or as innocent. Their silence doesn't generate sympathy or make us feel they are being bullied.

It looks like what it is: avoidance, contempt for the idea of their own accountability, and a lack of truthfulness and justification on their part. It looks like they aren't defending their position because it *is* indefensible. "No comment" or pure silence reads as guilt.

A populist, patriot, or decent ordinary person can give off the same vibe if refusing entirely to speak with the mainstream media.

Alinsky was as right on tactics as he was wrong morally. And following his advice would mean engaging with the media even when you know they are your enemy and everything they say will be a lie.

But you have to do it in a clever and controlled way. You have to do it selectively, with your emotions marshaled to maximum effect.

Dealing with these liars can and probably should provoke your anger. We should all be furious with the mainstream media. We should hate them, and we have enormous justification to hate them. They have been the primary enablers of Globalist tyranny and of the removal of both sane governance and individual liberty in the Western world. Their lies have cost lives. Their utter corruption is an affront to any decent person and a barrier to any recovery of a decent society.

But we must begin *knowing* that, not necessarily *saying* that. We must begin as if we do expect fairness from them, even while expecting the opposite. It is then that their attempts to trap us become a trap for them.

A few broad examples spring to mind here. Look at Donald Trump. Nobody has had more hatred poured on his head by the mainstream media than Trump has. Nobody knows better than Trump that when he goes into a mainstream TV studio or interview he is facing an enemy who hates him, an enemy who will be relentlessly attacking him, demonizing him, and providing false and damaging descriptions of him and his policies and actions.

Trump still invites the mainstream media to his rallies, he still conducts countless interviews with them, and he still takes questions from them. He is not afraid of facing them. And he looks on each media attack as an opportunity to mock them, to show what they are, even as they try to control the public perception of what he is.

Trump has been living the Alinsky rule regarding mockery for years, both as its primary target from the media and as a person turning that back on them, exposing just how biased they are and just how deserving of mockery their pretensions are.

And that in itself is one of the things which has drawn people who are not his most natural allies towards him. Robert F. Kennedy Jr. spoke at length about this contrast between Trump and Kamala, about how Trump gives interviews and talks to anyone, including his enemies, compared to the bunker mentality that both Biden and now Harris have displayed.

The best demeanor to adopt in relation to mainstream media or when being interviewed by them is an initial open friendliness. This is when they show that their bias can quickly give way to amused contempt and a growing steel core of anger, but anger that is rational, controlled, and calmly and succinctly explained. That's far more effective than silence or rage. It gives them the opportunity to hang themselves (for the British police, that's a figure of speech). It gives you the opportunity to point out their hypocrisy and their crimes as well.

Every attack and trap they try to spring on you is an opportunity to expose what they are and subject it to mockery, both from yourself and others. This is what Elon Musk did when agreeing to an interview with Don Lemon.

Nothing exposed the essential rigor and depth of Musk's thinking and the essential shallow malice of Lemon's thinking more than offering that interview and letting Lemon show himself for what he is while trying to nail Musk for what he is not. It's an interview that beautifully illustrates that Elon Musk is an intelligent individual and that Lemon is a rather stupid type (the mainstream media hack) without relying on the mere assertion of those truths. Everyone could see Lemon trying to dishonestly take down Musk and Musk trying in increasing exasperation to have an adult conversation with a real person.

So, the mainstream media are, of course, our enemies as much as the politicized police have become our enemies, and like our interactions with the police, our interactions with the media must be conducted on that basis of profound antagonism. But the rules of response are slightly different:

- Assume that the media will give the worst possible spin to everything you have ever said.
- Know that they will try and ambush you.
- Offer a friendly beginning. This makes you the victim, rather than the instigator, of the inevitable disagreement.
- Expect a straw man version of any position you have ever adopted.
- Do not accept any premise offered by their attacks.
- Calmly but firmly interrupt any lies in their questions.
- Hold them to their own rules (another Alinsky standard), and point out any racism, sexism, or lack of objectivity in their statements.
- Speak on behalf of the people their attitudes harm and make sure to mention those people. Ask them why they don't care about those people.
- Have specific instances of their crimes in mind.
- Mock what they are doing.
- Explain the social and cultural cost of what they are doing succinctly. This can be very effectively done in a tone of regret or even bewilderment.
- Anger is an energy, but should be mainly powering your delivery, which itself remains calm.
- In forming your own views, always favor alternate media over mainstream media.

Social Media

> "There are only two industries that call their customers 'users': illegal drugs and software."
>
> —Edward Tufte, statistician

"Elon Musk, in his effort to buy Twitter, signaled that under his ownership, the company would allow all speech that the First Amendment protects. 'By "free speech" I simply mean that which matches the law,' he tweeted on April 26. 'I am against censorship that goes far beyond the law.'"

Jeffrey Rosen, "Elon Musk is Right That Twitter Should Follow the First Amendment," *The Atlantic*, May 2, 2022

"The mogul's treatment of union organizers and whistleblowers suggested that 'free speech absolutism' was mostly code for a high tolerance for bigotry towards particular groups, a smoke screen that obscured an obvious hostility towards any speech that threatened his ability to make money."

Adam Serwer, "Elon Musk's Free Speech Charade is Over," *The Atlantic*, April 12, 2023

In this category, I am going to include all social media companies and organizations and all online interactions of any kind, including video and music content and platforms. This would include Facebook/Meta, Instagram, Google, Rumble, TikTok, Facebook Messenger, WhatsApp, YouTube, X, all email providers and messages, all communication platforms (Zoom, Teams etc.), and all website discussion or comment forums.

As with other areas, I have already described to an extent that most of the major companies running these are Globalist entities that are now aligned with Globalist-run nation-states in monitoring their citizens, spreading propaganda to their citizens, and policing the thoughts and speech of their citizens.

Following the investigative work of those rare former mainstream media journalists like Matt Taibbi who retain some integrity, Elon Musk's release of the Twitter Files, and the change of Twitter policies that so infuriated the Globalist pet hacks at *The Atlantic*, we have some basic confirmed information regarding the importance of social media and its place in the censorship-industrial complex:

We know that several of these companies were formed with DARPA US military technology and grants, and with *CIA funding*.

We know that several are heavily reliant on large state-provided contracts and funding, which makes them *subject to political control*.

We know that multiple administrations and companies have received direct and indirect *threats* from the Biden administration and from European governments, as well as from transnational bodies like the UN and the EU.

We know that since separating what was Twitter from the censorship complex, Musk and his companies have faced a raft of special investigations and legalized attacks, together with a personal campaign of vilification in the mainstream media rapidly becoming as hysterical as the one applied to Donald Trump.

The owners and chief executives of social media companies are, therefore, frequently in fear of the court ordered breakup of their social media empires if they fail to comply with state instructions (which include being ordered to spread lies and silence truths depending on the Globalist assessment of whether the truth is beneficial to the Globalist policy agenda). We know that monopoly laws have been used to threaten the owners of these private companies to the point where *the private company becomes the outsourced censorship arm of the State*.

A further frequently applied threat is the removal of protections that prevent a social media company being sued for posts made by a user of that platform (Section 230 of the Communications Decency Act 1996, in the US). The removal of Section 230 is only suggested when companies resist partisan-state direction (i.e., Democratic Party control) of what content is allowed on the platform, often accompanied by the demand that specific and truthful information be removed (like the Hunter Biden laptop story).

These companies are also often under direct assault from pressure groups, charities, NGOs, leading Globalist politicians, and bureaucratic officials from regulatory bodies, all pressing a Globalist mandate and a Globalist censorship agenda.

We know that Globalist billionaires fund the targeting of members of their class (particularly in the media and social media) who do not comply or support the same ideas, setting up and funding pressure groups (like "Hope Not Hate"), fact-checker groups (like Snopes), or activist individuals and organizations (like Just Stop Oil) who will flood social media companies with complaints and monitor and report the accounts they want removed.

We know that several of these companies had or still have close relationships with the FBI and CIA, including *shared FBI office space* and *senior executives at these companies with FBI and CIA backgrounds.*

We know that any social media company supporting free speech and resisting state demands for partisan treatment of content will be targeted with multi-pronged assaults, including anti-trust and monopolies investigations, *denial of service* by other companies integral to the provision of a social media platform, and direct cyberattacks also intended to deny service and take down rebellious platforms.

We know that Gab, Parler, Truth Social, and X have all been subjected to corporate Globalist denial of service and to various other legal and nonlegal assaults designed to drive them out of business or interrupt and disrupt the services they provide. Parler was subjected to a particularly lengthy and coordinated denial of service attack by companies like Amazon that was refusing to supply web hosting, for example, and specific alternative media events, including directly political ones (like the launch on X of the Ron DeSantis presidential campaign bid and the more recent Trump-Musk interview on X). These events have been the targets of cyber warfare assaults with zero mainstream media interest in these things as being forms of election rigging and electoral interference.

Really, the primary major companies active in social media or providing the services such companies themselves need to operate have functioned as a *Globalist cartel* seeking to drive non-Globalist competitors out of existence, all with the tacit or explicit support of the authorities and the State.

That cartel system received its greatest blow when the total conformity being imposed was broken by Elon Musk's purchase of Twitter, which has allowed much greater and much less partisan protections of free speech ever since (this is the primary reason Musk has become a figure of hate, second only to Donald Trump).

Most of us use social media, email, the cloud storage of data, search engines, websites, and the like every single day. We are interacting with multiple platforms, often with multiple personal accounts even on a single platform. And we are increasingly using these mediums in place of office meetings or telephone calls.

An ordinary person can withdraw from all these aspects of modern living, although to do so completely would require an independent means of income or a job that doesn't feature any of these things. Any kind of office job means, though, that you are using email and probably websites too.

Some general points to remember when interacting with these technologies, which apply in most instances and now have a direct political impact that could affect your civil liberties, are provided below:

- Everything you write online in any context can be recovered by the Globalist state and used against you.
- It doesn't matter if your comment is satirical. It will be judged as literal.
- Any non-PC comment in any work context can be reported and see you fired. It doesn't matter if your behavior or performance is in all other ways exemplary.
- Everything you write as an email, every browser search you conduct, every website you visit, and your entire online history can be recovered and used against you.
- Deleted posts and very old posts can and will be used against you. (One of the recently jailed British victims of Globalist tyranny was jailed for a post she had immediately deleted. One of the January

6 militia defendants was jailed partly for a message he received and never read.)
- If criminal action is not taken to imprison you, Globalist media outlets will be provided with your most incriminating posts and comments in order to smear you. These will routinely be taken out of context and used in hit pieces, should you be notable enough to attract that attention.
- Everything is permanent. Nothing is private. Unless you obey and conform.
- Favored groups know the system now favors them and are often eager to report you. Be particularly cautious in interactions with these groups (LGBTQ+ and especially trans activists, ethnic minorities, Muslims, leftists, and progressives).
- Purge your personal accounts of people who might report you.
- Use your privacy settings to protect you from people who might report you.
- Be aware that many seemingly patriotic or right-wing public groups and forums are either set up by or quickly taken over by leftists. These people then try to provoke responses they can report to the platform or to the police.
- Entrapment as described above will come from private individuals who are Globalist-progressive fanatics *and* from public institutions and bodies.
- You don't exist as an individual with privacy, free speech, and other rights in a Globalist-run system. You exist as a body and mind to be controlled and as a package of data to be sold.
- Avoid public discussion groups, local politics groups, and mainstream media comment threads.
- Build your own network of like-minded people you trust. Remember that anything you say to these people can also be accessed by the Globalist state and used against you.

Given the points above, it might seem that I am presenting a hopeless scenario where the only option available to a person with traditional conservative, patriotic views or with objections to mass immigration, open borders, and Globalist censorship is to shut up and withdraw from public comment and public life.

That is not what I am advocating.

This book is not intended as a black pill. It's not intended to make you despair. It's not just saying. "Let's be honest, tyranny is already here."

No. It is more about saying, "How can I be better and smarter at fighting back? How can I work towards freedom, be an example of freedom, retain my dignity? How can I defend truth and decency in the best possible way, the smartest way, without quickly ending up in a prison cell as another victim of this now sick, diseased authoritarian system that retains the outer forms and appearance of democracy while offering none of the freedoms we were born with?"

It begins in awareness. It begins in being honest, to ourselves, about what our countries now are. It begins in seeing the reality rather than the media fantasy or the excusatory lies. But this is a red pill, not a black one, and a red pill is still moderated by innate logic and reason rather than by some genuinely bizarre rabbit hole.

I'm not asking you here to believe something crazy or evil like the idea that the Jews control everything or the idea that famous people are clones or alien lizards. I despise the literal and alternative belief in nonsense just as I despise the mainstream beliefs, which are pure nonsense and on much the same grounds.

You can simultaneously know that the Globalist authorities and their puppet media use the term "conspiracy theory" to demonize truths that embarrass or threaten them *and* that some conspiracy theories really are nuts *and* that many now fashionable and respectable ideas are *also* nuts (like the Green doomsday cultism or like the race hate evils of critical race theory).

And you can do that in each case by logic and morality. Both of which don't require you to be a genius, but which have been perfected and honed over two-and-a-half thousand years in a Western world that only went mad relatively recently.

How should you interact with it all? As a sane man would with a mad, mad world. As a point of rational light in a sea of increasingly lunatic delusion.

As a person born free, who would like their children to be free as well.

WE CARE A LOT

ADDRESSING THE LIE OF GLOBALIST COMPASSION

This is a person who has spent her life fighting on behalf of people who need a voice and a champion. As you heard from Michelle, Kamala wasn't born into privilege. She had to work for what she's got, and she actually cares about what other people are going through. She's not the neighbor running the leaf blower—she's the neighbor rushing over to help when you need a hand.

As a prosecutor, Kamala stood up for children who had been victims of sexual abuse. As Attorney General of the most populous state in the country, she fought big banks and for-profit colleges, securing billions of dollars for the people they had scammed. After the home mortgage crisis, she pushed me and my administration hard to make sure homeowners got a fair settlement. Didn't matter that I was a Democrat. Didn't matter that she had knocked on doors for my campaign in Iowa—she was going to fight to get as much relief as possible for the families who deserved it.

As Vice President, she helped take on the drug companies to cap the cost of insulin, lower the cost of health care, and give families with kids a tax cut. And she's running for president with real plans to lower costs even more, protect

Medicare and Social Security, and sign a law to guarantee every woman's right to make her own health care decisions.

In other words, Kamala Harris won't be focused on her problems—she'll be focused on yours. As president, she won't just cater to her own supporters, punish those who refuse to kiss the ring or bend the knee. She'll work on behalf of every American.

—Barack Obama, 2024 Democratic National Convention Speech

It's possible that someone who has read this far considers this book a series of wild "far-right" accusations. Many people have been conditioned to see any pushback on Globalism, any traditional values, and any populist assertion of non-Globalist priorities as "far-right extremism" (even though the Left had a socially traditional wing too, in the past).

Most people who are conditioned and programmed this way won't engage with any populist or traditionalist on an equal footing, won't read any text like this, won't debate any of the key issues honestly, and will carry on mindlessly adopting whatever latest position suits the ruling class and is promoted through the mainstream media.

They might even believe that Globalists care a lot.

Many of those people will, sadly, be unreachable now. Indoctrination is effective, and when it has the kind of resources that are applied to modern twenty-four-hour news cycle, it's very effective.

Those who destroy your world and ruin your neighborhood, those who enrich themselves by destroying the country they were supposed to serve, are quick to offer you *immaterial rewards* of "hope," "joy," "change," and "a better way" when they have taken everything worthwhile and real for themselves. Their care is the care of an abuser, sidling up to the bruised and impoverished object of their false affections when they want a little extra after you have already given them way too much.

The pathology of welfarism, clientelism, patronage, and Globalist compassion is the pathology of abuse.

We saw during COVID with the placement of psychological warfare specialists like Professor Susan Michie on supposedly scientific advisory bodies, like the UK's Scientific Advisory Group for Emergencies, how effective a coordinated psychological warfare operation can be. Because that's what the mainstream messaging on COVID was—a planned, uniform, and relentless operation to shift the perceptions of the general public and get them to the point where they would accept huge infringements on their long-established basic rights and actually be angry and hateful towards those who did not.

All across the Western world, people were *swiftly brainwashed* into both bizarre affirmations of loyalty to the COVID restrictions (like the repeated late-night rituals of bashing pots and pans for the National Health Service in the UK) and doing things that made no sense at all (like wearing multiple useless masks and, particularly in the Far East, putting children in plastic bubbles).

All of the allegedly protective measures looked ridiculous and were things that previously signaled extreme mental collapse or psychologically damaged eccentricity. Think about the germophobic behavior of Howard Hughes, for instance, or the plastic bubbles, face masking, and oxygen tents of the more recent eccentric germophobe, Michael Jackson.

Those people were (rightly) considered more than a little unbalanced due to doing things that millions of us then copied, solely because the TV and the government were telling us to.

The truth is that the actual danger level of the virus never justified these responses at all, proper scientific awareness would quickly ascertain that most of these measures were utterly useless, and an honest medical establishment and government would have swiftly reversed or never engaged in such policies in the first place. Instead, long after the actual danger rates of COVID were known to be minimal and mainly focused on elderly vulnerable groups with multiple comorbidities, huge effort was expended both on exaggerating the danger and insisting on ever more masochistic, harmful, and authoritarian responses to it.

And most people, as psychological experiments going back decades already knew they would, accepted the word of authority figures with absolute trust, no matter how odd and ridiculous the demands became.

The famous Milgram experiments conducted in the early 1960s showed how respect for authority can be translated directly into getting ordinary people to do hideous things. In 1961, Yale University professor Stanley Milgram showed that a random selection of people would overwhelmingly agree to torture someone else so long as *a figure in a white coat told them to* and reassured them that it all made sense. Genuine participants were told that they were conducting beneficial research. They were shown a machine that they were told applied an electric current to a person in a chair. They met the "other volunteer" who would sit in the chair. They were told to keep applying current and increasing the voltage on command. Even when they heard sounds of distress or even screams, 65 percent of them would keep applying the current when instructed to do so and go up to levels that, if the experiment was real, would kill a person.

Milgram published his findings first in 1963 in the *Journal of Abnormal and Social Psychology* and then followed that up with a more detailed explanation in his 1974 book *Obedience to Authority: An Experimental View*. These findings were not explaining abnormal people committing horrible deeds after years of indoctrination in extremist ideologies. They were describing random selections of ordinary people and finding that the *majority* of them would do hideous things if reassured that everything was OK by a man in a white coat claiming to be a respectable scientist.

That's the context of putting psychological warfare specialists on a supposed pandemic advisory body (Michie, as an aside, is also a lifelong supporter of the Communist Party of Great Britain). Such people had known for fifty years that people can be made to do crazy things if respectable authority tells them to…and especially if that authority tells them that it is scientific, rational, and beneficial to others.

Ordinary people will ignore screams and focus on the white coat.

All of which makes the demonization of the unvaccinated and the extreme measures people tolerated a lot more understandable. They were told that this was being good. They were told that this made sense. They were told that those opposing it were selfish, dangerous vectors of disease.

All of these things were lies. All of them were instances of psychological manipulation towards a mass hysteria justifying mad actions.

But they knew it would work. Milgram had already told them it would…so long as the white coat, so long as the support of a trusted medical profession was there reassuring everyone as they accepted insane policies.

Of course, if COVID had been Ebola or something hugely dangerous to everyone, the measures could be more easily understood. If it had possessed fatality rates of 10 percent, 20 percent, or 30 percent, the panic and hysteria would be very understandable. The measures adopted were all ones that don't actually stop viral transmission, so they would still have been irrational in terms of efficacy, but at least they would be more rational than doing these things in response to a fairly mild virus.

The thing is the authorities knew it wasn't that dangerous. They must have realized that pretty quickly, and they knew, for example, that children were virtually immune to it. The rates of child fatality would be statistically zero, and no more threatening than a flu or a cold.

But still there was the huge disruption, the huge assault on civil liberties, the huge *transfer of trillions of dollars of wealth*, the huge economic damage to everyone except those with shares in pharmaceutical companies or ownership of such companies.

Almost as if that was the point, isn't it?

And this was achieved by three things: first, the ruling class being corrupt and crazy and unaccountable enough to do it, second, the psychological warfare experts directing the government and official and medical establishment messaging, and third, these people knowing after fifty years of research just how effective scientific authority combined with declared altruism is.

They told you that they were the ones who cared.

Tell people a scientist says it makes sense, and many will indeed think it makes sense. Tell people it's compassionate and caring and *for the greater good*…and they will hate the people opposing it.

COVID, though, in this and everything else, is only the most extreme recent example of a general trend.

That general trend can be described as Globalist authorities doing things that are harmful and that no rational person possessed of proper objective reporting would support, while claiming that everything they are doing is altruistic and good.

The claim of compassion by selfish authorities is another tool of oppression, and the people doing this have known that based on psychological research going back at least five decades.

When we think of how Globalists present themselves and present their actions and intentions, we see a total departure from the *actual risks and consequences*. We see a set of policies always couched as compassionate and caring ones. What these policies actually do is hurt people and enrich Globalists. But what Globalists present them as is the height of enlightened caring about the planet, about people, or about positive things like democracy and equality.

We see demands for ever more authority, wealth, and power concentrated in their hands and exclusively under their control, presented as necessary and caring defenses against diseases and viruses, lies and misinformation, the "far right," or the "threat to democracy."

We need these new laws, new powers, and gradual removal of your old rights, liberties, and way of life so that we can save you from Donald Trump, from a virus we manufactured, from Vladimir Putin, from archaic horrors like a secure border and the low crime rates that come with a homogeneous conservative population, or from a climate apocalypse that only exists in our garbage in, garbage out computer modeling junk data.

It's for the greater good that we inject you against your will, silence your opinion, or move increasingly towards a techno-feudal tyranny. It's for the greater good that we make your energy sources more expensive, more unreliable, and more ecologically damaging while calling that "Green" and "saving the planet."

It's *compassion* when we oppress you, and *caring* when we imprison you.

Every time the effects are bad, but the intentions (supposedly) are oh so *good*.

Respect the science and ignore the excess death rates. Follow the white coat and all will be well. Milgram told us you would fall for this.

Kamala is a *good person*. Don't you know that *she cares*?

The Globalist claim of compassion is the most effective political lie ever sold to a malleable public, and it is one built on psychological research and the tendency of many of us to act as the social animals we are and conform to the crowd.

The same instinct that makes someone stand facing the same way as other people in a lift is the one that makes us trust our nurse, doctor, scientific adviser, and government. This is even when we have evidence that they are financially profiting from lies or that (in the case of our real ruling elites and their chief political puppets) they have, through ideology and corruption, become what may accurately be described as functionally insane.

Look at any Globalist policy and you see the same patterns repeated.

Take the racial policies, something like affirmative action and race-based spending. For sixty years, affirmative action has been loading government spending towards US black communities. Trillions of dollars beyond normal spending has been earmarked for black communities. Enormous levels of welfare support have been directed primarily and sometimes exclusively at black America. No community has received more "support," more patronage, more consideration than black communities in the US—on the surface, at least. The money set aside for addressing black poverty and disparities of outcomes for black people could well have founded an entirely new nation and made it a rich one too.

What's the result of this money and concern, all this altruism and compassion? What have the people claiming to care about racism, inequality, and ethnic minorities delivered for black people in the US?

The worst performance of any demographic there is.

The most dangerous and crime ridden neighborhoods.

The highest number of criminals. The highest number of crack addicts and junkies.

This is occurring in the cities where death is commonplace, and life is lived as it would be lived in Batman's decaying Gotham.

Streets of squalor and despair, and tent cities of tramps and vagrants and broken people.

The cities under Democrat rule, the black majority cities where 80 or 90 percent of blacks vote Democrat, are invariably the *worst shitholes in America*. And yet these Democrats really care, don't they?

They care so much that they ruin lives for minor possession drug offenses when they want to look tough and release violent offenders onto the streets when they want to look kind. They care so much that they support the riots that burn black neighborhoods to the ground. They care so much that instead of breaking the gangs, they fund the broken families that breed the next generation of gang members.

The *people who care* have turned once strongly Christian black communities—once proud people with jobs, dignity, and self-reliance, people with families with fathers present and mothers raising children, people who genuinely wanted an equal chance to make something of themselves rather than special exemptions for barbaric behavior—into communities blighted with the worst rates of divorce, drug addiction, homelessness, and crime.

Black communities have been destroyed by Democrat patronage, almost as if all the money went into Democrat pockets instead of on improving things.

I do not think black people are too feckless and stupid to govern themselves in the truest sense, to have self-respect and limit their worst instincts. I think they are just as responsible for their actions as anyone else. I think they are just as capable of doing the right things as anyone else. I think they can pass the tests in school because they have good teachers rather than because the standards are lowered based on their skin color. I think black fathers *can* raise their kids and support them too.

The people who *care* and the people who "fight racism" don't think this way. They think black people are so stupid, so useless, so worthless that you have to turn them into dependent political pets being constantly fed scraps of attention, patronage, and special privileges that actually hurt them. Get them addicted to welfare so the moms raise children alone and the dads get girl after girl pregnant without supporting anyone.

Call anyone who sees how damaging to black people this all is a racist.

The second worst fate that can befall a demographic group is to be demonized and hated by Globalists.

The worst fate that can befall a demographic group is to be adopted, championed, and patronized by Globalists.

The first group will face relentless media attacks and active discrimination. But the second group will be treated as children robbed of agency, children raised by neglectful and abusive parents, children poisoned by the way their patrons think.

Those who believed the white coats were the ones who die the most in those excess death figures following COVID vaccinations. They were the ones who took the poison and took the boosters. They were the ones who posted about doing their bit and having their third booster before dropping dead in a "sudden and unexpected tragedy."

Those who believe the Democrats care about them are the ones who take in the poison of critical race theory and the attitudes that make people fail. It's their money, money supposedly going to them but mysteriously having no effect, that enriches the "community leaders" and the Machine politicians who make cities like Chicago such horrendous failures.

Those who care so much about Ukraine? Those are the people who deliver half a million deaths in Ukraine.

Those who care so much about the planet's finite resources and man's careless custodianship and pollution? Those are the people driving an electric vehicle that only exists because a cobalt mine in Africa is devastating an environment there and being mined by child slaves digging in the dirt.

The people who care so much that they want to eradicate polio in India? That was the Bill and Melinda Gates Foundation, probably responsible for half a million cases of a condition worse than polio (Non-Polio Acute Flaccid Paralysis).

The people worrying about temperature rises (which occur in natural cycles none of our technology can change) because they care so much about *man-made* climate change? Those are the people ready to make a *man-made deliberate* change to the atmosphere of the entire planet by blocking out the sun.

The *care* and *compassion* of a Globalist does more harm than the hardest-hearted pragmatism of any Populist ever will. Like an abusive husband, they harm the ones they claim to love even more than they harm anyone else.

FROM COMPASSION TO OPPRESSION

BEWARE OF GLOBALISTS BEARING GIFTS

The simple fact is that children are suffering because the U.S. welfare system has failed. Designed as a system to help children, it has ended up damaging and abusing the very children it was intended to save. The welfare system has failed because the ideas upon which it was founded are flawed. The current system is based on the assumption that higher welfare benefits and expanded welfare eligibility are good for children. According to this theory, welfare reduces poverty, and so will increase children's lifetime well-being and attainment. This is untrue. Higher welfare payments do not help children; they increase dependence and illegitimacy, which have a devastating effect on children's development.

It is welfare dependence, not poverty, that has the most negative effect on children. Recent research by Congressional Budget Office Director June O'Neill shows that increasing the length of time a child spends on welfare may reduce the child's IQ by as much as 20 percent.

> Welfare also plays a powerful role in promoting illegitimacy. Research by CBO Director O'Neill also shows, for example, that a 50 percent increase in monthly AFDC and food stamp benefit levels will cause a 43 percent increase in the number of illegitimate births within a state. Illegitimacy, in turn, has an enormous negative effect on children's development and on their behavior as adults. Being born outside of marriage and raised in single parent homes:
>
> - Triples the level of behavioral and emotional problems among children;
> - Nearly triples the level of teen sexual activity;
> - Doubles the probability a young woman will have children out of wedlock; and,
> - Doubles the probability a boy will become a threat to society, engage in criminal activity, and wind up in jail.
>
> Overall, welfare operates as a form of social toxin. The more of this toxin received by a child's family, the less successful the child will be as an adult. If America's children are to be saved, the current welfare system must be replaced.
>
> —Patrick Fagan and Robert Rector, "How Welfare Harms Kids," The Heritage Foundation, June 5, 1996

The most obvious example of the contradiction between noble and even *utopian intentions* and *devastating social and financial consequences* comes when we consider the "welfare state."

At the end of World War Two, Britain, followed swiftly by other Western nations, created the welfare state. The explanation was that populations that had undergone the horrors and sacrifices of the conflict deserved a better world. Veterans and their families deserved a better world. People who had risked their lives and people who had lost family members or suffered through aerial bombing campaigns, needed the rubble rebuilt. Why not build something better this time?

This was the offer that was irresistible. Because in many ways it was true.

People did deserve better.

And it is understandable that the promise of free healthcare (such as that provided by Britain's National Health Service) should be as attractive to populations that had just undergone vast suffering, populations that included many persons injured in the conflict, and millions of people deeply affected in other ways too.

Economies had been centralized and more controlled than before in order to fight the war, a repeat of the processes that occurred in World War One. Cooperative efforts between nations had been vital to win the war.

In some ways, the growth of transnational bodies managing international affairs and providing a global perspective on things like human rights or which wars were justified or unjustified were part of the exact same process, *a desire for a radical new settlement*, and a better way of doing things—both as a reward for recent sacrifices *and* as a preventative measure supposed to avoid a similar conflagration in the future.

The moral authority of the old way of doing things was utterly broken by two world wars and millions of dead in both of them. The old way was nation-based, nationalistic, and look at the harm German nationalism had done.

In another sense, this general feeling, quickly marshaled and directed by those who had radical plans in mind already, did two seemingly contradictory things.

At one and the same time, it *justified the rapid expansion of the State* and *the transfer of authority from the Nation to transnational bodies*. These two things seem contradictory but were driven by the same false conclusions at the end of World War Two.

The State, as reward and fulfillment of that desire for a better world, would expand into territories that were previously covered by private initiatives, the churches, and a private medical sector. The State would become not just the provider of law and order and military defense but also much more involved in things like the "health of the Nation" and much more proactive and immediate in tackling issues like poverty or what would become "social justice."

The State would not wait for private enterprise to enrich people and improve conditions, and it would not expect families to care for their own or charities to deal with social conditions that were hurting people. The State would become an idealist seeking to improve and save lives and even *manage lives* much more directly than it ever had before. It would be highly interventionist, and the private sphere would shrink.

If people were without work, the State should provide for them.

If people needed medical treatment, the State should provide it for "free."

In Britain—a Britain still affected by rationing and where everyone had lost something—these seemed like things ordinary people deserved, and they became enormously popular ideas.

Of course, the State should expand to fulfill these idealistic duties. *Of course*, that was compassionate and caring.

Of course, it was callous and uncaring to oppose such a thing.

People were encouraged to focus on the compassion, while ignoring the concentration and consolidation of power that comes with the expansion of the State. People were sold the vision of a fairer world where the State takes cares of you and not told how that makes you *dependent* on the State for things a real family and a real community should be supplying.

And in Europe, the conditions were perfect for huge state interventions. There was an enormous rebuilding project needed. There were shattered nations, orphaned children, and cities reduced to rubble. Only vast spending could quickly rebuild those nations.

So *vast spending* was normalized too. An economically dominant USA, one flushed with victory and with the vast economic potential of its huge nation finally unleashed by the efforts of the war economy and now the new manufacturer of the world, was ready to engage in that gigantic spending operation (although not ready to ignore all the debts allies like Britain had accumulated as war loans).

It was even very profitable to do so. US businesses boomed on the back of US government contracts for rebuilding Europe. The Marshall Plan installed a fatal lesson in the US mentality—bombing other nations could secure your greatness and then rebuilding those nations with vast spending could profit your private enterprises. That false lesson, as much as the active manipulations of the new military-industrial complex, would come to trap the USA in the posture of world's policeman entering one war after another.

It becomes somewhat difficult to tell people that vast government spending is not wise when they see the world's most powerful nation doing it. Just as it becomes impossible to tell the British public that healthcare should remain private when they are being offered it for "free" and this spending seems necessary and just and is still dwarfed by the European rebuilding project.

How do you tell voters that welfare payments for the victors of the war can't be afforded when the losers of that war are having vast spending lavished on them?

So vast spending was normalized even in nations bankrupted by World War Two. Radical new approaches were normalized and old cautions, old loyalties, and an old-world conservatism were tainted with Nazism. The rapid expansion of the State and its spending was normalized at the same time that the Nation and loyalty to the Nation was considered responsible for grotesque evils.

While Nazi socialism—the deep Nazi concern for "the greater good," for "the health of the Nation," and for State solutions to poverty and ill health, as well as the State management of doctors and nurses—was *conveniently forgotten*. (Globalists tend to support euthanasia, the State direction of medicine, and, in many cases, population control. They say this is for humane reasons. These are all things Nazis were also interested in and which led to some of their vilest crimes.)

The State should always, in reality, be subordinate to the people and the Nation. Every tyranny (Nazism, Communism, Globalism) inverts this relationship.

A "nation-state" is after all a hybrid. It's both nation (the instinctive, tribal loyalty of a specific people to a specific place built over time organically) and state (the specific government, the mechanisms of governance, and the agents of the government and official opposition—in a two-party system).

World War Two told the ruling class that the Nation part was suspicious and dangerous and could morph into Nazism and war and needed to be suppressed, while at the same time telling them that the State, the government, is more trustworthy than the people and all their archaic and now Nazism-tainted assumptions that the State only exists to serve them.

The people who built the National Health Service or built the UN were of the same class taking the same completely false lessons from World War Two. It was the total power of the State that allowed Nazism to do hideous things to people under its control. It was a utopian project controlling everything that excused, for Nazis, their actions. It was nationalism from other nations that defeated Nazism, and it was the old values that were morally horrified by Nazism.

And yet, the lesson taken was that the old values were to blame for Nazism, that nationalism was to blame for Nazism, and that the State should expand while the more instinctive loyalties to the Nation should be suppressed.

This is while also expanding the State massively to accommodate the State's intrusion into things, like paying the unemployed and delivering "free" healthcare. And this was done without any understanding that *nothing is free* and that the expanded state you have expanded to do good also has an expanded power to do evil.

This was especially when the ruling class were simultaneously teaching themselves that loyalty to their own people and prioritization of those people (the only thing that justifies a state having power in the first place) was dangerous, extremist, and sure to recreate a Nazi Germany.

What the "welfare state" promised then was this: The State will care for you and protect you. If you lose a job, you will have a safety net of welfare. If you are sick or injured, you will have a doctor and a hospital bed for free. If you are a single mother, the State will pay what a feckless father won't. If you are old, you will have a pension provided by the State. This is a better world. This is compassion.

What the welfare state did was this: Massively increase government spending. Transfer whole sectors of the economy into state management that was generally more incompetent than the private sector. Hugely expand the State. Provide *a mask of compassion for government intrusion* into areas of your life that the State should have no authority over. Create monopolies in the health sector. Encourage feckless and self-destructive behavior (because there's a safety net). Destroy the independence, positive attributes, self-reliance, and pride of large sections of the working class. Create and pay for an anti-social underclass. Fund huge amounts of fraud from people skilled at playing the system. Bring in a socialism that leads to Communism as a supposed antidote to Nazism. Make the medical profession beholden to the State. Fund feckless mothers having degenerate lifestyles where children by multiple fathers are born simply for the mother to remain in the welfare system. Allow feckless fathers to abandon their children more readily, and allow families to fragment while expecting the State to show a compassion and responsibility that they have *stopped showing themselves*.

And that's not even the worst of what welfarism (which extended worldwide becomes Globalist 'compassion'. leads to. Even if the proclaimed noble intentions are sincere, the practical consequences, the results of the policy, are harmful.

Remember that other false lesson drawn (with Communist prodding) from World War Two? Remember that the same people building these welfare systems are now learning that if they feel loyalty particularly to their own people, they should be ashamed of that? And if their people demand priority over others then those people are incipient Nazis?

Well, what that kind of psychological and ideological formation does is gradually turn this welfare state towards supporting *everyone except the majority*, except the people, except those of you who were originally told it was all being built for.

Those of us whose whole traditional moral framework was not shattered by two world wars and a lot of Communist and Globalist lies since those wars tend to think that it's perfectly normal and natural for the State, the government, to serve a specific people. We tend to think that if the government is going to spend vast sums of money on idealistic projects, utopian dreams, and showing *how much they care* then that spending should be on *us*.

Wasn't that what the original welfare state promise? Even setting aside the trap of just how badly and inefficiently government tends to operate things and how all these "free" things aren't free but built on debt, money printing, and high taxation that is a crippling burden on both present and future generations—wasn't it all supposed to be *for* a specific national population?

Wasn't it called the *National* Health Service in the UK? But now it services primarily people who were born abroad, and services people who have never contributed to it, who are both from abroad and born in the UK?

When war-weary populations were promised welfare as a reward, how popular would that have been if you had told them that it would be spent on people who had illegally invaded the country? That it would go to people who came here from other places, displaced them, and made their streets dangerous or beat their kids up or raped them?

When the welfare state was being proposed and sold and won an election, was anyone told that the bill would keep massively expanding forever, while the services provided became more and more incompetent and useless?

When the US Department of Education made education a federal rather than a state directed thing, was that great move sold on the basis that following its creation, the thousands of state bureaucrats employed would preside over a massive expansion of spending that, at the *same time*, enacted *a huge collapse of teaching standards* and educational results?

Americans tend to think they have avoided and escaped the welfare state because they are still charged directly and personally by a hospital when they are ill or sick. But, of course, with state-backed health provisions like Medicaid and with hospitals charging people personally, you haven't really escaped anything—instead you have the worst excesses of both private and public health provision *operating at the same time*.

And Americans, of course, have exactly the same problem with normalized vast spending—a high tax, high borrowing, welfare providing, all intrusive state spouting constantly about how much it cares while delivering ruin and decline.

Americans have the same problem with a Globalist ruling class turning welfare from perhaps sensible emergency support for the genuinely suffering of your own people into a vast machine of corruption spitting out incredibly negative social results.

And Americans have the same problem of all that *caring money* flowing back into the pockets of the kind of people who press for vast state spending in the first place.

Finally, Americans have the same problem of all this Globalist welfare compassion actually funding the destruction of the nation and being spent on everyone except decent Americans. They have these Globalist "leaders who care" spending their tax dollars and burdening their families with future debts in order to pay criminal and dangerous people who have invaded the nation.

It's the "caring" money that usually goes towards the State, and the directors of the State doing everything they can to destroy the Nation and make the people who *do* care about the Nation, as the ultimate insult, pay for it.

Across the Western world, people see their leaders arbitrarily assigning vast sums abroad (the UK has just given £11.6 billion for climate change provisions in other nations). This is because Globalists see caring about your own people as a very unsatisfying form of caring and probably the marker of a far-right extremist.

If the money is even spent at home, it must be spent on those who have invaded the home. That's what the welfare state combined with Cultural Marxist lessons on history ends up producing.

And that "compassion" is not compassion at all. It's *betrayal*, betrayal of the basic duties and responsibilities of government—betrayal of the existing majority of your population.

It is stealing from the majority to fund the death of that majority. It's taking what should be funds spent within the nation on basic and sensible services and appropriating all that spending and power for insane self-destructive policies.

In the UK, we have, with the new Labour government, a rapid succession of examples of what that pathological-sado-masochistic version of Globalist compassion looks like in operation.

We are told, for example, that it would be cruel and callous, racist and unjust…to deny welfare or housing to terrorists. Plans to exclude foreign terrorists from welfare and from housing lists are scrapped. So British taxpayers, under the rubrics of compassion and human rights, must pay for the people who want to blow them up.

We are also under various UN and European accords, of course, which say that we can only be a *civilized* and *compassionate* nation if we accept millions of invaders who see our women and children as easy meat. We are told that a civilized nation must have an asylum system and must welcome refugees, but many of these arrivals are not themselves civilized people. Knowingly importing people who threaten and harm your existing population is not really civilized at all.

In the US, UK, Germany, and other advanced Western nations, Globalists have perfected a *suicidal altruism* and a compassion towards the worst arrivals from elsewhere, which becomes a sadism towards the most innocent and vulnerable of the West's existing citizens. It's in California—the former "Sunshine State," that is now the most Third-World state of the USA—that we see Globalist "compassion" at its most devastatingly unjust.

Because in California, US citizens and state residents are now being told to fund state loans of up to $150,000 for foreign invaders who entered the country illegally. This is happening while California's leaders will also snatch ordinary citizens' children from them if those citizens try to protect their children from state-backed degenerates and perverts grooming their child to "transition."

It's a heady Globalist promise, isn't it? "Your kids aren't safe," and "we can steal them," combined with "we will also steal your money to pay for invaders to have what you are losing."

Globalist compassion always increases their power and the power of the State, enriches them and impoverishes you, and funds something obviously unjust and destructive. Every single time.

None of the spending goes to improving anything, none of it goes on you, and all of it goes to them and ruining the country or state you once loved.

All of it represents an assault on citizenship and any sense of mutual, reciprocal loyalty between the State and the individual citizen, because when *non-citizens are prioritized* and *citizens oppressed*, that's the end of a sane and functioning nation.

FROM DEPENDENCE TO SELF-RELIANCE

RECLAIMING YOUR CAPACITY FOR INDEPENDENT LIVING

A man is to carry himself in the presence of all opposition as if every thing were titular and ephemeral but he. I am ashamed to think how easily we capitulate to badges and names, to large societies and dead institutions. Every decent and well-spoken individual affects and sways me more than is right. I ought to go upright and vital, and speak the rude truth in all ways. If malice and vanity wear the coat of philanthropy, shall that pass? If an angry bigot assumes this bountiful cause of Abolition, and comes to me with his last news from Barbadoes, why should I not say to him, "Go love thy infant; love thy wood-chopper; be good-natured and modest; have that grace; and never varnish your hard, uncharitable ambition with this incredible tenderness for black folk a thousand miles off. Thy love afar is spite at home." Rough and graceless would be such greeting, but truth is handsomer than the affectation of love. Your goodness must have some edge to it,--else it is none. The doctrine of hatred must be preached, as the counteraction of

> the doctrine of love when that pules and whines.... Expect me not to show cause why I seek or why I exclude company. Then again, do not tell me, as a good man did to-day, of my obligation to put all poor men in good situations. Are they *my* poor? I tell thee thou foolish philanthropist that I grudge the dollar, the dime, the cent, I give to such men as do not belong to me and to whom I do not belong. There is a class of persons to whom by all spiritual affinity I am bought and sold; for them I will go to prison, if need be; but your miscellaneous popular charities; the education at college of fools; the building of meetinghouses to the vain end to which many now stand; alms to sots, and the thousand-fold Relief Societies;--though I confess with shame I sometimes succumb and give the dollar, it is a wicked dollar which by and by I shall have the manhood to withhold.
>
> —Ralph Waldo Emerson, "Self-Reliance"

Both the Globalist policies that claim to have a compassionate purpose and the ones that are more obviously about increasing Globalist control while eliminating political rivals operate by doing two things:

1. They place control of resources and decision-making in Globalist hands.
2. They make ordinary people dependent on the things Globalists control.

We can see this happening in both the "benevolent" things Globalists are very keen on and the "problematic" social ideas and groups they tend to attack.

Let's give some examples.

Globalists dislike nationalism and groups that prioritize their own nation and its interests. But why? Why do they want to weaken the nation and transfer power from the nation, continually, to transnational bodies like the EU or the UN?

Because their plans are not national. *The power they crave is not national.* The loyalties they feel are not national.

We are told that their love is universal. But really it is their *quest for power and control* that is universal. There is no institution, topic, or cause that they will not turn to the accumulation of power and the assertion of control. There is no boundary on what they or the State may do that they will recognize as sacred. The border of your nation is not sacred. The doorstep of your home is not sacred. The rights of the parent and child are not sacred. The border made by the bounds of your body is not sacred— there they will assume the authority to give you license to do that which harms you or another life within you and the power to insist that you take an experiment on their demand. The freedom of your speech is not sacred. And the privacy of your thoughts are not sacred, either.

As Emerson asserts, a man must find a point where he says to the Globalist, or any like-minded agent of the State, that he exists, that he possesses inalienable rights, and that the boundaries of thought and speech and what we may do without government control of everything are *still sacred.*

There comes a point where a man (or a woman) must say, "Who are these people you demand that I help?" Are they *my* people? Are their interests in accord with my own? Are their loves and battles mine as well?

Are you merely supporting them in order to *reduce me*, control me, and concentrate all power in all things into your hands?

Globalists want to operate globally in an unrestricted fashion. They want their power to cross all borders and their authority to affect all populations. They want to be able to move goods and workers wherever makes them, personally, the most money, and they don't want different rules or barriers getting in the way of that.

So, what happens when a nationalist leader putting the interests of his own nation and its existing citizens first is in power? Well, in that case, the Globalist faces a sudden barrier to doing whatever he pleases with whomever he pleases. He must negotiate separate deals with different nations, obey different rules in different places, and there's now a natural limit on the extent of power and influence he can accrue in a particular place that has a nationalist or populist party defending it.

The Globalist will talk about how damaging protectionism is and how sensible consistent rates of tax or consistent trading standards are, and he might even take a kernel of truth from some shared and consistent approaches as being a good thing. But what he's really worried about are limitations on his power and the barriers to him being able to get what he wants (total control of others and total freedom to do as he pleases) wherever he may be.

Transnational bodies, by being removed from the control of a specific nation and even more importantly *removed from accountability* to a specific set of citizens, allow the Globalist to impose *his* rules more broadly and, at the same time, free him from *old* rules decided by others.

Because of that, the Globalist will always insist that the rules must be ones determined globally, that is, by transnational bodies that aren't democratic, aren't elected, and aren't loyal to a single nation.

So, it's the UN that becomes the arbiter of which wars are just or unjust, not the voters. Or it's the EU that determines tariffs on trade or what products are legal, not specific EU nations. Or it's the International Monetary Fund that can determine whether a nation gets a life-saving loan in a moment of crisis or is refused that assistance (which comes with political demands).

And in each case, the Globalists can conduct small meetings in private with representatives of these bodies and reach agreements that no voter has prior awareness of or the ability to deny. Here, both sides know that it is their interests, rather than the interests of any national population, that are getting advanced.

The Globalist-run international banking system operates in this way (particularly with regard to poorer and more desperate nations), the same way a dealer would act towards an addict—both generous when getting the nation addicted and punishing and much less friendly if the addict looks like they're going clean or refusing to pay.

But, of course, the Globalists in general and the transnational institutions they created and dominate don't just want that kind of subservient dependency from nation-states. They want it from individuals too.

They obtain it in a very similar fashion: a "compassionate generosity" (with money taken from the public in the first place) for favored groups of clients and supporters, combined with an evermore contrasting stringency with the parts of the addicted populace that defy instructions, live and think independently, or otherwise threaten Globalist power and policies.

Look at who and what they attack: families and traditional fatherhood. A family represents the most stable building block of society as a whole. If you wanted a more stable society, you'd encourage marriage and child-rearing. If you wanted the best outcomes for children, you'd be honest about how devastating broken family backgrounds often are.

But a family is *a loyalty that the Globalist does not directly control*. And a protective traditional father is going to be standing up for his family, his children, and his community. He would be one of the first people to notice threats to them. A traditional male is going to be the person most likely to threaten a system that moves towards more and more open tyranny.

So, the Globalist intends to destroy that kind of connection and favors abortion, divorce, casual drug use, welfare, or casual or perverse sexual morals—anything that either breaks these units down or entangles them in state control and dependency on state control.

Throughout the Western world, there's been one very strong example of what the real agenda is: this is about control and dependency rather than anything else. That example is the treatment of farmers.

Under "net zero" rules, we are now told that farmers must pay excessive new fees or pay for upgrades to their equipment and practices to make farms carbon neutral. We are told that we should turn away from milk, dairy, and meat. We are told that herds need to be culled to "save the planet," and farmers are encouraged to turn their land from agricultural use to other uses (like fields of solar panel farms).

Why? It's not for the alleged "Green" reasons. Farmers have been custodians of the land a lot longer than politicians have. Farmers are the experts on nature and the countryside.

Farmers, though, have all the things that make people much more difficult to control and bully. They are one of the groups least likely to fall for urban myths and programming or to forget objective reality and spend more time worrying about micro-aggressions and trans rights. You won't find many farmers confused by the difference between male and female.

And these are the people who still possess the things you need for self-reliance: *Practical skills. Your own land. A real locally based community. An independent food supply.* And an independent energy supply too, most often. A farmer is far less dependent than a city dweller.

Both in terms of making individuals dependent on the State—therefore more easily controlled—and in terms of Globalists exclusively controlling key food, energy, water, and land resources, farmers are a natural point of potential resistance to Globalist plans. And in fact, farmers have been among the earliest people to actively and forcefully resist Globalist plans everywhere from Ireland to India and Holland to Africa.

Under Globalist rule, dependent client groups (welfare recipients, state employees, asylum seekers, low-skilled immigrants, the psychologically damaged, and the permanently offended) receive excuses, opportunities, and patronage. Society is shifted towards serving these groups and increasing their status and wealth. At the same time, self-reliant groups and individuals (like farmers, rural communities, traditional families and fathers, committed Christians whose faith gives them a spiritual independence grounded in a morality that the Globalists haven't written, the middle-class, and financially independent pensioners) are attacked.

The lesson of Globalist rule is that you can no longer rely on the basic institutions of civilization. You can't rely on them to enforce the rules fairly, to defend the innocent, to punish the guilty, to possess a shared loyalty—to do the things they were created to do. You can't rely on the media to be honest, the police to be impartial, the courts to be just, or the judges to be objective and politically neutral any more than you can rely on the elections to be free and fair.

And this applies to every institution in a Globalist system. It's not just the Department of Justice that becomes the opposite of what it is supposed to be.

It will also be something like a Catholic charity. You would expect it to be helping Catholics within your nation but it is actually run as a *progressive project* funneling dangerous migrants and helping them in illegal border crossings. It's the Royal National Lifeboat Institution of Great Britain, no longer voluntarily saving your own sailors and fishermen when they get into difficulties at sea, but now ferrying boatloads of fighting-age invaders onto your shores.

This means that you must recover your self-reliance.

The police aren't going to keep you safe on the streets. You need to keep away from the dangerous streets and the dangerous people (who are usually arrivals). You need to move out of the areas where the criminals and the unintegrated, often savage groups, congregate. It's insane for a white British person to keep living in Rochdale or Birmingham if they have any means of getting out, and its equally insane for a Republican to keep living in California or New York.

The political systems in these places are run by people who hate you, people who will lock you up if you defend yourself, and let your killers walk free if you don't.

But at the same time, white flight or Republican exodus is not going to keep currently safe areas safe in the future. It's not going to stop what Globalists are doing. It doesn't remove you from all the ways the federal government or the national government of a European nation being led by Globalists can ruin your country and your life.

You're still affected by the rampant inflation and the cost-of-living crisis. And most catastrophically of all, you are still going to probably be in a danger zone from a potential nuclear war if our utterly insane Globalist leaders manage to finally push Russia to the point where the Doomsday Clock strikes midnight.

You have to determine the extent to which you want to withdraw from an increasingly malign Globalist system. Do you have the financial resources and the family situation that allows you to go somewhere better? Can you at least get to a more rural location, a "red" state, or to a place that has shown some respect for the Constitution and for your freedom if you are in the US? Can you get to another, less freedom-averse nation if you are in Europe?

Or will you withdraw in terms of interaction with the institutions and the police and instead realize that you are more likely to need to avoid them than rely on them these days?

Making a retreat decision like this is not something that you should be ashamed of—it is a marker of shame regarding just how perverse, tyrannical, and malign our countries become under "respectable" Globalist rule.

You aren't a conspiracy theorist if you no longer trust any of our authorities, including supposedly benign ones like our medical authorities.

Given the nature of the authorities' behavior now and in recent years, you are a realist. And a realist takes steps to mitigate risk and protect themselves and their families.

It's not enough to complain anymore. Grumbles won't save you, and there are likely no "white hat saviors" riding to the rescue either. A Trump election victory is still possible, but who knows what levels of cheating will be applied this time? The rise of populist parties is very encouraging and the persistence of MAGA is too, but what will you do, as an individual, if the Globalists go ahead and *ban the only political movements* that listen to you?

You must think about your response before that day comes and plan for the best ways of protecting yourself and your family in the worst circumstances.

I do not mean by all this that we should all join militias, establish compounds, hoard food, and become survivalists sitting in bunkers. Some of us have done that. Some of us can do that. Some of us are still a long way away from that.

And I understand we have ordinary lives and ordinary commitments, and it all sounds very bleak and depressing. The temptation is to do nothing. The temptation is to hope for the best. The temptation is to hunker down not in a bunker but in a living room watching Netflix and grumbling about the race bullshit or the black elves or the LGBTQ+ film choices.

But the reality is that these Globalists aren't very sane and aren't very moral and are committed now to basically changing everything. And the changes they want aren't going to be good for you or your children, at all.

A few years back, there were virtually no gender reassignment clinics in the US. Today there are thousands. And the State can steal your kids if you try to stop them "transitioning." It's a big industry now, making lots of money.

A little longer ago than that, but as recently as 1992, all abortion was supposed to be "safe, legal, and rare" according to a Democrat president. Now, hundreds of thousands of babies are aborted (murdered) every year, their remains are used for medical procedures, and traded between medical institutions for profit. Planned Parenthood offered a travelling van of joyful abortion outside the DNC and have become one of the strongest pressure groups in the US. *Again*, a whole industry revolves around this. The current Democrat vice president pick has been personally responsible for the agonized deaths of babies who survived abortion procedures and were then, thanks to the policy he enacted, left to starve to death.

When I was born, fifty years ago, there were still very few mosques in the United Kingdom. Now, there are thousands of mosques, thousands of sharia courts, enforcing a separate theological system of law. There is now a Muslim mayor of London and millions of Muslims as part of the fastest growing religion and one of the fastest growing demographics in the UK. Up to a million white children have been raped and abused by Muslims for over thirty to forty years of abuse that the authorities covered up. Armed Muslims can rampage through city centers terrorizing white people with no condemnation at all or drive through a Jewish neighborhood threatening to rape Jewish girls with no condemnation and no charges at all while the media and the government talk about the scourge and evil of "white supremacism" and the "far right."

And people are put in prison for twenty months for shouting, "We want our country back."

The one thing (other than seizing and corrupting power) that Globalists are good at is making things worse and doing so quicker than you thought they could.

The America of the Biden administration, the Britain of the Keir Starmer regime, the Canada of Justin Trudeau, the France of Emmanuel Macron, and the Germany of Olaf Scholz—in their contempt for free speech, their contentment with corruption, electoral dishonesty, and fraud, their ideological hatred of their own people, and their complacency and complicity with the terrorism and demographic replacements they have welcomed—would have been inconceivable even thirty years ago, let alone fifty.

I never thought to find myself living in a nation that had less respect for the political diversity of opinion and free speech than Russia has, but I am.

I never thought that Western leaders would look admiringly on the tyranny, oppression, and total control of the populace that exists in Communist China, but they do.

I never thought that they could change that much and at the same time get away with presenting themselves as the moderates and the respectable people, but they do.

And it's in *this* context that I say that self-reliance, *being able to support and protect yourself and your family*, is utterly vital. It will make the difference between you being an unthinking agent or an unaware victim of Globalist leaders and policies and the difference between you being at least as prepared as you can be and your resources allowing for whatever hideous thing they do next.

It's been noted multiple times that survivors of horrible events tend to have a calm, pragmatic approach. They tend to start doing the things that save them quicker than other people do, but without fuss and hysteria. They don't waste time screaming and crying. They might be a bit better at seeing something deadly approach. But they act in a controlled way, quietly doing the best they can to increase their chances.

The same applies to points of political crisis and to living in countries that are corrupt and no longer offer the standards of safety and representation, of liberty and accountability, that applied when you were born.

A CAUTIOUS NOTE OF OPTIMISM

THE RED PILL IS NOT THE BLACK PILL

"Pills" feature prominently in the online chat rooms and forums dedicated to right-wing extremism. These are not actual pharmaceuticals; instead, each "pill" sends a message about a person's level of dedication to an extremist ideology or cause. Are they just beginning to learn about an ideology, or have they progressed further to embrace a nihilistic, potentially violent mindset? While online posts about "pills" can help outside audiences gauge individuals' states of mind, they are primarily used as a shorthand within extremist groups' internal conversations."

—The Anti-Defamation League, "The Extremist Medicine Cabinet: a Guide to Online 'Pills.'" (Because extremism is exclusively right wing, and popular culture references to film franchises are substantive proof of being a Nazi.)

Red pill and blue pill, symbols originating from the 1999 science-fiction film *The Matrix*. The pills represent a choice between remaining in a state of blissful ignorance (blue) or accepting a painful reality (red).... *The Matrix* depicts a futuristic world in which humans are kept in pods and used as batteries for a machine-ruled society. Under the influence of a reality-simulating computer system, called the Matrix, humans believe they are living their lives as usual. Computer hacker Neo (Keanu Reeves) meets the mysterious guru Morpheus (Laurence Fishburne), who presents him with the choice of the red pill or the blue pill. As Morpheus describes, "You take the blue pill, the story ends. You wake up in your bed and believe whatever you want to believe. You take the red pill, you stay in Wonderland. And I show you how deep the rabbit hole goes." Neo takes the red pill and wakes up in the real world.... Other colors of the pills have also emerged in the manosphere ["a vast network of websites and blogs frequented by online misogynist groups"]. The term *black pill*, first popularized in the 2010s on the incel blog Omega Virgin Revolt, refers to accepting the futility of fighting against a feminist system. Anarchist podcaster and writer Michael Malice has promoted the idea of the white pill, which expresses hope for a better political future. Less common references include the pink pill, purple pill, and green pill. In recent years the idea of "-pilling" has become a more mainstream online joke and a self-deprecating, ironic way to describe becoming interested in or influenced by something.

—Allison Rauch, *Red Pill and Blue Pill*, Britannica.com

There is wisdom in recognizing bleak and dangerous circumstances, in being aware of threats and dangers. There is no wisdom in succumbing to apathy and despair. Clearly, seeking a deeper understanding of what we are today experiencing—one which is more self-reliant as Emerson saw it and more in tune with objective reality once the intervening layers of mass media and mainstream media interpretations are discarded—is a good thing.

Giving way to genuine extremism that leads towards total despair (a.k.a. "the black pill"), resulting in either violence towards others or self-harm and suicide is just as obviously a bad thing.

Self-reliance means questioning the mainstream media and alternative media, based on logic, established facts, and traditional morality. Sadly, alternative media will increasingly tend towards accepting anything (no matter how ridiculous) as true if it comes from a non-mainstream source, just as the mainstream media will now assert anything (no matter how ridiculous) if it protects them and their paymasters' Globalist positions.

Both stop applying real standards and analysis regarding the truth of an assertion or the validity of a policy, whereas an already existing hinterland of logic or morality *in the individual* protects against the errors made by blindly trusting any source.

The Matrix formulation of "pills" is, therefore, both helpful and unhelpful. As any brief scan of mainstream sources reveals, it allows both a convenient shorthand for discussing differing levels of awareness and a convenient means by which the Globalist-progressive-dominated mainstream smears *all* conservative, right-wing, non-progressive and non-Globalist voices as ones linked to wacky conspiracy theories and extremist actions.

When encyclopedias treat left-wing anarchist use of this terminology as essentially politically neutral and even wholesome (ignoring, for example, that leftist anarchism has a very long history of violent action and terrorism stretching back into the nineteenth century and ultimately back to the French Revolution) but right-wing use of the same popular culture reference must be solely extremist, we can see the level of engrained and institutional bias we are now dealing with.

A Globalist discussion of *The Matrix* and "pill" symbology accidentally confirms the extent to which we do have a "matrix" in place, where the respectable voices are extremely selective in their discussions of just what extremism is.

For this reason, I should state that I'm using the terms purely as a shorthand (blue for unaware, red for aware, and black for despair) with no alliance with extremism from any source (including all those kinds of extremism and political violence Globalists end up supporting).

With that explanation offered, if we look at the power of Globalism and how far it has changed our societies and endangered the things we once took for granted, we can give in to despair. This is especially if we are an ordinary working-class person who doesn't have a lot of job security, social contacts and advantages, any personal power granted by an institutional role or independent wealth, or any of the other things that are most effective in creating change for the good or preventing the worst abuses from the maligned.

We are fighting people who can go after Donald Trump and Elon Musk. What can we do?

There are thousands of businesses, corporations, NGOs (nongovernmental organizations), transnational institutions, and corrupt politicians and media personalities on the other side—and the police, courts, judges, elections, and mainstream political parties. All of it.

Sometimes it seems as if everything is against you.

So yes, despair is easy.

What can we do about it?

We can change it. We can defy it. And over time, we can destroy it. The most powerless of us can do that, can contribute to that.

And this is, in fact, the true lesson of history. The true lesson of history is not just how easy it is for a country or several countries to *slip into tyranny*. It's not just that this happens with depressing regularity or that all times have been imperfect in various ways and that utopia is an illusion only offered by the most malign and the most destructive.

We aren't after utopia, just *better*.

The true lesson of history is that *better* is just as easy as *worse*.

The things that need to be done to reform and improve without insanity, fanaticism, and bloodshed are really not that complicated at all.

We need to *ditch obviously mad contemporary ideas* like critical race theory and "net zero." We need to greatly reduce government spending. We need to break the link between corporate monopolies and radical progressive social policies and activism. We need to *teach logic* and reduce the leftist and Globalist-progressive strangleholds on education and entertainment. We need to *listen more to ordinary people* and less to great foundations that only serve the interests of billionaires. We need to make the ruling and media classes *more accountable* and *more honest*. We need low taxes and strong borders.

None of these things are impossible for a government that actually wants to do them. None of these things come about, either, purely by some white hat government riding to the rescue.

They come about because the demand for them, from us, becomes greater than any propaganda can counteract, any censorship can silence, and any rulers can ignore.

The true lesson of history is that every tyranny falls. And some are strangled in their cribs, which is a good thing for all of us.

Think of the despair of a Soviet citizen in the period of Soviet dominance. Think of the astonishing and brutal crimes that went unpunished. The Soviet system was one of the most ruthless in history. It inspired devoted fanaticism. It got away with genocides and terror. It had people so brainwashed, at the height of Stalinism, that people imprisoned and tortured on Stalin's orders would write "Long live Stalin!" in their own blood on the walls of their cells.

As utterly irrational as many of the people who think all is well under Globalism are, we aren't in a place that bad, yet.

By the grand scheme of things, the two worst systems of the twentieth century did not last that long as active polities. *The Nazis managed just twelve years in power. The Soviets managed just sixty-nine years in power.* Both, of course, did incalculable damage in those periods, and late Soviet propaganda and demoralization techniques have a large historical impact on many of the problems the West is experiencing today (as explained by KGB defector Yuri Bezmenov in his astonishingly accurate 1984 interview with G. Edward Griffin titled *Soviet Subversion of the Free World Press*).

But within little more than a decade, people saw Nazism go from a global military threat to vanished, utterly defeated, and utterly discredited ideology that 99.9 percent of people would thereafter forever despise. And within one human lifespan, people saw the Soviet system go from fanatical loyalty to a despised joke, from a tyrannical superpower to a broken and beaten ideology that multiple nations were happy to discard.

Even the sheer stupidity of a large percentage of younger people saying in polling that Communism is the best system for America could actually have been easily avoided (along with Cultural Marxism and off-shoots of that like "wokeness," modern race politics, and an enthusiasm for Islamic terrorists designated as an "oppressed people") with a sterner and clearer understanding of what Bezmenov warned was happening.

We were told in 1984 what was going to happen and what changes would occur in the cultural landscape unless we addressed the radical leftist, Soviet-inspired dominance of culture. It could have been stopped then.

Tyrannies always fall.

The thing is, though, that we really don't want to go through years of suffering before this one does. We want to escape the worst horrors of Globalism before they become any more equivalent to early-mid twentieth century extremism than they already are (the Globalist casting of every opponent as a Nazi is, of course, a psychological projection).

The level of hate disguised as good, hate that says it has outlawed hate, within the woke and Globalist-progressive attitudes and within the elite class that is financially backing these attitudes is such that we can be thankful it hasn't yet led to more murderous consequences. But we only have to look at Antifa thugs chasing down people to attack, BLM thugs doing the same, or Muslim gangs rampaging through British city centers to see the true face of what Globalism is and what Globalism encourages. Combine that with the devastating reality of the millions of still unacknowledged deaths caused by the COVID vaccines, and we can see that Globalist "altruism" and "respectability" in some ways (and especially because it's still not *seen* as such a threat) is just as dangerous as Nazism and Communism…if not more.

Globalists can tinker with the world's DNA or fund "perfectly respectable" research at places like Harvard into the remote control of other humans (real experiments that sound like science fiction nightmares). They can plot mad Bond-villain schemes, like blocking out the sun.

If we had what we once had (reasonably honest institutions and media), then there would be an accounting for all these changes and for the more reckless things that Globalists have already done, as well as a halt to the crazier things they plan to do.

But in the absence of that *so far*, we should not despair.

Rather, and in a rather ironic way, we can take both hope and pragmatic lessons from just how much everything has declined. Globalist success in radically changing our societies for the worse oddly presents us with the awareness that *radical reversal* is also possible. And it does that if we recognize that the insanities we see enthroned in our society today were ones that were worked towards by people who used to have no power at all.

Globalists, progressives, Cultural Marxists, traditional Marxists, radical leftists, race- and sexual-orientation-identity obsessives, and people who hated the Western world once stood where traditionalists, libertarians, classical liberals, patriots, Christians, and genuine moderates stand today.

They were once as powerless as us.

Our values were once sitting at the top of society, and *they* were the people that the police would arrest, the judges would sneer at, and the teachers and the journalists would condemn and mock.

They were the Commies, the beatniks, the losers. The FBI did not serve them; it hated them.

The social and sexual revolution of the 1960s, the internal division and sense of collapse in the 1970s, and even the patriotic resurgence of the 1980s (since it gave a false confidence and blinded the Right to where the Left was winning in education and culture) were all steps in the ascent of the radical progressive worldview and the switch from people like us (ordinary people with sensible political instincts) being respectable to people like us being *deplorable*.

When the single greatest playbook of radical leftist attitudes was written, it was written from a place of defeat. It was written when that generation's useful idiots had *failed*. It was written when its writer, Saul Alinsky, thought that all his revolutionary dreams for the radical refiguring of the US had been crushed.

The playbook of how to take over was written because they kept being beaten.

It's just as the even more organized and cunning KGB demoralization psychological warfare, as described by Bezmenov, came because the Soviets knew they were economically losing and already had realized that they would probably lose the Cold War altogether.

If it is possible for them to totally change society, it is just as possible for us to do so as well. Counterrevolution is as possible as revolution is.

And let's look at some of the existing positives.

When enough of us powerless people respond en masse in simple ways that hurt the profits of the powerful, it does have an effect. The Bud Light effect is real. Some of the executives involved lost their jobs. The campaign messaging was shifted to be far less woke.

Alternative media is flourishing and delivering truth and the possibility of differing opinions to people instead of the controlled lies and constant propaganda of the mainstream media. The mainstream media is dying as a thing that people actually want and follow.

Trust in the mainstream media is at a record low.

Globalist leaders invariably face punishing popularity ratings, which tell us that these leaders and these policies do not have majority support. They only ever have ruling-class support.

Some nations are already defying the Globalist agenda. Russia, rather obviously, has strongly opposed it in multiple ways. The BRICS nations have tyranny of their own (both China and most of the rest), but their economic bloc does present a barrier to true global hegemony (unless Western Globalists and BRICS leaders reach a pro-tyranny accommodation, which is possible).

Sweden, though, offers a more hopeful example of a push back. Sweden defied the COVID Globalist madness and is now under a genuinely right-wing government, showing that, contrary to Globalist lies, the worst policies can be rapidly jettisoned and reversed with only positive rather than negative impacts from doing so. Sweden has reduced immigration to effectively zero very quickly. It has dumped the UN Sustainability Goals and "net zero" policies. It is offering governance that actually listens. It is dumping the Green taxes on air travel.

It turns out that it is possible to get governments that protect the interests of their own people.

Hungary under Orban continues to act sensibly and refuse EU punishment and Soros-backed agitation.

If at least some of the fraud is dealt with, Trump could win and return to the presidency. Globalists and Democrats have no morality limiting what they will do to prevent that, but practical options do reduce if measures are taken against fraud and against assassination.

The US does have red states (like Florida) that are governed sanely. The "Republican in name only" element, as well as the perpetual war lobby (McCain, Cheney, Bush family influence), has been more and more squeezed out of their controlling position within the Republican Party.

Both classical liberals and ethnic minorities who want a functioning nation and a sane environment for individual liberty and business prosperity are responding by moving more and more towards the Right and towards populism as their lives and their freedom are harmed by Globalist measures and attitudes.

Trump is gradually building a coalition against corruption that might survive, with wisdom from other MAGA figures, the end of his own period in active politics.

The world's richest man, Elon Musk, is firmly opposed to the worst elements of Globalist policy and genuinely seems to want to preserve free speech, political debate, and decent economic conditions. The X platform remains a place where free speech can be protected, and Musk has research and development capabilities with his companies that may make censorship efforts increasingly obsolete.

You are not divorced from all this—even if you have little money or status, even if you feel powerless. Your voice matters until you *agree* that it does not matter.

You can be more careful with who you vote for, who you believe, who you fund, and who you purchase from. There are books like *Woke-Proof Your Life* telling you how to make those judgments in a better way. You an even download apps that will let you scan a product and determine how woke, Globalist, and progressive the company connected to it is.

You can follow alternative media. Get active on X, Rumble, and Truth Social. You can stay informed even when mainstream media or Globalist leaders want you to be treating them as the only source of truth.

You can and must *do your own research* and laugh at those who pretend that your capacity to read and investigate is something to be ashamed of.

You can make sure that your money does not rest in a single bank and protect it from arbitrary seizure by using cash, keeping a store of cash, and keeping some asset or commodity that can be quickly converted into cash (like gold or vehicles that can be sold).

You can claim whatever welfare and support you are entitled to, knowing that this is money that otherwise would be going to your enemies and invaders to your nation, but strive to never ever be dependent on it.

As much as is possible, you must cultivate self-reliance. It is better to have land than not have land. It is better to know basic skills (of survival and defense) than not know them. It is better to be armed than unarmed. It is better to be cautious than trusting. It is better to be taciturn than loud-mouthed around people you don't trust.

It is better to be free than to be owned.

If you can work for yourself, do so.

If you have to work for a company or a boss, don't let them brainwash you. Be prepared to lose a job before you betray your values. Be prepared to resist attempts to frame your thinking in areas totally unrelated to your actual duties.

Use their ideas and rules against them. Alinsky said to always hold your enemy to their own standards. You can do that too. Record your interactions with the police. Know your lawyer and have a lawyer. Join organizations like the Free Speech Union. Apply policy documents and grand declarations of anti-racism, anti-sexism, and the like to how you are being treated. Force them to show that they denied such protections to people like you or force them to reluctantly extend them to you.

The more dependent on others you are, the more easily you are controlled. But the more alone you are, the more easily you are crushed. So, you must cultivate a balance of being a person who can survive by their own efforts and who will think and act independently and without fearing what their employer or their rulers will demand, while also being a person who has a community, a family, and a network of your own connections and allies, both political and nonpolitical.

If you find people politically aligned with you, make those connections social and real. If you have leadership skills or the ability to persuade others, online or in person, use them to assist the growth of populist movements.

Disengage from social contact that can only lead to your betrayal, defeat, or some harm to you, and vigorously engage with ones that build your community with the kind of people who will help you and help your country recover itself.

Their revolution is not fully accomplished. Your time is not fully passed.

You can claim back the future. You can still reverence the past.

And you are not alone in wanting to.

APPENDIX

GLOBALIST INSTITUTIONS

The majority of people across the world, but particularly in the Western world, remain blissfully unaware of the vast network of organizations that in, one way or another, govern them. They vote in elections, and they favor one political party or another. They might also be aware of and either support or distrust a few of the key transnational bodies and international organizations that have been most obvious and active in setting and supporting particular policies adopted globally.

But I don't think many of us stop and think that often about just how many politically active organizations exist, and how many of them now exist to push for exactly the same kinds of policies, no matter what their alleged area of focus is.

The Yearbook of International Organizations, for example, lists over twenty-five thousand international nongovernmental organizations (NGOs). It includes some that are now defunct, but even so, the collective resources of these groups are enormous and have an impact on every aspect of our lives, from fishery policies to sporting events.

Of course, there *are* instances where an international organization makes sense or where basic regulatory standards and working practices need to align. It seems pretty sensible that ships passing through different territorial waters refer to the same terms that apply to international shipping when discussing what they are doing. It seems pretty sensible that air traffic controllers coordinate, understand each other, or have similar basic training.

But at the same time, when a certain mindset, a way of looking at the world, pervades all of these institutions, no matter what their explicit purposes are, that represents a vast kind of soft power in operation and an extraordinary opportunity to *shift public perception* globally.

What happens when they aren't talking about the sensible stuff that makes sure planes don't hit each other, but instead are talking about how many trans pilots you must employ?

And the sheer scale of it all, once politically corrupted, is mind-boggling.

If we include NGOs that have internationalist and Globalist attitudes, but which are mainly operating within one nation, the numbers become even more astonishing. There are, for example, 1,300 NGOs associated with the United Nations Department of Global Communication. There are over 6,000 organizations in active consultative status with the United Nations Economic and Social Council. There are over 40,000 NGOs listed by the United Nations Development Programme.

According to data supplied by the US Department of State in 2021, there are *1.5 million NGOs* active in the USA.

That's roughly an NGO for every 224 people in the US.

Who funds them? Who controls them? Are they accountable to the public? Are they doing what they claim to have been created for? Are they imposing ideological and political messages? Can you ignore them? Can the public fire them in some democratically accountable way? Are they serving foreign interests? Are they serving malign private interests?

The late Labour member of Parliament and critic of the EU Tony Benn (a man whose politics was very much of the "Old Left" and not similar to mine except on this issue) used to have five questions (similar to those above) that he would ask when deciding whether an institution or organization was honest and accountable.

In most cases, in relation to even the most powerful transnational bodies and NGOs (even those *taking over* government policy and government tasks), nobody asks these questions. The mainstream media *refuse to ask* these questions, and the mainstream political establishment knows the answers but *wants* this unaccountable model of rule.

All of these organizations tend to accord with certain basic assumptions and work within similar legal frameworks. We have seen with international sporting organizations, in particular, how entirely innocent, non-political activities (indeed, activities that are supposedly an escape from politics) can be suborned for *vast messaging campaigns* and propaganda campaigns aimed at expressing Globalist attitudes or supporting progressive, woke, socially leftist causes.

The 2024 Olympics (similarly but even more obviously ideological than previous Olympics) showcased Globalist-progressive attitudes to the world. The International Olympic Committee clearly made ideological and political choices in the nature of the competition rules regarding gender participation and in the kind of "values" and attitudes receiving promotion in the opening and closing ceremonies.

These choices included promoting gender confusion, mocking Christianity, celebrating diversity, promoting obesity, joyously delighting in the bloodshed of the French Revolution, pushing a LGBTQ+ agenda in every possible way, pretending that Russia doesn't exist, and pretending that refugees, migrants and illegal aliens can compete under an imaginary flag in what was a competition previously defined by a contest between nations.

And that is the *least* political (on the surface) organizations that anyone could think of.

Many more of these organizations are directly political, can enforce policy on nation-states, can condemn or issue warrants for the arrest of national leaders, oversee vast areas of legislation, or define what is or is not legal globally. Some of them, of course, represent the pooling of large-scale military assets and can directly intervene in wars. Others determine the rules nations follow in their financial transactions and economic policy choices, with ever growing "harmony" and coordination (such as the agreed alignment even between Brexit Britain and the EU) that the public have no say in and are often not even aware of in any detail.

Nation-states transfer more and more power to these organizations. With citizens, in particular, nations have less and less say on that, and following such transfers, less and less influence even by voting patterns on what policies are followed. National leaders will cite commitments to these organizations and their rules as things tying their hands when dealing with certain issues (like asylum policy and mass immigration) and act as if withdrawing from such agreements is an *impossibility* or a *moral crime*. Globalist bodies will unite to condemn any attempt to gain some kind of national benefit from these bodies, make them pay their own way without being dependent on huge funding from nation-states that see little positive return from the investment, or in any way be skeptical towards what becomes an entangling power network that both citizens and whole nations can be trapped within against their will.

Many of these bodies will claim to represent "stakeholders" or "communities"—*but won't at any point represent ordinary people*. Many will claim to exist to protect people from abuse or exploitation or oppression—and then will *impose rules* and *spread propaganda* that the majority don't want and don't agree with.

Charitable foundations, in particular, have a certain status based on the idea of them being *nonprofit* and *nonpolitical*, about them being purely altruistic, and then will do and promote directly political things that are harmful and that ordinary people should have some power to refuse—but don't. One hundred seventy thousand global charities have tax exemptions based on them being purely altruistic, but very obviously take political sides and promote certain political values or receive funding from the State in various ways.

For these reasons, because these groups often do have a defined *agenda* that isn't really about the things they are supposed to care about, it's useful to list some of the most powerful and influential of them.

The groups listed below collectively push Globalist attitudes on every topic you can think of: race, gender, class, health, mental health, law, agriculture, the Ukraine war, technology, surveillance, climate, energy, and "social justice."

The investment banks, in particular, have successfully imposed *progressive social attitudes* on the business world and throughout thousands of companies by leveraging their power to make or break a business through the supply or withholding of loans for the *political purpose* of enforcing diversity, equity, and inclusion (DEI) and environmental, social, and governance (ESG) commitments. Companies have to sign up to Globalist-progressive policies or be starved of loans and ostracized in the business and banking system.

Similarly, the global banking system and the international "rule of law" will be applied aggressively on nation-states that resist Globalist policy choices, and this applies on everything from the G7 condemnation of Brexit to EU fines imposed on Hungary, right up to sanctions, exclusion from international banking and credit systems, and military supply and action against Russia.

These actions are all directed by organizations that have no accountability to the ordinary citizen of any *Western "democracy."*

What follows is a brief description of some of the most powerful of these Globalist bodies that are running (and ruining) the world you live in.

BlackRock

Along with The Vanguard Group and State Street, BlackRock, Inc. is one of the three most powerful investment banks in the world. It was founded by Robert S. Kapito, Larry Fink, and Susan Wagner in 1988.

BlackRock is the world's largest asset manager with over *$10 trillion* worth of assets under its management as of December 31, 2023.

Larry Fink's personal net worth sits at over $1.2 billion. He is on the boards of *both* the Council on Foreign Relations and the World Economic Forum.

In his 2018 open letter to CEOs, Fink declared that "corporations should play an active role in improving the environment, working to better their communities, and increasing the diversity of their work forces," according to the summary from JLL, an international property and investment consultancy company. Similar instructions followed in 2019, with Fink arguing that corporations "must step into a leadership vacuum to tackle social and political issues when governments fail to address these issues," according to the summary on Fink's Wikipedia page.

All of the obsessions held by Fink are the standard Globalist-progressive ones—Green climate change catastrophism, DEI, and radical leftist social engineering in the name of "social justice."

The power of BlackRock as the world's largest asset manager is enormous and Fink's political agenda is pivotal in the shift of the Western "business world" and corporate culture towards progressive activism.

BlackRock and its two main investment banking rivals all enforce DEI polices and ESG policies on the companies they deal with, making vital business investment and operating loans dependent on progressive and Globalist political stances.

BlackRock is also the world's largest investor in the US military-industrial complex (other than the US government), predisposing both it and the Western business world generally towards perpetual war policies and such measures as support for Ukraine, which then become the "sensible" and "moral" foreign policy stances of Globalist political parties.

Common Purpose

Common Purpose is a global nonprofit organization founded in 1989 by Julia Middleton in the UK. According to their "About" page, it claims that it "delivers transformative learning experiences for individuals and organizations who want to make a difference in their worlds, and the world around them."

If that sounds like a creepy cult message from bloviating Globalist bullshitters, you're not wrong.

The organization presents itself as a charity focused on developing leadership programs and skills.

Essentially, they take public funding and charitable donations and use them to indoctrinate people with Globalist values, particularly focusing on politically engaged young people and "future leaders" (just like the World Economic Forum do).

Common Purpose gains contracts to supply leadership courses and workshops across the local and national government and in bodies like the UK Civil Service. It has branches doing the same thing in the US, Singapore, Pakistan, Bangladesh, Nigeria, and Germany and is involved in projects in over one hundred countries in total. Eight thousand students per year go through their longest programs, while eighty-five thousand "leaders" have already taken part in their courses.

Common Purpose has also set up subsidiary lobbying groups with a media focus without acknowledging the relationship between themselves and these other organizations. Sir David Bell, a trustee of Common Purpose and a member of the Leveson public inquiry into UK press standards, also set up the Media Standards Trust (a lobbying group that presented evidence to the inquiry) and yet another lobbying group (Hacked Off), which also presented evidence to the inquiry.

The Leveson inquiry notably targeted media abuses from right-wing tabloids while generally ignoring equally shocking behavior from left-wing press outlets, and this expensive, official inquiry established the extraordinary practice of a series of "Russian doll" pressure groups presenting evidence to each other on which they then based recommendations (which they were set up to want in the first place). The whole thing was disguised as public accountability.

Both senior Blair-era politicians like David Blunkett and former Conservative Prime Minister David Cameron got into trouble for undeclared links with Common Purpose when its activities first came to wider public attention.

Despite such scandals, Common Purpose continues to be hired by Globalist institutions to deliver leadership training, creating a core of the administrative and political class (particularly in the UK) who have gone through a process of indoctrination even more intensive than they tend to receive in the university environment.

United Nations Department of Global Communication (DGC)

Previously called the United Nations Department of Public Information, the DGC was founded on February 13, 1946. It is the department of the UN Secretariat charged with raising public awareness and support for the UN (essentially the UN's propaganda ministry). It's claimed original objectives, when it was called the Department of Public Information, were "communicating the ideals and the work of the United Nations to the world; to interacting and partnering with diverse audiences; and to building support for peace, development and human rights for all."

All very noble sounding, as usual.

In reality, this means television broadcasts, control of journalists, release of articles, and associate connections with a vast number of other organizations all coordinating public perception of the UN and advancing Globalist approaches to every political issue.

United Nations Economic and Social Council (ECOSOC)

The ECOSOC is one of the main bodies of the UN, although rarely discussed, and established by the founding UN Charter in 1945. ECOSOC is responsible for the direction and coordination of the economic, social, humanitarian, and cultural activities carried out by the UN. According to its Britannia entry, "It is the UN's largest and most complex subsidiary body."

As with multiple UN agencies, ECOSOC covers vast areas that are broadly and vaguely defined, effectively letting it interfere in almost anything it chooses to. It establishes committees on human rights, narcotics, population, social development, statistics, the status of women, and science and technology.

These have a track record of selectivity when it comes to human rights, often hectoring Western nations while appointing or supporting representatives from Third World nations with worse records on such issues.

In a typical example of UN bureaucratic hypocrisy, the fifty-four ECOSOC members who guide it are appointed from the global political elite with little public awareness of even who these people are.

ECOSOC also helps coordinate the activities of more than 2,500 NGOs, which have consultative status.

North Atlantic Treaty Organization (NATO)

Ostensibly created to coordinate and promote the mutual military defense of member states, NATO's existence and purpose made some sense in the context of the Cold War and the postwar desire to avoid another Nazi Germany. On creation, it was very specifically about the protection of western Europe (nations with Atlantic proximity) and as the Cold War developed, very focused on that protection being a deterrent (along with nuclear arsenals) to Soviet aggression or expansion.

Since the end of the Cold War, NATO's purpose and limits have been increasingly blurred, arguably morphing it from a necessary deterrent to an active aggressor. The signatories have relentlessly expanded, the Atlantic part of the organization's name now being meaningless, and their attentions have remained focused on Russia after the fall of the Soviet Union.

Assurances given during the Clinton administration regarding NATO expansion were abandoned, and Russian inquiries about joining in the early period of Putin's ascension were rebuffed.

Russian security concerns regarding a hostile military alliance potentially placing nuclear missiles on their border and being encircled by that alliance are not unfounded ones and contributed to the Ukraine war, regardless of how dishonest both NATO and the Western media have been about this. Just as the US would not accept such a scenario during the Cuban missile crisis, Russia has persistently described NATO membership for Ukraine and similar former Soviet satellites as a security red line for them.

NATO generals and leaders have been, however, enthusiastically belligerent in their language and "warnings," which seem more designed to provoke Russia than seek peace, and all this comes in the context of

Russians remembering pivotal NATO air strikes against their traditional ally Serbia at the end of the Yugoslav Wars.

It's hard to continue to justify a mutual *defense* pact that militarily intervenes in conflicts not involving member states.

Open Society Foundations

The personal legacy of the ninety-four-year-old (as of 2024) billionaire financial speculator George Soros, the Open Society Foundations, now largely directed by his children, consist of a huge network of influence pushing Globalist and progressive attitudes through private meetings, direct funding of political candidates, lobbying campaigns, and advertising propaganda. The Soros organization is banned in Hungary due to repeated efforts to interfere in Hungarian elections and force progressive policies on the Hungarian government.

George Soros is a rapacious capitalist who "broke the Bank of England" with ruthless and highly profitable assaults on the British pound, leading to a British recession. This one example of his approach to currency trading did huge damage to British pension funds and the savings of ordinary people, while making Soros himself even richer.

Earlier than that, as a teenager in an occupied nation during World War Two, Soros hid his Jewish ancestry (very understandable), collaborated with the Nazi seizures of Jewish property (a lot less understandable), and infamously later expressed a complete lack of regret or guilt for that participation in Nazi crimes (outright evil, and he manifested the same attitude whenever asked about the economic damage caused by his financial speculations).

The foundation he established, in typical Globalist fashion, claims the highest ideals again. It claims to promote an "open society" of greater freedom, diversity, tolerance, and empathy, as well as higher standards of democracy and accountability. What that means, in effect, is the funding of radical hard left social pressure groups and establishing corrupt influence over Democrat politicians in the US and their equivalents elsewhere.

Soros's foundations, along with the UN, have been the biggest promoter of open borders and mass migration, wrapping this destructive policy in the language of compassion for refugees and asylum seekers and having no regard for the effect on Western nations.

It has also funded many of the most corrupt politicians, district attorneys, and prosecutors in the US. Soros's money has backed these politicians in their campaigns, and they have then enacted their master's policy choices, such as the mass release of violent criminals; the decriminalization of rioting, shoplifting, looting, and violence from favored groups; the introduction of racial bias and agendas in law and policing; and the pursuit of trumped up charges against non-Globalist political opponents.

As a greedy financial speculator, Soros did enormous damage to others while profiting himself. But as "philanthropists," he and his children have played a key part in the promotion of the most ruinous policies imaginable, directly harming the fabric of Western civilization, helping to turn the US into a banana republic, and harming huge numbers of ordinary people.

Atlantic Council

The Atlantic Council was founded in 1961. It is a think tank that supposedly promotes cooperation between North America and Europe. Although founded sixteen years after the end of World War Two, its ethos and purpose centers on continuing the transnational "rules-based international order" established at the end of World War Two, like the UN. In another similarity to the UN, it can only be properly understood as a Globalist attempt to fix global geopolitics based on the understanding of the world and politics of which sees nationalism as the primary threat to global peace and security. It works particularly closely with NATO.

The members of the Atlantic Council have primarily been engaged in foreign policy direction, trying to shape an aggressively Globalist approach using the resources of both the US and European nations to enforce conformity and back the perpetual war policy of US neocons and the military-industrial complex. In foreign policy military adventurism, the Atlantic Council drafts advise and policy approaches justifying intervention, while the UN rubber stamps such actions and gives them the moral authority of being "international" (even though the primary resourcing is drawn from the US).

More recently, the Atlantic Council has also been very keen on climate change hysteria and pushing for North American and European unity on the wealth transfer opportunities deriving from a radical energy supply shift.

Notably, the Atlantic Council tried to draw Hungary deeper into Globalist alignment by partnering with the Hungary Foundation. Criticisms of the "state of democracy" in Hungary led the Orban government to realize that this was just another attempted method of control and the relationship was severed.

The Atlantic Council receives funding from twenty-five or more foreign governments, with the United Arab Emirates being a particularly consistent funder (a distant nation oddly concerned about cross-Atlantic cooperation). The UK is another big funder through the Foreign, Commonwealth and Development Office. Its wider funding serves almost as a roll call of the "usual suspects," which feature in both anti-establishment "conspiracy theories" and Globalist lists of the great and the good: Goldman Sachs, The Rockefeller Foundation, Facebook/Meta, private donors like the multimillionaire US funder Adrienne Arsht or the Lebanese billionaire Bahaa Hariri, and, in terms of corruption, most notably the Ukrainian oligarch outfit Burisma Holdings (the same Burisma Holdings tied to the Biden family).

During the Obama administration, the Atlantic Council figures moved into the administration and were particularly powerful figures within it, the most notable of these being Susan Rice (Obama's ambassador to the UN), Richard Holbrooke, and Anne-Marie Slaughter. Chairman of the Atlantic Council James L. Jones became Obama's national security adviser in 2009.

Bilderberg Group

The Bilderburg Group was established in 1954 and is named after the Hotel de Bilderberg near the village of Oosterbeek in the Netherlands, where its first meeting took place. Its first attendees represented a mix of Belgian government figures and private industrialists with a declared interest in opposing anti-American sentiment in Europe. It's since become yet another private, invite-only annual meeting place, clearing house, and policy discussion forum for powerful American and European political figures.

The group is again tied to the postwar rules-based international order and again pushes generally Globalist approaches and policies in a range of areas. As such, it has become one of the organizations most focused on by various conspiracy theories (some of which are a lot more sensible than others, and some of which are a lot crazier than others).

Mainstream media and sites like RationalWiki tend to dismiss all criticism of the Bilderberg Group or link *all* criticism to extremist versions that include discussions of the Illuminati, alien lizards, or vile Jew-hating ideas, without acknowledging the democratic deficit and lack of accountability inherent in this private meeting model of policy discussion and formation.

What is fair to say is that the views and policies pushed by this group will always favor internationalism over nationalism and the transnational bodies that share its attitudes over traditional barriers to transnational authority. They will also automatically favor the now standard prejudices and opinions of an international elite over loyalty to those citizens and their key concerns, because that elite have far more in common with each other than they have with the ordinary citizens of their respective nations.

So, despite how ridiculous some conspiracy theories may be, the Bilderberg Group is just one of multiple organizations that, even without deliberate conspiracy, by being present would, *by its very nature, act like a conspiracy in meeting secretly and imposing policies that are not put to the test of public opinion*. A conspiracy of assumptions and class prejudices would be enough to exclude the voices and best interests of ordinary people when the powerful regularly gather in these private groups that do have a shared agenda.

Bill & Melinda Gates Foundation (BMGF)

Possibly the most notorious billionaire on the Globalist side of the political equation and Microsoft founder, Bill Gates has become, through the foundation he established in 2000, the world's biggest private donor in the fields of medicine, vaccination, and medical research. An explanation of the Gates transition from ruthless capitalist accused of unfair monopoly practices to the world's foremost philanthropist can be found in my previous book *Gates of Hell: Why Bill Gates is the Most Dangerous Man in the World*.

The explicitly declared aims of the BMGF are to fund medical and vaccine research, eliminate childhood diseases and poverty, support Third World development, protect against global pandemics, and develop better agricultural practices and greener energy sources. The foundation is the most powerful private body involved in both global health policy and climate and net zero policy.

It's also the most successful advocate of "philanthrocapitalism," where the interests of private donors and state funding supposedly cohere around allegedly noble intentions. The personal wealth of Bill Gates has grown enormously by investing in the companies and medicines he promotes as a "philanthropist" and by engaging in public-private partnerships where national governments match large donations made by the Gates Foundation.

The BMGF effectively controlled global health responses to the COVID pandemic, and BMGF senior staff were consulted on a weekly basis by most Western governments during COVID. Gates personally contacted multiple world leaders in private calls and meetings, which aligned with policy announcements and changes.

Gates and his foundation exert enormous (some might say controlling) influence on the UN's World Health Organization (WHO) as its largest private donor, with 11–13 percent of the WHO annual budget coming directly from the foundation and with the current WHO leader, Dr. Tedros Ghebreyesus, being a handpicked close Gates ally and personal friend.

Effectively, Bill Gates and his foundation exert more influence on global health policies affecting billions of people than almost any national government does. They also have a sizable say in the world of scientific research and in the opinions of thousands of scientists at least dependent on foundation funding. Many of the national scientific advisers during COVID (Patrick Vallance and Chris Whitty in the UK, Anthony Fauci in the US, and the Imperial College team headed by Professor Niall Ferguson—which became the Imperial College COVID-19 Response Team) provided the statistical "evidence" via computer modeling that "justified" harsh COVID measures and was the key scientific support for persuading the US Congress and administration that it faced a major pandemic threat. Ferguson and the Imperial team had received multiple BMGF donations and grants.

Private foundations avoid monopoly laws that apply to private companies and tax laws that apply to both companies and private individuals. They exert huge lobbying influence with far less oversight of their activities and have, therefore, become an obvious choice for the very wealthy wishing to direct public policy without standing for office.

Council on Foreign Relations (CFR)

Founded in 1921, the Council on Foreign Relations may be the most influential think tank in US history. It has been referred to as "Wall Street's think tank" for its strong banking and financial connections, while Louise Shelley, director of the Terrorism, Transnational Crime and Corruption Center at George Mason University, said: "If you want to target the political establishment, there is nothing more central to the political elite of this country than the Council on Foreign Relations."

Emerging from the elements of Woodrow Wilson's World War One collection of scholars and experts (known as "the Inquiry"), the CFR was an early and vocal proponent of the internationalism and interventionism that has dominated US foreign policy ever since. Academics and scholars were quickly joined by financiers, bankers, and lawyers, and from the start, the organization had high-level political connections, beginning with Theodore Roosevelt's Secretary of State Elihu Root.

The Council on Foreign Relations is one of the oldest and most prestigious Globalist organizations. Wilsonian internationalism has since become the standard foreign policy template for all subsequent US administrations. Combined with the efforts of the military-industrial complex, Wilsonian interventionist idealism has shaped the entire course of US foreign policy ever since.

The CFR has been publishing the bimonthly *Foreign Affairs* journal since 1922, which has featured countless journalists, politicians, and thinkers of a hawkish, aggressive foreign policy persuasion (the kind of policy much later described as "neocon").

Its membership has included US presidents (notably Eisenhower, who would ironically issue one of the most anti-Globalist and anti-perpetual war warnings ever issued by a departing president), CIA directors, and media figures, along with bankers and business magnates. In a 1993 *Washington Post* article ("Ruling Class Journalists"), Richard Harwood described the CFR membership as "the nearest thing we have to a ruling establishment in the United States."

The CFR is an example of the US elite deciding that imperial military adventurism and the destabilization of foreign regime change is a deeply moral project that can be described as saving and spreading democracy.

From the 1930s on, the CFR has closely advised all US presidents and received funding from the Ford Foundation and the Rockefeller Foundation. David Rockefeller chaired the CFR for fifteen years. Its efforts, though span, the entire twentieth century. World War One saw the Wilsonian doctrine of global-forced conversion to "American values" first enacted, while World War Two helped the Wilsonians frame less aggressive foreign policy as appeasement or being "too friendly with dictators" (a narrative that still dominates US foreign policy, for example, with regard to Trump's more realistic approach).

Wilsonian internationalism was effectively the precursor of contemporary neocon positions, extending a Monroe Doctrine–sense of "protective" imperial mission disguised as high ideals from interventionism in South America to similar engagement in Europe and the wider globe.

Modern foreign policy disasters of US military adventurism in Afghanistan, Iraq, Syria, and Libya, together with the idea that the US has a sacred duty to support Ukraine against Russia, cannot be fully understood without recognizing the vast influence CFR policies and members have had on what's considered respectable, sensible, and necessary in US foreign policy.

CFR influence remains very high. Seventeen of the thirty-four highest ranking initial appointments of the Biden administration were people who have been CFR members or have immediate family members who were CFR members. The socialist magazine *Monthly Review* (not a source I'd usually find myself in agreement with) provided a list of Biden team connections that indicates the extent of their contemporary influence:

The CFR Group on the Biden Team

- Kamala Harris, Vice President (CFR through family; Harvard; DLA Piper; Uber through family)
- Antony Blinken, Secretary of State (CFR member; Harvard and Columbia; WestExec)
- Janet Yellen, Secretary of the Treasury (CFR member; Yale and Harvard; Brookings)
- Lloyd Austin, Secretary of Defense (CFR member; WestExec; Raytheon)
- Linda Thomas-Greenfield, UN Ambassador (CFR member; Albright Stonebridge)
- Cecilia Rouse, Council of Economic Advisors (CFR director; Princeton; Rowe Price)
- Alejandro Mayorkas, Secretary of Homeland Security (CFR member; Wilmer Hale)

- Jake Sullivan, National Security Advisor (CFR author; Yale and Oxford; Carnegie)
- Ron Klain, Chief of Staff (CFR through family; Harvard; O'Melveny and Meyers)
- John Kerry, Special Envoy for Climate (CFR member; Yale)
- Susan Rice, Chief of Domestic Council (CFR member; Harvard, Oxford, and Stanford)
- William J. Burns, Director of Central Intelligence (CFR member; Oxford; Carnegie)
- Kurt M. Campbell, Indo-Pacific Tsar (CFR member; Harvard and Oxford; Asia Group)
- Thomas Vilsack, Secretary of Agriculture (CFR member; Dairy Export Council)
- Gina Raimondo, Secretary of Commerce (CFR member; Oxford; Point Judith Capital)
- Eric S. Lander, Director of Office of Science and Technology (CFR member; Harvard)
- Jeffery Zients, Counselor to the President (CFR member; Cranemere)

—Data is as of March 1, 2021. Council on Foreign Relations, *Annual Report 2018* (Washington DC: Council on Foreign Relations, 2018), 48–71; "Celebrating a Century," Council on Foreign Relations, January 2021; biographies from websites of think tanks, corporations, and strategic policy groups.

The CFR, of course, features in several conspiracy theory narratives, but again the problems of its influence are true regardless of whether or not the more lurid claims are believed. It's a membership organization that gathers some of the most powerful people in the US, that pushes a set Globalist agenda, and that wields unaccountable influence through private and undisclosed meetings. As well as these cozy and private meetings with policy formers, it controls about $100 million per annum in revenue to apply to lobbying and propaganda.

The CFR has also been prone to a series of scandals. Between 1995 to 2009, Jeffrey Epstein was a member and he donated $350,000 to the organization in that period. In 2019, the CFR accepted a $12 million donation from Leonard "Len" Blavatnik, the Ukrainian billionaire oligarch. (He has also funded neocon war hawks in the Republican Party, principally the late John McCain and South Carolina Senator Lindsey Graham. He has also contributed to Democrats, including Kamala, Chuck Schumer, Hillary Clinton, Pete Buttigieg, and Joe Biden.)

Clinton Foundation

The Clinton Foundation was created in 2001 as yet another supposedly nonprofit, supposedly benign, vanity philanthropic foundation following the standard template for these organizations already established by similar entities. It's initial mission statement declared an unabashedly Globalist focus with a declared aim to "strengthen the capacity of people in the United States and throughout the world to meet the challenges of global interdependence." It had an endowment in 2018 of $292.4 million and a revenue during the same year of $20 million, making it—despite the ongoing close involvement of a former president (Bill Clinton), a former US secretary of state and presidential candidate (Hillary Clinton), and their well-known daughter (Chelsea Clinton)—smaller than many of the other organizations mentioned here. Nevertheless, it controls significant wealth and employs two thousand people. Its power derives as much from the personal contacts Bill and Hillary Clinton can call on as it does from the resources of the foundation itself. By 2016, the Clinton Foundation raised over $2 billion in donations.

It's also been involved in multiple scandals. In 2016, Bill Barr opened an investigation into the foundation in relation to the FBI Crossfire Hurricane scandal/conspiracy. During Hillary Clinton's period as secretary of state, she had over eighty-five private meetings with donors to the foundation who had gifted the foundation a total of $156 million. The allegations that these meetings involved the sale of influence and affected policy decisions as secretary of state have never been fully investigated.

The Clinton Foundation also received significant grants from multiple foreign powers, including Saudi Arabia, Australia, and Germany, again while one of its founding board members was serving in office. Bill Clinton received speaking fees of up to $750,000 for each talk during the same period while advocating the Globalist aims of the foundation.

Huma Abedin, the longtime Hillary Clinton aide and ally who was vice-chairperson of her 2016 presidential campaign, at one point held four jobs simultaneously in both government and for the Clinton Foundation, leading to obvious potential conflicts of interest. She failed to disclose her consultancy work for Teneo (a strategic consulting firm) while serving as Hillary's closest staff adviser. In 2012, Abedin was accused of family ties to the Muslim Brotherhood (claims disputed by fellow Globalists from across the aisle such as John McCain). Abedin was also involved in the Hillary email scandal and in the investigation of the Benghazi debacle. In her private life, she previously dated US Democratic Representative Anthony Wiener (she is currently the fiancée of Alex Soros).

Perhaps the most significant scandal involving the Clinton Foundation pertains to the decision of the Obama administration to allow the sale of the uranium mining company Uranium One to the Russian Rosatom company in 2010. The sale of such a company represents the sale of huge quantities of uranium, with obvious national security implications. For this reason, the sale had to be approved by the State Department, with Hillary Clinton as the ultimate decision-maker. Uranium One's complicated ownership trail led to the Russian sale following and perhaps being facilitated by a period in which Uranium One purchased another company, UrAsia Energy, from Frank Giustra. Giustra accompanied Bill Clinton and participated in meetings with him in 2005 in Kazakhstan, followed that up with an initial donation of $31.3 million to the Clinton Foundation, and followed that by a second donation of at least $100 million in 2007.

Fact-checkers and mainstream media today assert that these connections are purely coincidental and that Giustra's private meetings and interests could not have benefited from the subsequent sale of Uranium One. That might be true if the benefit is solely from share price and ownership. But by this reckoning, it is also perfectly normal for a secretary of state's husband to be visiting foreign leaders where uranium mines are situated in the company of a foreign billionaire with uranium interests. It is also perfectly normal for that secretary of state to then approve a national security issue sale of a uranium mining company while sitting on the board of a foundation that received somewhere between $131 to 145 million from the same uranium industry billionaire.

The Clintons and the Clinton Foundation have also had strong ties to Haiti. They visited the nation as newlyweds in 1975. While president, Bill Clinton lobbied for agricultural reforms in Haiti. He also, of course, launched a US military invasion to oust a military junta and restore democracy in Haiti. Following the 2010 Haitian earthquake disaster, the Clinton Foundation became the main private coordinator of Western relief efforts and one of Haiti's largest benefactors, with more than thirty-four projects running in the country. As secretary of state, Hillary oversaw $4.4 billion of US aid. Bill Clinton became a UN special representative on Haiti and codirector of relief efforts. Both the Clinton Foundation and the US government promised that this aid and the money raised in disaster relief donations by the foundation would repair the earthquake damage, provide emergency food and medical assistance, and build significant new infrastructure such as a major new hospital, a hotel complex, and an entire new port.

None of these promised developments exist today, although many Haitians were evicted and displaced for the hotel complex. There is no new port or hospital. It's hard to tell exactly where all the money has gone. Recently, Haiti's president had to flee the capitol as it was taken over by cannibal crime gangs. The Biden administration has flown three hundred thousand Haitians into the US and dumped twenty-five thousand of them on a single sixty thousand-population town in Ohio.

Clearly, Clinton Foundation philanthropy isn't very successful at improving the lives it allegedly exists to improve. Such a contrast between noble ideals and claims and huge spending resulting in no discernible benefits could be described as one of the defining features of Globalist initiatives.

Club of Rome

Currently based in Winterthur, Switzerland, the Club of Rome was founded in 1968 at the Accademia dei Lincei in Rome by the Italian industrialist Aurelio Peccei and British chemist Alexander King. The club is another non-profit Globalist NGO described on its Wikipedia entry as an "organization of intellectuals and business leaders whose goal is a critical discussion of pressing global issues." It is composed of one hundred full members "selected from current and former heads of state and government, UN administrators, high-level politicians and government officials, diplomats, scientists, economists, and business leaders from around the globe." (Remember the idea that powerful people gather together to privately shape the world is a ridiculous conspiracy theory?)

Looking at its own website immediately confronts you with standard Globalist positions: climate catastrophism, "Humanity is facing its greatest emergency.... At present humanity has no way to deal with such a crisis—and a global plan of action is urgently needed"; chilling authoritarianism masquerading as public consultation and environmental care, "Causing environmental damage should be a criminal offence, say 72% of people in G20 countries surveyed" (What bodies define this damage and enforce the punishments?); and social engineering virtue signaling on gender politics, "empowering female leadership in times of global crisis."

The Club of Rome's primary influence has been to define one of the standard tropes of Globalism, which is that current population levels and social and technological complexity are unsustainable. Essentially the idea is that the resources of the Earth are finite and that we have reached or are about to reach their limits. The first point of that idea is perfectly sensible, but the second is deeply sinister. Because belief in it justifies a depopulation agenda, radical measures, and societal changes enforced from above to "save the world" from industrialized nations (modernity) and "too many people" (the human species).

This potentially disastrous doctrine has been pressed by the Club of Rome since at least the publication of the 1972 book *The Limits of Growth*. It underpins the entire concept of sustainable development (beloved by the UN), which might encompass some sensible limits on things like environmental damage and pollution, but which in its current form uses noble language to plot massive societal, energy, and food changes without consultation and without the least concern for possible risks ("net zero" is the culmination of this thinking).

Council of Europe

Another body founded in the immediate aftermath of World War Two (1949), the Council of Europe is described by its advocates and supporters as the most important human rights organization in Europe. Its alleged purposes are the standard ones always claimed by Globalist organizations: upholding human rights, democracy, and the rule of law. As ever, these things, when put into practice, mean *defining* human rights (often in ways that harm ordinary citizens and favor violent criminals), accumulating power to an *unelected* body, and imposing laws that have had *zero democratic input* from citizens and zero direct *accountability* to citizens.

Typically, the council preserves democratic-seeming forms (a two-body structure with the Committee of Ministers from member states and the Parliamentary Assembly of the Council of Europe). However, the ministers are selected by member governments, and public awareness of who these representatives are is even more minimal than would be the case for selected appointees in some obscure branch of local government. An entire bureaucratic structure apes representative democracy while most citizens aren't even aware of its existence, let alone taking or capable of taking any active role in affecting its policies.

While it does not have law-making powers, it pushes for the enforcement of international agreements reached by member states. (There are forty-six members, including all EU member states. No state has ever joined the EU without also joining the Council of Europe.) It controls a budget of around €500 million per annum and is headquartered in Strasbourg.

The Council of Europe drafted the European Convention on Human Rights and uses its power and influence today to hold member states to this and other "shared values." It's under the terms of such agreements that many member states have found themselves effectively powerless (even if they had the intent to buck Globalist instructions) to deal with mass immigration effectively, since the entire human rights structure being enforced demands asylum quotas, payments, and welfare to refugees and all the other measures that act as injustices against existing citizens and lures for illegal immigration.

While enforcing and drafting "human rights" legislation that directly harms citizens in member states, the Council of Europe has also been involved in multiple corruption scandals typical of such unaccountable, self-policing bodies and equally typical of the "caviar diplomacy" the body engages in. A 2024 Follow the Money investigation found that one in four representatives were engaged in corruption of some form. In 2022, "Qatargate" exposed Qatar's purchase of influence via gifts and bribes, while a similar corruption scandal involving Azerbaijan in 2018 resulted eventually in the expulsion of thirteen members of the Parliamentary Assembly of the Council of Europe. The bribes and corruption in that case amounted to $2.9 billion.

European Court of Human Rights (ECHR)

Also based in Strasbourg is the European Court of Human Rights, which is an international court. It hears cases regarding alleged human rights abuses from all forty-six member states where plaintiffs argue that the State in question has breached the European Convention on Human Rights or the UN Universal Declaration of Human Rights. The court issues both judgments and advisory opinions.

Judges are "elected" by the Parliamentary Assembly of the Council of Europe, with each body referring to the other for their supposed democratic accountability. ("It's OK, citizen. This other authority you have no interest in supports me.") This is what the transnational Globalist model of democracy is—various bureaucracies all endorsing each other, but with legal teeth over citizens.

The court expects national legal systems and governments in member states to comply with its judgments and advisory opinions. It can also issue damages/fines as punishments. Its effectively pursued judicial activism in the areas of definition of the family, treatment of same-sex relationships and gender identity, and Globalist attitudes to race and citizenship.

The court has insisted that prisoners have the right to vote (resisted by the UK), ruled against a Moscow ban of Pride festivals, and generally pursued a progressive social agenda.

In April 2024, the court ruled that Switzerland had infringed on the human rights of women by not doing enough to mitigate the effects of climate change, an absurd ruling that encapsulates the "seriousness" of the verdicts it passes and the use of human rights to serve other clearly political and ideological positions.

European Union (EU)

The EU is probably the second-most powerful Globalist institution after the UN, and, in some ways, closer to being the beginning of world government than the UN is. It covers twenty-seven member states and a population of around 450 million people. It has its own flag, parliament, anthem, and pooled military resources (with plans for a full and permanent EU army). All member states are subordinate to its legal mechanisms, the international courts it favors, the gigantic quantity of legislation, guidelines, and rulings it produces, and its claimed dominion over agricultural policies, fishery policies, social policies, climate policies, and economic policies. The entirety of the legislation of a member state must align with existing EU legislation, and the majority of the legislation of a member state will originate at the EU level.

From my birth in 1974 to 2016, my country was a subordinate vassal of the EU, paying vast tribute every year, subjected to European court rulings, and following EU dictates on every policy and every regulatory measure. There was no opportunity provided to me or millions of others to reject its power and oversight. Brexit in 2016 saw the UK leave the EU, at which point the malignancy of its grasp and its lack of respect for democracy became even more apparent as Britain was entangled in a drawn-out leaving process following EU rules. The EU demanded a special additional payment, the continuation of membership payments, and continued legislative and economic alignment destroying all the potential benefits of leaving.

Supporters of the EU (in the UK, these are the Remainers and establishment figures) claim it is a voluntary trade alliance that benefits every member state and that being outside this alliance is economically ruinous and morally contemptible, given how the institution represents togetherness, cooperation, peace, and European fellowship and understanding. Most of these arguments are, of course, irrational and emotional distortions. In reality, EU policy is dominated by Germany and France, while Britain paid an enormous sum with little influence gained in return. The institution is fundamentally undemocratic, as it gives power to people that citizens in most of the member states cannot vote for or against or remove from their positions. Nor has it been of much economic benefit since its creation. It has burdened Europe with regulatory bloat and inefficient aims, and the period of its existence has seen European nations relentlessly out-competed by foreign competitors. The European/EU share of world trade and world GDP has declined steadily. Membership bars full access to other, more successful trade areas and prevents competitive economic, tax, and trade policies being adopted. At best, it is an anachronistic, outdated, bureaucratic 1950s solution to the problems of the 1930s and a huge, parasitic drag on Western nation-states.

Corruption is endemic in this European model of over-mighty bureaucrats and a ruling class more loyal to each other than to the citizens of any specific nation. Senior EU figures have been well-known fraudsters and crooks or politicians already rejected democratically by voters in their home nations.

In 1999, the entire Santer Commission (the commission being the twenty-highest officials of the EU, its primary executive arm) was forced to resign in response to corruption and budgetary incompetence revelations. In 2006, the Galvin Report into the members of the European Parliament's expenses was so damning that it was completely suppressed. In 2011, former Austrian member of European Parliament Ernst Strasser was found guilty in a cash-for-influence scandal. In 2022, the European Public Prosecutor's Office opened an investigation into European Commission President Ursula von der Leyen's private negotiation of a €35 billion deal with Pfizer, which was conducted by private texts and meetings rather than by official teams of negotiators. Von der Layen had previously been accused of destroying evidence relating to possible corruption when she served as the German minister of defense. She was reelected (by the EU Parliament, not by voters directly) for a second term as commission president in 2024.

Group of Twenty (G20)

One of the more recent Globalist institutions, the Group of Twenty G20 was founded in 1999 primarily at the instigation of German finance minister Hans Eichel and Canadian finance minister (later prime minister of Canada) Paul Martin. It is an international forum engaged in the typical Globalist activities of schmoozing, network forming, glad-handing counterparts while enjoying five-star, taxpayer-funded hospitality, and fostering social networks between like-minded Globalist leaders, who all then tend to follow the same policy platforms in their respective nations.

Since the global financial crash of 2008, G20 summits have been held at least annually and sometimes more frequently than that. They have become the focus of anti-Globalist protest and require a considerable security budget. The G20 is also closely aligned with the similar but more exclusive G7 and G8 groups.

G20 refers to the top twenty economies in the world but actually consists of nineteen nation-states, plus the EU and the African Union.

Controversy has circulated regarding the treatment of the EU president as if they were the head of a nation-state.

The G20 has no enforcement powers of its own and likes to talk about doing things but not actually do them, but still has considerable influence based on the power of the nation-states that attend. The fact is that the finance ministers and heads of government of these nations are now regularly meeting and aligning their policies based on G20 discussions. Taken collectively, the nations present at G20 summits represent about 80 percent of the global GDP, 75 percent of all international trade, and rule over two-thirds of the planet's population and 60 percent of global land mass.

In 2016 and 2017, the G20 took an active role in opposing Brexit, with G20 leaders and representatives issuing repeated warnings regarding the alleged damage Brexit would inflict on Britain and the global economy. These statements were a direct interference in an internal British democratic decision-making process, and, like many other dire forecasts, it turned out to be completely inaccurate. The "cost of Brexit" fallacy continues, however, to be pushed by Remainers in Britain and Globalist EU enthusiasts elsewhere.

G20 summits during the COVID hysteria saw leaders observing masking and social distancing for photo opportunities and then mingling and socializing in close contact without masks when they thought that they were not being filmed or photographed. Staff serving at these functions tended to remain masked, and the leak of these images expressed the social, class-based hypocrisies of COVID measures even before their complete lack of efficacy was widely acknowledged.

Group of Seven (G7)

Essentially a more exclusive precursor version of the G20, the Group of Seven is an international and economic forum composed of Canada, France, Germany, Italy, Japan, the UK and the US, with the EU as a special additional member. G7 members are International Monetary Fund–advanced economies. The heads of state of the member nations meet annually, while high-level bureaucrats, finance ministers, and civil servants meet more regularly. Founded in 1973 (prompted by the 1973 oil crisis), the G7 also included Russia as a member (the group was called the G8 accordingly) from 1997 until its expulsion in 2014.

The presidency of the G7 rotates annually among the member nations. Once again, it claims to address global challenges and spread democracy and trade. Like every Globalist institution, it presses a climate change agenda. The G7 has taken a strong anti-Russian, pro-Ukrainian line consistent with that of other Globalist institutions and has likewise demanded all the usual Globalist obsessions. As with NATO and other Globalist institutions, there's a constant call for expansion with several proposals to invite new members currently ongoing.

Gavi, the Vaccine Alliance

Founded in 2000 as the Global Alliance for Vaccines and Immunization, Gavi was the brainchild primarily of Bill Gates. It's a public-private global health partnership with the aim of increasing access to immunization in poor countries. In reality, it is a lobby group of pharmaceutical- and medical-industry voices formed to push for large-scale global vaccination programs at the expense of Western taxpayers. The public-private nature consists of private interests developing new vaccines, public money matching "philanthropic" investment, and then the philanthropists (who have shares in the vaccine-developing companies) persuading governments to spend vast sums on these products because in doing so they are saving the world from infectious diseases.

It's just a fortunate by-product, honestly, that this develops vast profits for pharmaceutical companies and investors, and Western governments frequently end up underwriting all the costs to the extent that there is zero risk involved for the companies developing new vaccines. The business-oriented merger of vaccine development with huge public spending (in other words, the private-public partnership) has even been termed the "Gates model."

Between 2016 to 2020, Gavi received $9.3 billion of funding, with over half of this coming from the largest three donors (the UK, the US, and the Bill and Melinda Gates Foundation). Gavi has become the world's main operator in terms of vaccination programs in low- and middle-income countries, primarily transferring funds from UK and US taxpayers to pharmaceutical investors on a vast scale under the guise of allegedly saving millions of lives in the Third World. COVID policies saw Gavi take a prominent role within the West itself. Supporters claim that Gavi programs are vital in the fight against viruses and diseases in the developing world, but little public consultation occurs before debt-laden Western governments pledge billions to these causes. In 2023, *The New York Times* reported that Gavi-aligned vaccine developers were keeping $1.4 billion in payments for COVID supplies that were unwanted and never used. Vaccine critics also pointed to the vast extension of vaccination since Gavi's formation, the health crisis in heavily vaccinated Western populations in terms of autism rates and multiple other conditions, and the correlation of major Gavi-backed vaccine rollouts with serious harmful conditions in the Third World (particularly the five hundred thousand non-polio acute flaccid paralysis cases following Gates- and Gavi-backed polio vaccinations).

International Criminal Court (ICC)

While the UN's International Court of Justice hears cases based on disputes between nation-states, the International Criminal Court, based in The Hague, Netherlands, is the first and only permanent international court with jurisdiction to prosecute individuals for the international crimes of genocide, war crimes, crimes against humanity, and the crime of aggression. The court was established by the Rome Statute and has been operating since 2002. There are 124 ICC member states who recognize the authority of the court.

Like the UN, the ICC is funded by direct payments from member states assessed for their ability to pay.

The key issue regarding the IPCC is the standard one that applies to Globalist organizations—it is a body that can directly impact the rights of an individual citizen, and it is a body that individual citizens have no say over. It has power without democratic accountability. At the same time, it impinges on national sovereignty. Both an individual and a nation might be justified in asking, "By what right does this court judge me? Should this foreign court have sway over me?"

This becomes a particularly significant issue when the court makes judgments that are as much political choices as they are matters of law or justice. Both the war crimes and the crimes of aggression (things like invasion, military occupation, annexation, bombardment, and blockade) the court covers have huge implications for both national sovereignty and in terms of the court being used for a political purpose, backing one side or another within a conflict.

For Globalists, these concerns don't register or matter, since they automatically consider transnational bodies, international courts, and global responses better than individual rights more locally defined, national sovereignty distinct from overriding international agreements, and traditional moralities not put into a legislative framework at all.

The ICC has, however, strayed into obviously political and controversial territory. It has been accused of a close relationship with the anti-Israel BDS (Boycott, Divestment and Sanctions) movement. It has followed that by pursuing war crimes and genocide cases against Israeli leaders such as Benjamin Netanyahu, a move which seems to favor Hamas terrorists and severely infringes on a state's right to defend itself and wage war against terrorist organizations. Perhaps less controversially, but also in a way that impacts national sovereignty generally, the ICC has also issued verdicts against Russia and Vladimir Putin.

Nor has the ICC been free of scandals regarding more general corruption. Former chief prosecutor of the ICC, Luis Moreno Ocampo, was involved in a scandal in 2023 when forty thousand leaked documents revealed a close business relationship with a son of former Libyan dictator Muammar Gaddafi, together with consultancy work for various nefarious individuals (focused on tax havens) and ties with the Armenian government.

International Monetary Fund (IMF)

The International Monetary Fund is a financial agency of the United Nations. It is headquartered in Washington DC, and is the global lender of last resort to national governments. It's claimed purpose is essentially two-fold: first, to provide financial stability to Western nations via exchange-rate stability and promotion of confidence and trade and second, to assist developing nations in difficulty by providing loans and advice backed by the more developed nations. (The idea that these two things might contradict each other or saddle Western nations with extreme debt levels does not seem to register.)

The IMF was established in 1945 at the Bretton Woods Conference and is a key part of the global banking and finance system. Its membership consists of 191 countries, all of whom make contributions on a quota system. This provides a pool of funds, allowing loans to react to national and international crises. Its budget in 2023 was $1,295 million.

The former managing director of the IMF Dominique Strauss-Kahn was arrested in relation to charges of sexual assault in 2011. He was succeeded by Christine Lagarde, who served two terms as director, despite herself being convicted by a French court of fraud and misconduct in office. The conviction was related to a €403 million scandal illegally favoring businessman Bernard Tapie when she was the French finance minister. The current director is Kristalina Georgieva, a Bulgarian who has been praised (surprise, surprise) for her focus on perennial Globalist noble causes, climate change, and gender equality.

As BlackRock enforces Globalist social attitudes on companies in return for lending, the IMF has the power to do effectively the same in their lending conditions to national governments.

Following the 2008 financial crash and a particularly severe crisis in Greece from 2009, the IMF conspired with the European Central Bank and the EU to impose undemocratic rule by selecting technocrats over an elected Greek government, which forced Greece to comply with strict technocratic instructions in return for outstanding loan forgiveness (effectively bypassing Greek election results).

The Intergovernmental Panel on Climate Change (IPCC)

The UN's Intergovernmental Panel on Climate Change (the IPCC), established in 1988, is probably the most influential Globalist body in transforming climate apocalypse rhetoric from the fringe activity of extreme environmentalists into one of the standard policy assumptions of our times. It produces both large five-year reports and an ongoing series of smaller reports assessing climate change. These reports advance the argument that climate change is both man-made and potentially catastrophic, and advocate for increased spending and radically altered food and energy policies supposedly designed to prevent the coming climate apocalypse (things like "net zero").

More than any other body or individual measure, IPCC reports have given institutional and global scientific legitimacy to those advocating for radical Green taxes, subsidies, and policy choices, with repeated IPCC reports calling for urgent and extensive action to mitigate global temperature rises.

Without going into full arguments on climate change issues, the entire project is riddled with contradictions and problems the IPCC reports do not address. (Such issues are the ecological impact of mining for the rare minerals needed for electric vehicles, the pollution footprint of supposedly Green energy sources like solar farms and wind farms, and the land use required for these inefficient energy sources, etc.)

But the primary problem regarding the IPCC reports that are taken as the scientific consensus, the authoritative and respectable voice on climate change, and as the firm scientific evidence of the need for radical Green measures is that all of these reports rely almost totally on computer modeling based on debatable assumptions. Similar computer modeling systems have been wildly inaccurate with regards to pandemics and viruses and tend to posit a range of apocalyptic future scenarios for which no real-world evidence exists. Nobel Prize–winning scientists have been among those pointing out that relying on computer models to read the future is dependent on the input of information being both accurate and comprehensive, while many of the boundless variables involved in predicting climate are still beyond our full understanding.

Nevertheless, the IPCC has been very successful in making climate apocalypse rhetoric respectable and extreme and expensive climate policies a standard feature of Globalist policy platforms in every Western-developed nation.

Obama Foundation

One day, perhaps, a full and honest accounting of one of the very worst American presidencies in history will take place, together with an analysis of the extent to which Obama shaped the Biden era as well. For now, Obama represents possibly the most successful individual Globalist politician there has been in terms of covering up what he is, disguising the extraordinary damage he has done, and being generally perceived as respectable, successful, and moderate. His period really coincides with the takeover of the mainstream by ideas and policies that not that long ago would have been considered obviously mad. In some ways, the Obama-era shift of the Overton window and its radicalization of the mainstream with radical progressive views (particularly the capture of "Big Business") represents a more damaging and total destruction of traditional Western morals and virtues than even the 1960s social and sexual revolution accomplished.

Founded in 2014, the Obama Foundation is the nonprofit organization intended to secure the "Obama legacy." It has net assets of $925 million and has raised over $1.1 billion in contributions and gifts since 2017, including a $100 million gift from Airbnb cofounder and CEO Brian Chesky. (This went towards the Voyager Scholarship scheme where the foundation picks up the university tuition fees and supplies additional cash and mentorship to young students identified as potential future Globalist leaders.) Its interest in education scholarships include the My Brother's Keeper Alliance, which continues the My Brother's Keeper

Challenge Obama launched when still president (essentially race-based priority and funding for black students).

The main focus of the Obama Foundation, though, has been on the vast vanity project called the Barack Obama Presidential Center in Chicago, which, typical for a Globalist grand project, has swallowed up vast resources while taking longer than originally envisaged to actually build anything. The intention seems to be to create a sort of Smithsonian of Obama hubris, which will include a museum of US history divided into BO (before Obama) and AO (after Obama) eras. (I'm joking, but in a truthful way.)

Organisation for Economic Co-operation and Development (OECD)

Originally founded in 1948 as the Organisation for European Economic Cooperation, the OECD took its modern name in 1961 as an intergovernmental organization with thirty-eight member countries. It is yet another transnational body that claims to promote democracy, the market economy, and economic and social progress (one would think if one of these organizations was truly successful, we wouldn't need all the others doing the same thing). The OECD is funded by its member nation-states and had an operating budget of €383.4 million for 2023.

The most powerful aspect of the OECD's remit is as the organization that sets the rules governing international taxation. Its power in this area has been used to set minimum tax levels on multinational corporations, which, of course, directly impinges on the tax setting and raising powers of supposedly sovereign nations. Effectively, nations are barred by the OECD from being especially tax efficient and from outcompeting other nations via very low tax levels on major business enterprises (there's still some flexibility, but less than if the OECD did not exist). The OECD also acts as an internationally recognized statistics agency through its numerous reports and studies.

Former Australian Finance Minister Mathias Cormann (current secretary-general of the OECD) was embroiled in scandal in 2023 when investigations revealed that Cormann received equity in a hidden trust provided by Luke Sayers, then CEO of PwC Australia. Cormann oversaw a vast expansion of the Australian government, outsourcing previously public sector jobs to accountancy and consultancy service firms (such as PwC). This outsourcing increased by more than 400 percent while Cormann was the Australian finance minister and was so extensive that over AUD 1.2 billion was spent on it in 2021–22. In the same decade, the "Big Four" consultancy firms made over $10 billion total from such work, while Sayers personally took home $30 million between 2012 and 2020 as a direct result of Cormann's largesse.

The Rockefeller Foundation

If we are talking about major long-term influence on global(ist) policies and developments from any body that is not itself a national government, the Rockefeller Foundation (current website motto "to make opportunity universal and sustainable") has to be a strong contender for the title of the most important Globalist institution in private hands.

The Gates Foundation may today arguably be more active, but that and every supposedly philanthropic foundation in the world (the Soros, Obama, and Clinton ones mentioned here, for instance) follow a precedent established by the Rockefeller Foundation.

The Rockefeller dynasty built up enormous wealth via Standard Oil and its monopolistic practices. That made John Rockefeller both extraordinarily rich and widely detested. When the family needed to rescue their reputation, they helped birth the entire modern discipline of public relations (hiring the earliest masters of these dark arts) and showed the purely selfish advantages of philanthropy (its usefulness for whitewashing a reputation, for avoiding inheritance taxes, for avoiding company based monopoly laws, for retaining generational family influence, and for influencing and even directing social and cultural policy from the government according to the views of the people in charge of these foundations).

The Rockefeller Foundation is one of the very oldest Globalist institutions there is (founded May 14, 1913) and is still enormously wealthy (controlling an endowment of $6.3 billion as of 2022). It has had international reach since at least the 1930s, and many other Globalist institutions were founded with its support or based on models and precedents it had set. The World Health Organization was purposely structured to ape the Rockefeller Foundation's International Health Division. It was an early proponent of the establishment of the United Nations. The US National Science Foundation and even more importantly the National Institutes of Health (Dr. Fauci's power base) were modeled on Rockefeller initiatives. William Gates Sr. was a Rockefeller lawyer, and the young Bill Gates read admiring biographies of the Rockefellers in his childhood.

There is a reason that the Rockefellers feature heavily in some of the most lurid conspiracy theories, particularly ones which talk about the five families controlling the world. While much of this stuff is nonsense, the fact remains that many modern Globalist policy platforms, the vast network of NGOs which exist today, and subsequent politically active foundations are all following what were originally Rockefeller moves. Buying influence and reputation and accumulating vast wealth too all existed before the Rockefellers, but "philanthrocapitalism" in its modern form is as much John Rockefeller Jr.'s legacy as it is the legacy of Bill Gates.

The Rockefeller Foundation's influence is cited positively by those who believe it helped (or was largely responsible for), such as in the elimination of certain diseases, but is also cited for numerous negative impacts, particularly in the Third World. Perhaps the most sinister of its activities for most negative commentators is the long interest the organization has shown in fertility, depopulation, abortion, "sustainability" (the modern version of "there are too many people on the planet"), contraception, and population-control measures.

The Trilateral Commission

In some ways an extension of the Rockefeller Foundation, the Trilateral Commission often features in the same extreme discussions about hidden influence and secret organizations. (The reality being instead that the organizations are not exactly hidden but a curious mix of being both known and unaccountable, social extensions of private power networks masquerading as official bodies, which is the real issue.)

The commission was the brainchild of David Rockefeller, with the assistance of President Jimmy Carter's National Security Advisor Zbigniew Brzezinski and Jimmy Carter himself. It was founded in 1973. Alan Greenspan and Paul Volcker (both former heads of the Federal Reserve System) were also founder members.

The commission consists of around four hundred members. It states that it exists to promote cooperation and understanding between North America, Europe, and the Far East (originally Japan, but expanded now to include other nations from that region). As with all Globalist institutions, it presses for the rule of law (law drafted by these Globalist bodies), open economies (resulting in open borders), and democratic principles (only those governments following Globalist policies being deemed democratic).

United Nations (UN)

The UN is undoubtedly the centerpiece of the post–World War global political settlement and the body more than any other that would presumably form the core of any genuine "One World government."

It's current byline (the banner on the UN website) is a cloying example of the saccharine nature of Globalist self-description: "peace, dignity and equality on a healthy planet." What does such a motto really encompass? The positives are so broad as to be meaningless, almost as a sort of positive baby language for a bureaucracy trying to assert how nice it is.

Nevertheless, this simpering set of "values" describes one of the most important organizations on the planet. Founded by the UN Charter on June 26, 1945, it encompasses 193 member states and two observer states. Its charter objectives center primarily on maintaining international peace and security, preventing future world wars, protecting human rights, delivering humanitarian aid, upholding international law, and promoting sustainable development.

The UN is the parent body of an enormous number of other powerful Globalist organizations: the World Health Organization, the International

Panel on Climate Change, the World Bank, the International Court of Justice, the World Food Programme, UNESCO, UNICEF, and the UNHCR (the UN Refugee Agency).

All of which, of course, sound noble, but actually encompass a great deal of negative actions. The UN has acted as a rubber stamp conferring legitimacy on unnecessary wars (in the name of reestablishing peace). It has put the heads of barbaric non-Western regimes on committees supposedly advising and admonishing others on human rights. It has long shown an adversarial and biased attitude towards Israel. It has produced reports that continuously criticize and admonish Western governments whenever they have patriotic, populist, or conservative leaders, especially on human rights issues and the adherence to Globalist-progressive social values on issues like trans rights and women's rights (while being far more reticent about criticizing Islamic nations). It has taken to labeling any populist movement as "far right," a habit it shares with the mainstream media and established political parties.

The UN's seventeen Sustainable Development Goals and its outlined 2030 and 2050 strategies have been massively influential on moves towards radically altering the existing energy and food supplies of Western nations, advocating "net zero," promoting Green apocalypse and pandemic apocalypse hysteria, and backing increasingly authoritarian moves and power-centralizing moves related to these projects (also known as "excuses"). Many of the things described as sustainable or positive represent the birth of a techno-feudal system where basic human rights are actually denied to the people in the most developed nations.

In 2014, semi-official UN "peacekeepers" acting under the authority of the UN's Security Council were found to be sexually abusing children in the Central African Republic. Some of the victims were as young as eight.

Multiple reports have confirmed UN peacekeeper troops' involvement in shocking cases of sexual abuse, exploitation, coercion, bribery, and rape in Haiti, with an academic paper from the journal *International Peacekeeping* describing these abuses in detail in 2023.

In 2021, the UN withdrew 450 peacekeepers supplied by the African nation of Gabon following fresh allegations of abuse.

Such cases, however, go back much further. In *The Impact of Armed Conflict on Children*, a UN report from 1996, it was stated that in half of the conflicts, the arrival of peacekeeping forces coincided with sharp rises in child prostitution.

In 2010, UN aid workers from Nepal reintroduced cholera to Haiti, resulting in ten thousand deaths, while the UN denied any responsibility and initially refused any form of compensation.

In 2018, the documentary *UN Sex Abuse Scandal* aired, citing more than two thousand victims of abuse by UN peacekeepers. In the same year, on August 16, Nicole Einbinder for *Frontline* stated, "humanitarian aid workers are speaking out about what they describe as a culture of sexual misconduct within the UN and other major humanitarian organizations."

In 2023, UN employees took part in the Oct 7 Hamas terrorist atrocities, with at least twelve members of the UN agency for Palestinian refugees (UNRWA) confirmed as being active terrorists involved in the brutal torture, rape, murder, and kidnap of Israeli civilians (including men, women, and children). A later Israeli report stated that thirteen UN employees took part in the attack, with one providing logistic support and one tasked with setting up a Hamas operations center.

World Economic Forum (WEF)

The WEF (website "We bring together government, businesses and civil society to improve the state of the world") is perhaps now the first organization people think of when they talk about unaccountable elites gathering together to decide the fate of the world without the slightest interaction with ordinary people.

Founded in 1971 by Klaus Schwab (who is still the executive chairman) and based in Switzerland, the WEF has one thousand member companies, all of whom typically have an annual turnover of more than $5 billion. As such, it represents the largest business interest lobby group in the world.

F*ck the Planet

It has become most famous (or infamous) for hosting annual meetings in the Swiss mountain resort of Davos. The Davos gatherings consist of representatives of the member companies, together with invited politicians, world leaders, charity heads, NGO executives, and of course billionaires and the politically active superrich. Its combination of luxury and lack of transparency makes it a byword now, at least in alternative media, for a sort of ancient regime class of techno-bureaucratic nobility.

Both Schwab and the WEF itself have done little to dispel concerns regarding their seemingly antidemocratic (in the real sense) idea of how the world should be run. Unashamedly focused on the profit and prejudices of the "great and the good," the WEF has come up with clumsy slogans like "you will have nothing and be happy," while also framing narratives of a "Great Reset" in ways that the voting public see suddenly mirrored by every Globalist Western leader there is. Schwab has spoken about disasters and crises as windows of opportunities for the radical societal shifts the WEF favors, a tendency that rather naturally leads many to wonder whether the crises are manufactured to provide the windows of opportunity rather than being the events the WEF is merely responding to.

Supporters describe the WEF as either a useful place for networking and getting things done, or less flatteringly as nothing more than a place to just talk and vanity-based social gathering. But the fact remains that the initiatives and policies the WEF push forward can have enormous impact, while at the same time the organization has no accountability whatsoever to any portion of the general public. Chancellors, senior ministers, prime ministers, and presidents have all made the trek to Davos, while many of them were groomed and assisted early in their careers by the WEF young leaders program.

Current British Prime Minister Keir Starmer instantly answered that he prefers Davos to Westminster when the question was posed to him, explaining that at Davos there is a unity of purpose and a chance to get things done that is absent from Westminster. US Democratic presidential candidate and vice president Kamala Harris partnered with Schwab and the WEF in a call-to-action initiative promoting "inclusive and sustainable economic development" in Latin America. Kamala's husband, Doug Emhoff, attended the 2024 Davos gathering in January and gave speeches on anti-Semitism, Islamophobia, and "other forms of hate," no doubt closely connected to the Globalist general push for more and more controls on speech and more and more censorship mechanisms.

The influence of the WEF and Schwab is often even more powerful than some of the strongest critics of the organization present it as being. Schwab led a WEF delegation that advised China on integrating itself into the world economy as long ago as the 1970s, with the WEF playing just as active a role in China's global rehabilitation and embrace of some elements of capitalism as Henry Kissinger or Richard Nixon did.

World Health Organization (WHO)

The World Health Organization was founded on April 7, 1948. It's a subsidiary organization of the United Nations. It has responsibility for international public health and is an authority covering pandemic responses, vaccines, medical research, and public health policy. It sets international health standards, provides technical assistance to countries, acts as a forum for public discussion of health policies (i.e., propaganda and the promotion of Globalist health initiatives), and collects data on health issues.

Its budget for 2024–25 stands at $6.83 billion. Major Western nation-states are the majority of the primary funders of the WHO (particularly the US and the UK), but the Gates Foundation/Bill Gates contributes between 11 to 13 percent of the WHO budget in any given year. The Gates contribution is greater than that of most nation-states and comes with massive influence on WHO policy and recommendations. While the WHO is nominally governed by the World Health Assembly, to some extent it is accurate to say that the current director general of the WHO is a hand-picked long-term Gates ally and that Bill Gates is at least partly in control of what is supposed to be a major branch of the UN.

During COVID, the WHO entirely followed the same directions that Bill Gates did and that the Gates Foundation advocated. The organization gave global legitimacy to the most useless and indeed dangerous policy choices during COVID. As with national establishment medical figures like Dr. Fauci, its advice on masking changed and contradicted itself, with this first being described as unnecessary (accurate) and then being described as a vital safety measure to prevent viral spread (inaccurate). The WHO gave an air of global authority and respectability to the policies of lockdowns (economically ruinous and useless for preventing viral spread), masking, and social distancing (which had no scientific basis).

Under the proposed "pandemic treaty" that nation-states are being asked to sign, the WHO would gain authority to override all national sovereignty on the issue of pandemics, based on pandemics being declared with the very loosest and broadest definitions of the term. The WHO would then be legally entitled to enforce severe lockdowns, curfews, travel restrictions, and other measures without any democratic input and even against the preferred responses of a national government. This would be the reward, apparently, for the WHO getting every single aspect of the previous pandemic response wrong.

World Bank

One of the key organizations at the heart of the global macroeconomic order (working in concert with the IMF and the World Trade Organization), the World Bank was one of the first parts of the post–World War Two settlement to be put in place. (It was created in 1944, even before World War Two ended, at the Bretton Woods Conference.)

Affiliated with the UN, the World Bank is the world's largest source of financial assistance to developing nations. As well as providing technical assistance and policy advice (such advice always being linked to the adoption of Globalist principles), it supervises the implementation of alleged free-market reforms (which more and more seem like corporatism and conditions favorable to multinationals rather than a genuinely free market).

The World Bank has 189 member countries, each of whom have representation on its Board of Governors. Various branches of the World Bank provide loans to developing nations, while others offer insurance to the creditors providing those loans. The Board of Governors possess minimal authority, with decision-making and real power concentrated in the World Bank's twenty-five executive directors. The president of the World Bank has considerable power and influence.

The longest-serving president and the single individual most responsible for shaping its policies and attitudes was Robert McNamara (the Kennedy- and Johnson-era US secretary of defense) who served as the president of the World Bank from 1968 to 1981. McNamara, originally appointed by Lyndon Johnson, had the kind of length of service and influence over the World Bank's direction that might be compared with, for example, J. Edgar Hoover's dominance of the FBI.

McNamara was a very early advocate (a contender for the title of originator of the idea) of "sustainable development," long before the UN itself was issuing the Sustainable Development Goals. The concept as pushed by McNamara applied to the development of Third World nations that needed to industrialize and modernize to advance their economies and general standard of living. At that time, it may even have made some sense in terms of asking how these nations could do that without causing extensive damage to their environment. Since then, however, both the meaning and direction of "sustainable development" has changed, with it now being entirely shackled to an extreme form of environmentalism and to a series of apocalypse theories with no firm evidential basis.

The original argument seems to have been that the gap between the richest and poorest nations should be closed by the development of the poorest, whereas today the means of closing that gap seems to be the punishment of developed nations in ways that threaten their energy security and general affluence.

Sustainable development is now applied to First World nations that the UN and others would like to see completely deindustrialized as a "solution" to the apocalyptic climate change models cooked up by the computer nerds at the IPCC.

World Trade Organization (WTO)

Based in Geneva, Switzerland, (conveniently close to the WEF) the WTO has been described as the referee of international trade. It is the body that sets the rules by which international trade is conducted. It then arbitrates disputes between nation-states when it comes to trade between them or the sanctions, tariffs, and embargoes they impose on each other (short of ones deemed part of aggression crimes).

As ever, even the briefest glance at the website of such an organization is dispiriting. In this case, I was greeted with "Trade and Environment Week 2024 to focus on inclusive shift to sustainability." It seems like some entrance in a Globalist bingo competition of meaningless waffle. It has an operating annual budget in excess of $220 million, with 623 full-time staff as of 2023.

This august body with the penchant for mindless buzz words is the world's largest international economic organization, with its 166 member countries covering an astonishing 98 percent of global trade and GDP. Somehow, it is said that nations traded with each other before the existence of the WTO, which was founded in 1995.

It provides a framework for dispute resolution and officially prohibits discrimination between trading partners (but provides exemptions on environmental and national security grounds).

In recent years, a lasting dispute with the US led to a US block on the appointment of WTO judges, severely impacting the ability of the WTO to pass judgments and render decisions relating to its areas of competence. Donald Trump startled the international establishment through his skepticism regarding the fairness and efficacy of the WTO (combined with similar attitudes towards the UN and NATO, this represented a significant challenge to the sacred articles of Globalism).

The Forum of Young Global Leaders

The Forum of Young Global Leaders was established by the WEF and Klaus Schwab in 2004. It represents perhaps the creepiest and most cult-like activities of the WEF as it centers on finding, developing (a.k.a. grooming), and promoting young people into positions of authority in the wider world after having first put them through an intensive program of training in correct Globalist, social, and political stances.

It runs three-year training packages for those the WEF has identified as potential future leaders and is described in this almost messianic fashion by its former Chair Nicole Schwab:

"For the past 20 years, we have embarked on a journey to identify, support and facilitate connections between young leaders who are committed to improving the state of the world. Amid these complex times, the YGL community has demonstrated resilience, unity and a vision for a sustainable and inclusive world."

Meanwhile her father, referring to the success of such efforts to develop Globalist-trained leaders of the future, said this:

"What we are very proud of now is that the young generation like Prime Minster Trudeau and the president of Argentina and so on, that we penetrate the cabinets [with our Young Global Leaders]."

WEF Young Global Leaders have included Alexander Soros, Mark Zuckerberg, Daniel Crenshaw (has publicly denied membership), Tulsi Gabbard, John Dutton, Sebastian Kurz, Jens Spahn, Justin Trudeau, Ed Balls, Marc Benioff, Sergey Brin, Yvette Cooper, Chrystia Freeland, Larry Page, Paul Meyer, Gavin Newsom, Samantha Power, Mikheil Saakashvili, Shami Chakrabarti, Alessandra Galloni, Kate Garvey, Sheryl Sandberg, Rajiv Shah, Peter Thiel, Jimmy Wales, Ellana Lee, Mark Leonard, Rory Stewart, Boris Nikolic, Ben Goldsmith, Dr. Sanjay Gupta, Ricken Patel, Nathan Wolfe, Nikki Haley, Huma Abedin, Daniel Bahr, Martha Lane Fox, Matteo Renzi, Chelsea Clinton, Catherine Howarth, Jacinda Ardern, Rebecca Weintraub, Alexander De Croo, Emmanuel Macron, Leana Wen, Jagmeet Singh, Peter Buttigieg, Carlos Alvarado Quesada, Annika Saarikko, Jack Conte, Sanna Marin, Alicia Garza, and Ibram X. Kendi.

ABOUT THE AUTHOR

Daniel Jupp is a populist writer from Essex, UK. He is a former host of a politics radio show with 100,000 listeners on Expat Radio, and has been published in *Spiked*, *The Spectator*, *Country Squire* magazine, and Politicalite. His previous books are *A Gift for Treason: The Cultural Marxist Assault on Western Civilization* and *Gates of Hell: Why Bill Gates Is the Most Dangerous Man in the World*.

Printed in Great Britain
by Amazon